Mr Newport: The Story of Aubrey Hames

Mr Newport

The Story of Aubrey Hames

By Dominic Hames

First published by Arena Books in 2023
www.arenabooks.co.uk

Dominic Hames
Mr Newport: The Story of Aubrey Hames

ISBN 978-1-914390-19-7 Paperback
ISBN 978-1-914390-24-1 Hardback
ISBN 978-1-914390-20-3 eBook

A CIP catalogue record for this book is available from the British Library.

Thema: DNBH; NHTB; 1DDU-GB-WS; 3MP; JPHL; JPHV; JPWB; JPR; JPZ; 3MPB; 3MPQ; NHWR7; 3MPBLB.

Distributed by *Ingram International, One Ingram Blvd., P.O. Box 3006, La Vergne, TN 37086-1985, USA.*

Cover design by Arena Books, photography by Robin Weaver.

To all those who would have liked to have read this book, but for whom it is unfortunately too late.

"HONOUR HIM"

How do you take the measure of a man?

Do you, with tape and plumb-line,

Gauge the length of his arms, and straightness of his back,

Or, with scales and callipers,

Determine the weight of his heart, and width of his mind?

No, for hearts are not constant,

Minds are variable,

Backs bend beneath burdens,

Arms stretch no further than their shoulders.

Measure a man by the affection held for him by others.

And should you discover a man that has given of his best,

and enjoyed the giving,

Found satisfaction in that, and sought nothing else,

Honour him,

For he will be loved by many.

Honour Him is a poem about Aubrey written by Newport Town Poet Goff Morgan, and read out by him at Aubrey's Freedom of Newport ceremony on 19th February 1998 and at his funeral on 12th June 1998.

Aubrey Hames

1923 - 1998

CONTENTS

FOREWORD

I have real pleasure in introducing this very fine biography of Aubrey Hames written by his son, Dominic.

I knew Aubrey for at least twenty-five years. He was a truly remarkable man in many respects – a great socialist, community leader and council leader. To me, he was always "Mr Newport." With his famous and distinctive moustache, Aubrey possessed a great speaking ability and intelligence which was always recognised by those of us in the Labour Party in Gwent. He was invariably courteous and very kind to me personally. I would often attend Mass in St Mary's Catholic Church, Stow Hill, with him and his beloved wife, Mary.

Dominic has written a wonderful account of his father's life. It has been meticulously researched and is splendidly detailed and comprehensive. He takes us through Aubrey's life – from his birth in my former constituency of Torfaen in Sebastopol, near Pontypool, in 1923, through his time in Newtown, mid Wales, and his eventful and colourful time in the army in India and Palestine. He then gives us a really scholarly and excellent description of his long political life in Newport where Aubrey became Leader of the Council, Mayor in Jubilee Year, and, in my view, the most significant figure in Welsh local government.

Dominic, rightly, spends quite some time discussing the allegations made against his father. Aubrey had been a senior official with the British Transport Docks Board and had been accused of minor corruption. He was, of course, completely vindicated, and he won the largest compensation awarded by an industrial tribunal (for wrongful dismissal). Anyone who knew Aubrey knew that the charges were spurious.

When he was made a Freeman of Newport, not long before he died, he was recognized for the huge contributions he made to the lives of the people of Newport. He was honoured for ensuring that the town was not cut in two by a motorway, for building a new leisure and cultural centre, for significantly increasing the housing stock of Newport, and for many more achievements that benefited the town. Above all, he was personally committed to the people, as testified by the many charities with which he was involved even after he had left frontline politics.

He had attempted to represent Newport in the House of Commons but never quite made it. I can firmly say, as a Parliamentarian for thirty-six years, that

Aubrey would have been a first-class MP, and very probably a Minister. But it was Newport that benefitted, and as a consequence he left a greater mark on his town, now a city, as a result of his singular and outstanding career in local government.

by Paul Murphy, Rt Hon. Lord Murphy of Torfaen, former Secretary of State for Wales and Northern Ireland, and MP for Torfaen, 1987 to 2015. *May 2023.*

PREFACE

When I decided to write this biography of my father towards the end of 2009, I knew that it was going to take me a long time. With a background in dealing with numbers and making future predictions based on those numbers – as opposed to reading political texts and analysing the past – I also readily accepted that I would struggle to understand or appreciate the various nuances of different political and historical events. At the very start I therefore decided to look at the possibility of sponsoring a PhD student to study the politics of Newport in the 2nd half of the 20th century – with the idea that this would help me uncover and understand the events of interest, resulting in a much more balanced and robust book.

As such, the first person I identified to contact was Professor Duncan Tanner, history professor and research director at Bangor University who was arguably the country's leading expert on the British Labour Party. By chance, he was also someone born and brought up in Newport when Aubrey was at his political peak. Unfortunately, searching for him on the internet brought up his obituary rather than his contact details; he had died unexpectedly a few weeks before at the ridiculously young age of 51. Contacting the University of South Wales, I then met Dr Richard Allen and Professor Ray Howell, and after various discussions over a period of more than three years, identified the perfect student, Jim Criddle, a retired teacher and councillor from Pontllanfraith. Working with Dr Richard Allen, Jim threw himself into his PhD studies and started to uncover many of the political events of Newport's past. Unfortunately though, two years into his studies Jim died of prostate cancer, the same disease that had taken Aubrey. Also lost was about a year of Jim's research, stored on a pen drive that could not be found (and no hard copies).

With subsequent redundancies at the University of South Wales, and other organisational changes, including significant increases in student fees, I therefore made the decision to carry on my research without the help of a PhD student. Having taken 4 years from contacting the University to Jim starting his studies, time was no longer on my side.

Many events from Aubrey's past were either undocumented, or there was little known about them, so the interviews were to be a key aspect of this book. As soon as possible, I started the process of identifying, finding, and interviewing as many people as possible, starting with those people who knew Aubrey from the earliest time in his life. The obvious person to start with was my mother Mary, Aubrey's wife. However, suffering from dementia that would soon take her life and although she enjoyed talking about the past, I gained little information from her. At this time Aubrey's Uncle Mervyn, his mother's brother, was also alive, but like my mother, he was also suffering from dementia and was no longer able to recall any events from the past. However, Aubrey's sister-in-law Nell Hames, and Mary's sister June Williams were invaluable with their insights, and as always, it was a pleasure to have an excuse to talk with them.

Outside family members, my first interview took place in April 2010 with Newport West MP, Paul Flynn, and his wife Sam. Paul introduced me to Reginald Silas Tyack, Labour's first "ex officio" council leader, who became such a key figure in this book that he even has a chapter based around him. Paul and Sam also gave me my first insight into the selection conference for the Labour candidate for the 1966 General Election, where Aubrey was expected to secure the nomination but allegedly choked. Thirteen years later I now know that the nomination was lost before the conference began, and if he had choked, it probably would have had something to do with my first appearance into the world four days previously. This interview was followed up by one with Connie and Clive Evans in Newtown. Connie married Aubrey during the 2nd World War, and was also the mother of Carole, the sister I never knew, who died before her 2nd birthday in 1950. It was wonderful to see Connie again having met her almost by accident in the late 1980s, as well as her husband Clive and their children Linda and Phillip, with whom I shared a half-sister. Unfortunately, just like my mother and my Great Uncle Mervyn, Connie was also suffering from dementia, although Clive and their daughter provided many details about Aubrey and Carole that I didn't know, as well as photos of Carole, that I hadn't previously seen. In 2013 when Connie died, Linda rang me on the morning of her death, and I attended her funeral where I was introduced to cousins and nephews and nieces of Connie. None of them had seen Aubrey since the 1940s, yet the love and affection, as well as the memories of Aubrey, were remarkable from people all of whom were children when they knew him. This was best demonstrated by Margaret Crew, Connie's niece. When I first met her and introduced myself, the first thing she said before I even entered her house was "Oh I loved him." This was a sentiment I was to hear often.

Most interviews for this book took place over the period 2011-2014. They included all the major political figures in Newport who had known Aubrey in the 1970s, as well as people who knew him during the war. The interviewee with the earliest memories of Aubrey was Chris Brawn, a friend of Aubrey's from his time in Newtown in the early 1940s and the wife of Aubrey's best friend in the Army. I interviewed people who had known Aubrey in every decade from the 1940s, but could find surprisingly few people who knew him in the 1960s, the decade where most stories in this book took place. This means that there are more uncertainties in this book from that period than I anticipated. However, I found Labour Party minutes and newspaper reports from this time to be remarkably candid, giving the circumstances and personal opinions around events, rather than just the facts. Interviews took place as far north as Sunderland, and as far south as Plymouth. The furthest I travelled for an interview was to Israel. The shortest I travelled was a quarter mile walk to the bowls club at the top of my road where I interviewed someone I had being trying to find for twelve years.

I was determined that I wasn't going to start this biography with the phrase "Aubrey was born …", and it turns out that if I had, the first line may well have been incorrect. Everyone knew him as Aubrey, Aub or in correspondence A.E. Hames. However, nobody, including myself or my brother or sisters knew that he was christened E.A. Hames – Edward Aubrey Hames. The only other place where I have found Edward before Aubrey apart from on his birth certificate was on an application for a job in the 1980s, although schoolboy rugby team sheets from the 1930s also refer to him as E.A. Hames. However, having started at the beginning, I soon found out my first and very important lesson when writing a biography; you start with the chapters you can work on, and when you get stuck, you move onto the next chapter you can work on. As you find out more, you move to new material, or return to previous chapters, and gradually, over a long period of time, chapters get finalised, and missing facts are uncovered. But having said that, chapters (or the book as a whole) can never be regarded as completely finished – especially when considering the most controversial or "interesting" parts of the story. I also made the decision very early on in my research to just use the phrase "the council" or "Newport Council". The various name changes of the council over the years – from the "Corporation", to the "Borough" of Newport (but not the "City" of Newport in Aubrey's lifetime) meant that I could have spent a considerable period of time trying to get this right depending on the time period I was talking about. I undoubtedly would have got this wrong several times, and it would have served no purpose beyond confusing most readers. I also suspect few people would worry.

Having started at the beginning, and while waiting for further material to be uncovered, I soon moved on to the chapter on Aubrey's time with the British Transport Docks Board (BTDB). He was employed with the BTDB from 1950 until he was sacked in 1979. The reason for his dismissal was because of spurious criminal charges that were brought against him, and that made national headlines. Ultimately, his case was thrown out of court. A television documentary was made, questions were raised in Parliament, and Aubrey was awarded record damages for unfair dismissal. With several thousand pages of notes, police witness statements, and various bits of BTDB paperwork in my possession, it was a relatively easy task to put this chapter together despite a significant number of people refusing to be interviewed about it. Most people ignored my requests, some said they couldn't remember, or that it was a long time ago. Others got a relative to respond on their behalf. In many cases, they would have been telling the truth about their inability to participate, although I do know that efforts were made by former members of the British Transport Police and the BTDB to stop people talking to me, just as efforts were made to stop people talking to the television documentary team in 1983. However, the one former member of the British Transport Police who worked on Aubrey's case, and who I most wanted to talk to, did talk to me – Maurice Woodman. Formally the most senior investigating officer of the British Transport Police, he had led the investigation, and the relatively short interview I had with him was invaluable. Subsequently, I tracked down and talked to his successor, Graham Satchwell, who knew nothing of Aubrey's case but who has written extensively about corruption in the British Transport Police in recent years. He is now persona non grata among many of his ex-colleagues and proved to be invaluable in helping to write this chapter. His last book is about Detective Sergeant Derek Ridgewell, who is probably responsible for more individual miscarriage of justice cases that have since been overturned than any other police officer in British history. Satchwell's research also revealed a link between Ridgewell and Maurice Woodman, and others, investigating Aubrey's case. Many people mentioned in this chapter come out with little credit, and I suggest that this number includes a few people who had, or ended up with, knighthoods.

As the first draft of the chapter on Aubrey's time on the BTDB was finished, I continued to work on the chapters that were easiest to write while simultaneously working my way through various Labour Party and council minutes, as well as newspaper reports and archived material across the UK. Many researchers provided invaluable help, particularly members from the Newport Reference Library. As further chapters were written, I also felt an obligation to tell the story of each event, not just Aubrey's role in them. This was particularly the case for events relating to Newport about which little, if anything, has been written. Background reading for these events was also based on versions of books relevant to the time, not necessarily the latest versions which may have been updated to cover a different time period. For events on the bigger stage, such as the situation faced by Aubrey when he served with the British Army in India and Palestine towards the end of the 1940s, I have assumed that the reader is unfamiliar with the background to these events, so have covered these accordingly. This has inherently made the book longer, but hopefully more interesting.

Unfortunately, one aspect of trying to write about events from the past is the attribution of praise or blame for whatever happened. Many people interviewed for this book talked about Aubrey's intelligence, honesty, financial acumen, and intimate knowledge of government policy, as well as his remarkable ability to turn people around to his way of thinking. But only council decisions are noted in minutes and debates are lost to time. In many cases therefore, it is not possible to ascertain what role, if any, Aubrey played. However, Labour party minutes give more details. They often record who said what, who instigated what and any debate or argument that ensued. As such, Aubrey's role in the Labour Party from the 1950s is clear. By a considerable margin, he played the most significant role in the evolution of the Labour Party in Newport in its history, and in the process, turned it from an institution that prioritised the interests of its aldermen and councillors, to one that prioritised the interests of its constituents. It would not surprise me if no individual across the UK has ever revolutionised a local Labour Party the way he did. This meant that by the 1970s it was 20 years ahead of other Labour groups in Gwent, as well as probably every other Labour group across Wales. His first minuted action as a councillor, Labour's youngest in Newport since the war, was a vote of no confidence in the leader of the Labour group, the dominant group on the council. Since the war, this was by far the most controversial event recorded in the Labour Party minutes in Newport, until he launched his second (and this time successful) attempt to remove the same person as leader nine years later. His attempt to remove the leader of the Labour group was all the more remarkable during this time when new councillors were expected to keep quiet and pay heed to the more senior members of the party. Because of Aubrey, by the time Dame Rosemary Butler and Paul Flynn were elected as councillors in Newport in the early 1970s, matters were debated, decisions made by consensus, and Labour Party members were equal regardless of age or experience. Across the rest of Gwent, and probably elsewhere, this was not the case; matters were not debated, seniority dominated the decision-making process, and new councillors had no say in the running of the party or the decisions made. This was to change from 1974 onwards with the creation of Gwent County Council and the influence that the Newport councillors – shaped by Aubrey's actions over the previous 20 years – had on this council.

Despite this, as mentioned above, there are still some events where Aubrey's role is unclear. Several people I have talked to have used the phrase "the man who saved Tredegar House," yet I have found little evidence that he played any more significant a role than anybody else. The decision to buy Tredegar House was at his instigation and without Aubrey it would no longer exist. However, the same could probably be said of several people, some of whom may ultimately have played a more significant role. Consequently, there will be instances where I have underplayed Aubrey's role, but equally others where I have probably given him more credit than he deserves. The obvious one may be the role he played in stopping what was to become the M4 motorway passing right through the middle of Newport, tunnelling under Maesglas and segmenting Newport into four. He may have had no influence in stopping this, or he may have played the key role. However, as this was the first event that he mentioned in his acceptance speech for the Freedom of Newport, it suggests the latter. I do though have a better idea of the role he had in building the Newport Centre – an event that I remember at the time. Although the original idea wasn't his, he convinced the council that they could afford it, and he got the national government to pay for most of it taking advantage of loopholes in government legislation. This meant that he successfully avoided saddling Newport ratepayers with a long-lasting debt. The disappointing decision to demolish the Newport Centre in 2021, just 36 years after it was built – due to a lack of proper maintenance – had nothing to do with Aubrey or with the council at the time it was built.

By the time Aubrey died in 1998, he was without doubt the best known and most respected citizen of Newport. A man who had turned down every honour offered to him, ended up being possibly the most honoured individual within Newport, by the people of Newport, in its history. He had turned down the offer of the Freedom of Newport multiple times, finally agreeing to accept it in his dying days when he was asked to accept it for his family rather than for himself. He was made an Honorary Alderman without being asked, and the decision to name a road after him was passed in a council meeting without his knowledge after being proposed by the Conservative group. He even had a poem written about him. It would surprise nobody that he had previously turned down national honours.

ACKNOWLEDGMENTS

In writing this book I have had to rely on the help and generosity of a significant number of people. Most of these knew Aubrey well, although others had never met nor heard of him. Regardless of whether they knew him or not, they willingly offered their time and patience to answer the many questions and queries that I asked. Unfortunately many of these people have since passed away, something that I realised was inevitable when I started my research. Some would have enjoyed reading this book, and it is a great sadness that I was unable to finish it sooner.

First of all I have to thank my wife Ruth, who over the last thirteen years has travelled with me to attend numerous interviews, as well as trips to various archives and libraries all over the UK in the hope of finding bits of information that may, or may not be of use. She has suffered hours of solitude as I have carried out my research in the evenings, as well as the presence of the large and ugly microfilm viewer used to look at various documents. Over the last eight years she has sometimes had to amuse our son and daughter as I "popped into a library" for an hour or two. In her professional capacity, Ruth identified my half-sister Carole's medical condition at birth, as well as the likely cause of her death and details of Aubrey's cancer treatment towards the end of his life. I also owe a debt of gratitude to other family members including my mother, my brother Robin and sisters Annette and Janine and brother-in-law Ian who answered whatever questions I put to them. I also owe an additional thanks to Annette for offering to proof-read the first draft of this book and correcting the many grammatical mistakes that I would never have spotted. My nieces Eleanor and Su were also a great help in typing up copies of their grandfather's early diaries for what was a pittance, even though it appeared a fortune to young teenagers. It was also a pleasure to talk to my two aunts, Nell and June about their recollections as well as to Aubrey's cousin, John Craven-Griffiths, who over the years had done a remarkable job of putting together Aubrey's mother's family tree. To this list I will also add Carol Collins my sister-in-law and her father John Wright. John was at the selection conference for the Labour candidate for Newport in 1966 at a time when he did not know Aubrey, yet many years later was to share their first grandchild.

Paul Flynn was invaluable in getting me started on this biography. He had an encyclopaedic knowledge of the history of the Newport Labour Party unsurpassed by anybody else I interviewed. He helped identify the early questions that I should ask, together with some of the answers, and even though the passage of time may have meant he got a date or name slightly wrong, his recollections meant I knew what to look for, where to find it, and if necessary, how to identify the correct details. Paul and his wife Sam were always welcoming when I called, even though I often just turned up on their doorstep unannounced. Paul was even willing to answer questions in his dying days. Apart from Paul, many other of Newport's current and former Labour and Conservative councillors or members willingly submitted to an interview or helped me in my research. This included former leaders of the council Bob Bright, Sir Harry Jones, Trevor Warren and Matthew Evans, the current (at the time) Presiding Officer of the Welsh Assembly Dame Rosemary Butler and her husband Derek, Ron Jones, Harry Williams, Clive Shakesheff, Gerald Davies, David Mayer, Joshua Worrad, Debbie Harvey, Pat Drewett and Paul Cockeram. It was also a pleasure to get to talk to Shirley Newnham and Marion Marsh many years after I had last seen them. Shirley, who regularly used to babysit me on Sunday mornings as my father did his ward rounds had a knowledge of the Labour Party in Newport that most closely matched Paul Flynn's. Marion, a family friend and wife of Aubrey's best friend in politics John Marsh knew Aubrey longer than most and provided recollections of my father back to the early 1950s, one of the few people I interviewed who knew him at that time. Marion died a few weeks after I interviewed her, and this was a sad reminder of what I knew would happen in some cases, and a difficult thing to absorb at the time.

These various interviews with members of both the Newport Labour and Conservative parties also introduced me to someone called Stewart Watson, who preceded Aubrey as leader of the council in Newport. Although Stewart Watson was no longer alive when I started this book, I interviewed his daughter Mary Evans, and his wife Patricia Watson, 91 at the time, the oldest person I interviewed. Mary over several years has provided me with lots of useful information about her father, including details of his relationship with my father unknown to those who knew them politically.

Outside the scores of books read for background material, as well as the Newport Labour Party minutes that kept my microfilm viewer busy, the main body of information was contained in numerous archives and libraries across the UK. The main source of information came from Newport Reference Library where first Ryan Pimm and later Lionel Clauzon carried out hundreds of hours of research for me. Lionel as a result probably now has a knowledge of the South Wales Argus in the 2nd half of the 20th century unmatched by anybody else. Many others from the Reference Library in Newport helped, some of whom I would have been unaware of. However they include Alex

Jarvis, Helen Griffiths, Tracey Paddon and Jessica Harding. Similar thanks also have to be given to staff at Gwent Archives including Colin Gibson, Kai Michael, Angela Saunderson, Frances Younson and Gareth Thomas, who answered my queries, carried out research for me and looked after me on my trips to Ebbw Vale. Other people whom I owe thanks to from different libraries or similar organisations across the UK include Elaine Arthurs (STEAM Museum of the GWR), Mark Beswick (Archive Information Officer, Met. Office), Beryl George (Lincolnshire Family History Society), Sonia Gomes (London School of Economics), Wendy Hawke (London Metropolitan Archives), Richard Head (Assault Glider Trust), Paul Hendriks (Exhibition Glider Collection, Wolfheze), Mike Houle (BRS historian), Bruce Kennedy (former researcher for HTV Wales), Dr. Christopher Knowles (visiting research fellow, King's College London), Paul Lowe (Palestine Remembered), Brigadier Andrew Paviour (Museum of Army Flying, Middle Wallop), Ken Pearce (Uxbridge Local History and Archives Society), Bob Rust (BRS historian), Peter Strong (Gwent County History Association), Kate Trenbath (Assistant Branch Librarian, Newtown), Jessamy Wilsdon (research assistant, Dorset History Group), Joanne David and Chris Davies (Newport Live) and Dave Pasley (Glider Pilot Regiment Family Members Group). I also need to thank the many independent researchers, historians and genealogists who spent many hours digging around in archives that I was unable to visit. These were Charlotte Austin, Clive Beardsmore, Sara Fox, Christopher Gardner, Kate McCaffrey, Sara McMahon (The Family History Company), Mike Sharpe, Derek Tait and Sabina Von Thuemmler. I am particularly indebted to Sabina as my inability to read German was one of many reasons I would have been unable to carry out research into various German archives.

For Aubrey's time in the army and his life in the 2nd World War, my greatest thanks must go to Connie and Clive Evans and they daughter Linda Tinker, as well as various relatives of Connie Evans. These include Margaret Crew, Mair Jones, Ray Jones, David Lewis and Ruth Lewis, all of whom made my wife and I very welcome when we visited them. Chris Brawn, a friend of Aubrey's in the 1940s and wife of Aubrey's best friend Fred Brawn provided invaluable information on Aubrey's time with Connie, information that nobody else could have known. Ken Kirkham, a Glider Pilot in the 2nd World War and a friend of Aubrey was a pleasure to meet, and someone I would have loved to have met in my younger days. It was a very sad moment for both my wife and I when I read of the announcement of his death in the Glider Pilot Regiment Society Magazine. Mark Smith, formerly curator of the Royal Artillery Museum Woolwich, now better known as the resident medal expert on the Antiques Roadshow was always welcoming when I went to see him as he made sense of various army documents, including my father's war record. Others who I have to thank for their help during Aubrey's time in the war are Chris Brawn (Fred and Chris' son), Bill Brunskill (colleague of Aubrey in the Glider Pilot Regiment), Ken Mead (Second World War Glider Pilot), Des Page (Second World War Glider Pilot), Phillip Barber (pre-war trumpeter in the Royal Artillery) and Paul Evans (Librarian, Royal Artillery Museum Woolwich). I also need to add local Newtown historian David Pugh to this list who helped dig out many details of Aubrey's time in Newtown, the type of information that only local historians know how to find.

For all the help and assistance I received in writing this book, there was one chapter where I knew from the start that I was likely to find few people who would give me any help, with some even making efforts to hinder my research efforts. Aubrey's time at the BTDB and the subsequent events that led to his dismissal would have been difficult for some and awkward for many. As such, great credit must go to Maurice Woodman, former Det. Chief Superintendent of the British Transport Police and the person who led the investigation into Aubrey's case. He had little to gain from talking to me, but still made the effort to ring me up.

One person who I was very keen to identify and interview for this book was a senior member of a police force in the 1970s, preferably someone who knew Aubrey. This was to get a feel for what the culture and practices of the British Transport Police would have been at this time. I thought I would struggle to find someone to talk to, but in my wildest dreams, I never expected to be able to find and talk to Maurice Woodman's successor, someone who knew him well and worked under him. Graham Satchwell has been invaluable in helping to write this book. He has been extremely candid when I have talked to him, and his subsequent book that outlines the crimes of the corrupt policeman Derek Ridgewell and the role Maurice Woodman played in hiding these crimes has completely changed the complexion of the chapter on Aubrey's time at the BTDB. His offers to read drafts of the chapter on Aubrey's time on the BTDB, as well as providing contacts that I could never have expected to find means that this chapter is considerably better than I could have imagined, and I am extremely grateful to him. Putting me in contact with John Jones, Head of Investigations at the Criminal Cases Review Commission also helped me uncover details of the law that existed at the time, something that I was struggling to work out. I therefore also owe a large debt of gratitude to John Jones. Another key interview carried out for this chapter was with Derek Mason, one of Aubrey's co-accused and the shortest distance I had to travel for an interview, which took place on the road that I lived. Derek cleared up many details of this case that I could not understand and I am extremely grateful to him for that. I also owe a debt of gratitude to Hana Ichilov, the former wife of Lihu Ichilov, the other man charged in this case. Although my interview with Hana had to be abandoned as she fell ill just before I travelled to Israel, talking to her on the phone before I left provided me with unrivalled information on Aubrey's past stretching back to his childhood, as well, of course, the details of his court case.

Others I would like to thank are the following. Michael Cole for providing a digital copy of an aerial photograph of Raglan Barracks used by Luftwaffe pilots during the Second World War to enable them to identify their targets. Fr. Michael Doyle of St. Mary's Church in Newport for enabling me to find out information on my parents' marriage. Iris Dyer for her recollections from working with my father at the Dock's Board. Francesca Gillett and Kevin Ward for facilitating an article in the South Wales Argus to help me find information on my father. I also have to thank Kevin Ward for his help in promoting this book, much of which will have taken place after it was published. Arena Books for their careful editing and all their help in getting this book to print. Professor Madeleine Gray at the University of South Wales for helping me track down information on life in Pontypool in the 1920s. Meg Gurney for telling me all about the house where my father was born. Adrian Guthrie, Rector St. Giles Church in Ickenham for trying to help me find school records from Swakely School in the 1930s. Anne Hobbs and Jeanette Webb for providing access to historic Brynglas School records. Anne Gardner, daughter of Staff Sergeant Alec Williams, for providing photographs and some details from her father's time in the Glider Pilot Regiment. David Hughes for memories of his time as a child in 1920s and 1930s Pontypool. Dianne Huntley for memories of my father's first election contest in Baneswell in 1953. Professors Dick Leonard and David Marquand for their memories from standing as parliamentary candidates in the 1960s. Andrew Miller for memories of his grandfather, Sydney Teece Miller, a former leader of Newport Borough Council. Paul Murphy and Don Touhig, former members of Tony Blair's government and current members of the House of Lords for finally making me realise how significant and influential my father was in the national Labour party. I also owe additional thanks to Paul Murphy for agreeing to write the forward for this book. Ella Mutha for all the photographs she provided to me taken by her mother Tish when my father was Mayor of Newport. Bryan Roden and James Skinner for providing original copies of photographs from their books on Pontypool and the surrounding areas and Ickenham and Hillingdon respectively. Kathy Rustell for her sterling, and continuing work on the website about my father.

Alan Shewring for his memories of my father when they were establishing St. Joseph's school. Robin Weaver, former photographer at the South Wales Argus, for permission to use some of his photographs in this book, particularly the wonderful image on the front cover. Mike Buckingham for memories of my father when he was a reporter on the South Wales Argus. Ian Wheeler for details and photographs of the Horsa glider once used as a house in Cholsey, where I lived when I started this book. David Williams, former reporter for HTV Wales for his insights into the television documentary on my father's court case. Gary Stuart for his recollections of his uncle Owen "Herbie" Andrews, my father's best friend at school. Richard Frame for his recollections of working with my father in his later life. Alison Powell and Sharon Challingsworth for their recollections of the redevelopment of Pill in the 1970s. David Brightmore for details of the Housing Action Areas and General Improvement Areas which he managed between 1975 and 1982, as well as John Bader who was Newport's Housing manager when redevelopment and rehabilitation was at its height in Newport. David and John were instrumental in helping out with arguably the most difficult chapter to write, and one still fresh in the minds of many residents of Newport.

Finally, I cannot finish these acknowledgments without mentioning Dr Richard Allen, formally at the University of South Wales and Jim Criddle. I really appreciate Richard for first engaging with me in identifying a suitable PhD student to cover the post-war political scene in Newport, and acting as Jim's supervisor. Subsequently Jim threw himself into his studies and I have little doubt that if fate had allowed him to finish, this book would have been immeasurably better as a result.

For any others I have missed off I most sincerely apologize. Despite my best intentions to keep track of everybody who helped me write this book, I did not keep as good a record as I had hoped.

CHAPTER 1

CHILDHOOD

Arthur Hames arrives in South Wales

By the time Aubrey's father, Arthur Hames, moved to Griffithstown in Pontypool from Dorchester towards the end of 1920, South Wales was at the start of an economic downturn that was to lead to mass unemployment and poverty without parallel in contemporary Britain.[1,2] At the centre of this downturn were the coalfields and the industries that depended on them. This included Pontypool Road Railway Station, in Griffithstown, which was the primary source of employment and development in the area, and the location of Arthur's new job as a railway goods porter.[3]

However, when Arthur first moved to Griffithstown there was initially little evidence of the economic problems that were to blight the area over much of the 1920s and 1930s. This was evidenced, for example, in the optimism displayed by the claim made by the South Wales miners for a 30% wage increase in March 1919.[4] Arriving at his new lodgings – 81 Commercial Street in Griffithstown – Arthur therefore probably saw a bright future ahead of him and, with no family ties, the opportunity to embark on a new and

---

[1] The Dorset electoral register of 1920 has Arthur registered to vote in Melcombe Regis. However, by the spring of 1921 the Monmouthshire County Council register of electors has him as registered to vote in Griffithstown. Having to be resident for 6 months before being eligible to vote, this suggests that Arthur probably moved to Griffithstown in the latter half of 1920.

[2] Morgan, K.O. *Rebirth of a nation: Wales, 1880-1980.* Oxford University Press, 1982.

[3] Lloyd, W.G. *Sebastopol. A local history.* Newport: Starling Press, 1992.

[4] Morgan, K.O.

hopefully secure career at one of the largest and busiest railway junctions in the country.

Arthur and Eleanor

Born in Weymouth in 1894, Arthur had not had an easy start to life. One of two illegitimate children born to Alice Hames, he spent little if any time in the care of his mother, who like her father before her suffered from long periods of depression.[5] Unable to look after either of her two children due to her mental health problems, Arthur was therefore initially brought up by his great uncle – his grandmother's brother – John Hames.[6] It is not known who Arthur's sibling was, or what happened to them.[7] At the age of eleven, his mother tried to commit suicide by jumping down a well, and was subsequently sectioned to the Herrison Hospital in Charminster. She died there two years later, thirty years after her own father, Arthur's grandfather, had died in the same institution. His guardian John Hames had died just one month earlier, and so Arthur was then taken into the care of his aunt Kathleen, Alice's sister.[8] These events undoubtedly affected Arthur; he was quiet and reserved, and like his mother and grandfather prone to periods of depression.[9] By the time he moved to Griffithstown this had already resulted in him having at least one nervous breakdown which had occurred shortly after leaving the navy at the end of the First World War.[10]

The house that Arthur moved into in 1920 was a typical Victorian terraced house of the period. He sublet a room there from William and Arthurena Davies – known as Bill and Lena respectively – who lived there with six

---

[5] Dorset History Centre. Herrison hospital female casebook 1904-1906. Ref: NG/HH/CMR/4/14B/8, and, Herrison Hospital casebook male & female 1873-1880. Ref: NG/HH/CMR/ 4/14/2.

[6] By sheer coincidence, Alice's parents John and Catherine Hames were the children of two different and unrelated couples both called John and Ann Hames.

[7] An extensive search of birth records of potential children has not identified who Arthur's sibling was. This suggests that they either died as an infant, or more likely were brought up by their father, or their father's family, taking his surname.

[8] In the 1901 census, Arthur is described as John Hames' son. 'John Rowland Hames' (1907). Certified copy of death certificate for John Rowland Hames, 8 February 1907. Sturminster Register Office.

[9] The Herrison hospital female casebook 1904-1906 described Arthur's mother Alice as someone who had never been a strong woman, always rather depressed and weakly. Similarly, the Herrison hospital male and female casebook 1873-1880 noted that Arthur's grandfather John was deeply depressed when admitted, and that this was a condition that he had suffered before.

[10] Private communication with Mary Hames, Aubrey's wife.

or seven children.[11] Poverty and rent arrears often forced families to sublet property at this time; Monmouthshire County Council registers of electors from this period indicate that it was quite common for two, or possibly even three families to live side by side in the small terrace houses of Griffithstown. Bill and Lena's household included the eldest and only girl, Eleanor, who was Lena's daughter from her first marriage to Frederick Craven-Griffiths, a theatre manager.[12] Despite Lena having a rich and successful merchant as an uncle – Thomas Cooke, who had twice been Mayor of Much Wenlock in Shropshire in the 1890s, and who later left £75,000 in his will when he died in 1931 – Bill and Lena struggled to provide the basic amenities for their family.[13,14] Their circumstances had already forced Lena to give up one child for adoption for financial reasons, and by the 1911 census, while married to Frederick, Lena was in Newington workhouse where Charlie Chaplin had stayed 15 years earlier.[15] While in the workhouse, she had given birth to a son while her daughter Eleanor was looked after by an aunt, and two other siblings by their grandmother.[16,17] Frederick's whereabouts were unknown. Soon after, Lena and Frederick were divorced and Lena returned to Monmouthshire, the county of her birth, where she married Bill Davies and moved to Griffithstown in early 1920.

Although Arthur, the lodger, and Eleanor, the daughter of the primary tenants, both shared the fact that they'd had difficult starts in life, they appeared to have little else in common. At twenty-six, Arthur was twelve years older than Eleanor, and was shy and reserved. Eleanor on the other hand was a confident and ambitious young lady, determined to make her own way in life. Eleanor was also a Baptist who liked to play the piano, whereas Arthur was a smoker who liked an occasional drink and a flutter on the horses – something that he had in common with Eleanor's stepfather, Bill. However, despite the differences between them, it appears that Arthur soon became very fond of Eleanor and wanted to marry her. These feelings weren't reciprocated by Eleanor who in later life described him as a "creepy

---

[11] She was called Arthurena as her parents wanted a boy whom they were going to call Arthur.

[12] Based on 1911 census records.

[13] Burial record in the English cemetery in Funchal, Madeira.

[14] Various sources, including private communication with John Craven-Griffiths, Aubrey's first cousin by his mother Eleanor. This is equivalent to about £4 million today.

[15] Private communication with Nell Hames, Aubrey's sister-in-law.

[16] Newington Workhouse Admission, Discharge and Creed Registers Jan 1907 to Dec 1913. Ref: SOBG. London Metropolitan Archives.

[17] Based on 1911 census records.

old man."[18] However, with Lena and Bill on poor relief and struggling to feed their family, not helped by Bill often spending his wages down the pub, they wanted Eleanor out of the house and encouraged the relationship.[19] Ultimately, Eleanor's mother forced her to marry Arthur.[20] The marriage took place on 16th April 1922 in Dorchester, the town where Arthur greup.[21,22] The marriage certificate, witnessed by Eleanor's stepfather Bill Davies, indicates that Eleanor's father probably did not approve of the marriage as he was incorrectly described on the certificate as deceased. Even though she was legally able to marry at this age without her parents' permission, Eleanor gave her age as 18 instead of 16, presumably to avoid potentially awkward questions. Arthur, obviously embarrassed by being illegitimate, gave his father's name as Arthur Charles Hames, a deceased Ironmonger. Six days before they were married, an Eleanor Davies in the same age range as Eleanor was discharged from the workhouse in Griffithstown.[23] It is not known if this was the same Eleanor (Eleanor was known as Davies at this time),[24] but if so, it highlights the impossible situation that this young woman was placed under. The life of a vagrant, or marriage to a man she now hated.

After the marriage, Arthur and Eleanor returned to Griffithstown and moved to 115 Greenhill Road, in the nearby suburb of Sebastopol, where Edward Aubrey Hames was born nine months later on 19th January 1923.[25] This was a good time for a future socialist and the future Mr Newport to be born. Just four months earlier, the famous 1922 by-election in Newport had, for the first time in history, led directly to the overthrow of a government.[26] This in turn, led to the first Labour government being unexpectedly formed in January 1924 – one year almost to the day after Aubrey was born. This was also only

---

[18] Interview with Robin Hames, Aubrey's eldest son and Eleanor's grandson, 29 November, 2022.

[19] Based on records from the poor relief order books, Panteg District searched from 1920. Gwent Archives.

[20] Private communication with Robin Hames, Aubrey's eldest son.

[21] "Arthur Charles Hames and Eleanor Maud Griffiths" Certified copy of marriage certificate of Arthur Charles Hames and Eleanor Maud Griffiths, 16 April, 1922. Baptist Chapel Dorchester.

[22] Various sources, including 1901 and 1911 census'.

[23] Pontypool Workhouse Administration Admission and Discharge Registers, Feb 1920-Jun 1924. Reference CSWBGP/I/238. Gwent Archives.

[24] From Aubrey's birth announcement in the South Wales Argus, 2nd February 1923.

[25] "Edward Aubrey Hames" Certified copy of birth certificate for Edward Aubrey Hames, 19 January 1923. Pontypool Register Office.

[26] Cook, C. and Ramsden, J. eds., *By-elections in British politics*. 2nd edition. London. Macmillan, 1997.

six years after the Labour Party had announced itself as a national political force at the 1918 General Election; with Griffithstown being represented for the first time (and ever since) by a Labour MP.[27]

The double-fronted house on the right of this photograph is 115 Greenhill Road in Sebastopol, where Aubrey was born in 1923, and lived for the first 2 years of his life. Built in 1855, this house no longer exists having been demolished in the 1960s.[28] Photograph courtesy of Bryan Roden.

Life in Griffithstown

Life for Arthur and Eleanor, like most people in Pontypool at this time, would have been difficult and many people were desperately poor.[29] With work scarce, the local workhouse had a steady stream of admissions who included the many vagrants who trawled the countryside at the time looking for work – including several members of the Regan family. Among these were the future uncle and great uncle of Aubrey's future wife Mary, who had not yet been born. Pontypool Road Railway station, which was the main loading

---

[27] Pontypool had returned a Labour MP since the constituency was founded in 1918. From the 1923 election until it was disbanded in 1983, more than 50% of the votes cast in every general election poll went to the Labour candidate.

[28] *Monmouthshire Merlin*. 15 July, 1855.

[29] Armstrong, E. *A Pontypool childhood in the 1920s*. Gwent County History Association, 2001.

5

point for coal for warships in the First World War, had lost about 30% of its coal trade since the end of the war, despite a short-lived localised economic boom in 1923.[30,31] As a result, railwaymen including Arthur, had been forced to take pay cuts which further exacerbating levels of poverty in the area.[32] However, despite the levels of squalor and deprivation that prevailed, people were generally law abiding, and the streets of Griffithstown, in daylight hours at least, would have been perfectly safe.[33] Few people owned their own property and the terraced houses in Griffithstown were mainly built for the expanding railway industry. As with Bill and Lena's house, these houses often had two families living side by side in cramped conditions. Yet even for the cramped conditions at the time, 115 Greenhill Road was small; with just four rooms, it had a total living area of about 20m² – probably less than half that of the typical terraced house.[34] Moreover, they likely shared it with another family and it was damp and prone to flooding from the rear during periods of heavy rain.[35,36] A typical house of the worst kind described by George Orwell in his famous book, *The Road to Wigan Pier*, this was clearly not a suitable environment to bring up a small child. Therefore, with the imminent birth of Aubrey's brother, Russell, they moved to 14 Florence Place in 1925. This was just a few roads away in nearby Griffithstown, and a two-minute walk from Eleanor's mother's house and her younger brothers, including Mervyn who was just a year older than Aubrey.

While living in Griffithstown, Aubrey received an elementary education at Griffithstown Infant's School (a short walk away on Oxford Street) and from the age of eight at the Junior School on Florence Place.[37] Here, he was one

[30] Wragg, D. *Wartime on the Railways*. Stroud. The History Press, 2006.

[31] A long running miners' strike in America in 1922 and the disruption to the German coal industry in 1923-24 due to the French seizure of the Ruhr Valley resulted in huge international demand for South Wales coal in 1923. This resulted in a lower unemployment rate in Wales than in any other part of the UK. However, this prosperity was short-lived, and by 1925 unemployment rates in the coal mining areas were rising, and economic conditions had worsened compared to their pre-1923 level (see Davies, J. A history of Wales).

[32] Wragg, D. *Wartime on the Railways*. Stroud. The History Press, 2006.

[33] Armstrong, E. *A Pontypool childhood in the 1920s*. Gwent County History Association, 2001.

[34] Hames, D. Conversation with Meg Gurney, resident of 113 Greenhill Road in the 1950s, 27 October, 2012.

[35] Various Monmouthshire County Council register of electors from spring 1923. Gwent Archives.

[36] Hames, D. Conversation with Meg Gurney, resident of 113 Greenhill Road in the 1950s, 27 October, 2012.

[37] Gwent Archives. School admission register for Griffithstown Junior School, 1923-1933. Reference CEA80/07.

of over four hundred students, over sixty of whom were in his year.[38] These were the same schools attended by his brother Russell, as well as his Uncle Mervyn.[37] Entries in the school logbook indicate that school life for Aubrey appeared to be little different from many of today's schools with, for example, lessons in English, Maths, History and Geography, school assemblies, and regular spelling tests.[39] Several entries in the logbook also highlight events that were considered of significance in both Griffithstown and the wider world at the time – of which easily the most prominent were the aviation feats of Amy Johnson in the 1930s. They include an entry celebrating the first solo flight of a woman from the UK to Australia; and the schoolchildren were assembled to mark the event during which the headteacher read out "Miss Johnson's message of account of this flight as it appeared in the columns of the Daily Mail."[40] Aubrey, like most of the children, probably listened in awe as he leant of Miss Johnson's feats, unaware that within fifteen years he too would be flying the same type of biplane as that flown by Amy Johnson. Overall, there are few entries that give evidence of what school life would have been like in Griffithstown. School holidays were little different to what they are now, with the school also closed for local and national elections. But one entry every year gave an indication of a certain local event of importance, namely the Baptist teas. On these days the school was closed "by order," presumably so that people could attend the event. This demonstrated the strong influence of the non-conformist churches on populations during this time, particularly in Griffithstown, where membership of the Baptist Church was one-tenth of the population (and was still growing, contrary to most areas in Wales).

The Baptist Church was certainly a major part of Aubrey's life as he grew up. His grandmother and mother were among those residents of Griffithstown who were members of the local Baptist Church, and entries in his diaries indicate that he was a Baptist as a child.[41,42] With many socialist pioneers emerging from a religious background, especially from the non-conformist churches, it may have been here that Aubrey was first exposed to his socialist ideals.[43]

---

[38] Gwent Archives. School logbook for Griffithstown Junior School, 1927-1949. Reference CEA80/03.

[39] Gwent Archives. School logbook for Griffithstown Junior School, 1927-1949. Reference CEA80/03.

[40] Gwent Archives. Reference CEA80/07.

[41] Hopkins, T. (2000) *A history of Griffithstown Baptist Church 1875-2000*. Griffithstown. Griffithstown Baptist Church.

[42] On 5th September 1943, one of Aubrey's diary entries reads "Shall I change to Baptist again?"

[43] Pugh, M. *Speak for Britain!: A new history of the Labour Party*. London. Vintage, 2011.

This was the same background from which the brilliant young orator and MP, Aneurin Bevan, emerged just 15 miles away in Ebbw Vale. Bevan was one of the most charismatic politicians of the 20th century and an inspiration to many future Labour politicians including Newport's two longest serving MPs, Roy Hughes and Paul Flynn.[44,45,46] The non-conformists' anti-smoking attitude was also one that Aubrey was to fall foul of later. Having been found smoking by his father, his "punishment" was to be treated to a cigar and a whisky. Promptly becoming sick, he never smoked again and rarely drank alcohol after that. The punishment had worked. Aubrey also had a great love for the cinema which was across the road from his grandmother's house. With his mother Eleanor playing the piano to accompany the silent movies of this time, it is likely that Aubrey went on a regular basis in his early childhood.[47]

However, these years of Aubrey's childhood were dominated by the economic conditions, and the disintegration of his parents' marriage. The Wall Street Crash of 1929 had plunged Britain into the longest and most widespread depression of the 20th century. South-East Wales, which relied heavily on the hard-hit coal and iron industries, was one of the worst affected areas of the country with unemployment rates in the region twice the national average, and little prospect of future work for the long-term unemployed.[48] This enhanced a widespread identification with, and loyalty to, the Labour Party across Industrial Wales.[49] Unemployment benefit was reduced to a level that only just prevented a family from outright starvation, and means testing introduced in 1931 meant that it was only available to those who had no other source of income such as savings.[50,] Wages were cut and some of

---

[44] It should be noted that Roy Hughes was MP for Newport before 1983, and Newport West after 1983. Paul Flynn was only MP for Newport East.

[45] Hughes, R. *Seek fairer skies*. Spennymoor. The Memoir Club, 2003.

[46] Flynn, P. *It must be Christmas*, 4 July, 2008. Available at: http://paulflynnmp.typepad.com/my_weblog/2008/07/it-must-be-christmas.html. Date accessed: 14/05/15.

[47] Around this time, approximately half the population went to the cinema at least once a week (see Stevenson, J. *Social history of Great Britain*).

[48] The Special Areas (Development and Improvement) Act of 1934 was brought in to deal with four "special" or "distressed" areas including South East Wales, which had been identified as having the highest unemployment rates in the 1930s, which was 44.5% at the time of the Act.

[49] Wrigley, C. ed., *A companion to early twentieth century Britain*. Oxford. Wiley-Blackwell, 2003.

[50] Unemployment rates in this period are usually based on the insured population, so therefore typically exclude categories such as the self-employed, agricultural labourers and married women who were not insured against unemployment. As a result, the total unemployed was almost certainly higher than given by the official figures.

8

the first to suffer were railwayman, including Aubrey's father, Arthur. This was at least the second cut in his wage since moving to Griffithstown.[51] As a railways' goods porter, he would have earned a basic wage of about 46 shillings (£2.30) in 1929, and by 1931 these wages were reduced by about 10%.[52] With the closure of the goods section of Pontypool Road in June 1930, and a 20% reduction in passenger income over the period 1929-1931, it is likely that Arthur as with many other railway workers in Griffithstown, took a much greater cut in his wage and was probably laid off for periods due to lack of work.[53] Already a relatively low paid profession (in about the lower 20 percentile for wages), by 1931 Arthur's wage would probably not have been more than 50% above unemployment benefit for a family of his size.[54] Based on figures published by Seebohm Rowntree it would have been comfortably below the probable poverty line.[55] Even with Eleanor's wages from the cinema, it is likely that Aubrey's parents struggled to maintain an acceptable standard of living which probably led to malnutrition for both Aubrey and Russell. Despite this, as they were both in employment at least some of the time, they were probably still better off than many in the Pontypool area. This poverty was noted to visibly shock Edward VIII when he visited South Wales in 1936.[56] Many of the children's clothes were ragged, ill-fitting and of poor quality, and with widespread malnutrition, many did not survive their childhoods. Out of economic necessity, attendance at school also suffered when children were sent to work to supplement their parents' meagre wages, especially during the hop-picking season in September.[57]

Move to London

Considering Eleanor's dislike for Arthur, it was inevitable that they would have problems in their marriage. As a result, it is believed that Eleanor left Arthur not long after Aubrey was born. They got back together shortly after,

---

[51] Approximately 70% of men who had been unemployed for more than a year in 1929 were coalminers (see Pilgrim Trust. Men without work).

[52] Branson, N. and Heinemann, M. *Britain in the nineteen thirties.* St. Albans. Granada, 1973.

[53] Hames, D. Email from Elaine Arthurs, STEAM museum of the GWR, Swindon, 31 May, 2013.

[54] This is based on an estimate for 1935 by Clarke, C. (1937) *Condition of Britain.* p. 258.

[55] Seebohm Rowntree was a sociological researcher and social reformer, who investigated poverty in York over several periods, including 1935. From his work, he established a minimum weekly wage necessary to secure the necessities for a healthy life.

[56] Morgan, K.O. *Rebirth of a nation: Wales, 1880-1980.* Oxford: Oxford University Press, 1982.

[57] Hughes, D. *Pontypool memories 1929-1947.* Bristol: Azimuth Print, 2010.

before moving to 14 Florence Place just before Russell was born in 1926, but the reconciliation was not long-lasting. Although 14 Florence Place remained Arthur's home for the next 10 years, Eleanor lived in a succession of houses within Griffithstown (but not back to her mother's house). Eleanor first returned to 115 Greenhill Road (just after Russell was born), where records indicate that she may have received poor relief.[58],[59] She did move back in with Arthur on at least two occasions, including one period of about four years between 1929 and 1933, however, with two young children to provide for, this was probably out of a need to avoid the workhouse, rather than out of choice. Although Eleanor worked in one of the few growth industries of the depression years, with approximately 50% more people working in cinemas in 1934 compared to 1930, this growth was to a great extent linked to the advent of sound movies.[60] With little need for a pianist, it is likely that Eleanor was a casualty of this growth rather than a beneficiary, and she probably lost her job. Any relationship between Eleanor and Arthur though was never going to last, and in 1934 Eleanor left Arthur completely and moved to Southall – a common destination for Welsh migrants in the 1930s.

Although the reasons for Eleanor leaving Griffithstown are not known, the almost certain loss of her job, coming at a time when unemployment reached its highest ever level, as well as her desire to get away from Arthur, probably meant that she had little choice.[61] With unemployment among the insured population in Pontypool around 45%, opportunities for alternative employment were limited, particularly for women in industrial South Wales where they comprised just 16% of the workforce compared to a UK average of 39%.[62] Eleanor was therefore one of approximately 115,000 people who left South Wales during the period 1931 to 1938 – which was the highest de-population of any region in the UK. Within the urban areas of Pontypool,

---

[58] The Monmouthshire County Council register of electors (Gwent Archives) suggests that Arthur lived at 14 Florence Place from at least the Autumn of 1925 until 1936. However, Griffithstown Baptist Church records show Eleanor living at 2-3 different addresses over the period 1927-1934.

[59] Panteg poor relief order books (Gwent Archives) that cover 1926 note an Ellie Griffiths receiving poor relief in 1926. This may have been Eleanor, particularly as it was rare for poor relief to be granted to a woman.

[60] Marquand, H. *The second industrial survey of South Wales*. Cardiff. National Industrial Development Council of Wales and Monmouthshire, 1937.

[61] Unemployment was almost 3 million amongst the insured workers in the winter of 1932/33, the highest unemployment since records began in 1881 (based on data from the Office for National Statistics).

[62] Davies, J. *A history of Wales*. London. Penguin, 2007.

this led to an annual reduction in population of about 1.5% per year.[63] Many of these emigrants moved to London where the unemployment rate was about a quarter of that of Pontypool, and an area that experienced a 14% increase in the insured population over the period 1932 to 1937.[64] However, Eleanor's move to Southall appeared to be quite sudden, as she went without taking Aubrey and Russell. When she later wrote to Arthur asking him to send the children, he initially refused but later relented.[65] Aubrey and Russell therefore left Griffithstown Junior School on 17th May 1934.[66] By this time, it is believed that Eleanor had moved to 82 Victoria Avenue, Uxbridge, in Hillingdon, to live with her father, Frederick, and stepmother. With a father who was a theatre manager, and with an apparent love of the expanding entertainment business, this would have been an obvious move for Eleanor. In this London borough of Hillingdon, unemployment rates were about a third of what they were in Wales, and with cinemas and theatres springing up like mushrooms in the area, this not only improved Eleanor's opportunities for employment in general, but also potentially for employment specifically in the entertainment business.[67,68] For Aubrey and Russell, the contrast between their new home and the bleak environment where they had been born, could not have been starker. Between 1932 and 1937, 80% of all new factories built were in Greater London, with 66% of new employment also created in these areas.[69] Those in employment enjoyed a richer life than previously known, including longer holidays, shorter hours, and higher wages.[70] When Aubrey attended the recently-opened Swakeleys School in Ickenham (a short five-minute walk from his grandfather's house), he would have seen many of his fellow pupils picked up by their parents in their motor cars and observed the radios and electrical appliances inside their houses, as well as the Sony Records shop where his mother worked for a while.[71,72] If he wasn't a socialist when he arrived in Hillingdon, the contrast between this

---

[63] Marquand, H. *The second industrial survey of South Wales*. Cardiff. National Industrial Development Council of Wales and Monmouthshire, 1937.

[64] Branson, N. and Heinemann, M.

[65] Private communication with Mary Hames, Aubrey's wife.

[66] Gwent Archives. Reference CEA80/07.

[67] Stevenson, J. and Cook, C. *Britain in the depression: Society and politics, 1929-1939.* London. Longman, 1994.

[68] Skinner, J. *Images of London - Hillingdon cinemas*. Stroud. Tempus, 2002.

[69] Branson, N. and Heinemann, M.

[70] Taylor, A.J.P. *English history 1914-1945*. Oxford. Clarendon., 1965.

[71] This comes from a job application of Aubrey's in the 1980s, where he states he went to Swakeleys School in Hillingdon in the 1930s.

[72] Private communication with Nell Hames, Aubrey's sister-in-law.

area and Pontypool, probably meant that he was by the time he left.

As for Eleanor, despite the opportunities, she struggled to keep hold of a job and maintain a living in Hillingdon – probably not helped by the reluctance of many public authorities and firms to employ women who had children as well as the lower wages for women even when they were doing the same jobs as men.[73,74] Therefore, with the depression biting, she returned to South Wales in 1935 and moved back in with Arthur. With the continuing decline in income from passengers at Pontypool Road, Arthur was now living in Newport, in a flat at 8 Hollybush Crescent in Malpas (now 373 Malpas Road), above the Post Office.[75] Apart from his time in the army and a brief period living in Newtown, this was to remain Aubrey's home for the next 20 years.

Aubrey arrives in Newport

A return to Arthur was probably a difficult decision for Eleanor, born out of necessity rather than any other reason. However, Eleanor did not stay with Arthur long, leaving him about a year later for one of the lodgers who shared their flat.[76] This time, Aubrey and Russell stayed with Arthur, and Eleanor never returned. Arthur and Eleanor never saw each other again although they never divorced.[77] Left to look after the two boys on his own, Arthur found it a struggle, and just as with his mother and grandfather at a similar age in their lives, he became noticeably more depressed. This came to a head one day, when returning home from work he found an old railway sleeper that he took home for firewood.[78] After being questioned by the police over this incident, his mental health appeared to deteriorate rapidly and he suffered another nervous breakdown.[79] Although it is believed he was not charged, Arthur never got over this incident and over the next 20 to 30 years he was regularly admitted to the St. Cadoc's Psychiatric Hospital in Caerleon.[80]

---

[73] Thorpe, A. (1992) *Britain in the 1930s*. Historical Association Studies. Oxford. Blackwell.

[74] Women in the 1930s were typically paid two-thirds of male wage rates for the same job.

[75] Branson, N. and Heinemann, M.

[76] Private communication with Mary Hames, Aubrey's wife.

[77] Only one of them would attend future family events.

[78] Private communication with Annette Hames, Aubrey's eldest surviving daughter.

[79] Ibid.

[80] Mental health issues resulted in Arthur being admitted to St. Cadocs Hospital in Caerleon several times over the years. Although admission records show that he was admitted at least twice in the 1960s, it is believed that he was initially admitted shortly after the accusation of theft, and effectively became a permanent resident in about 1951.

Much of the responsibility for looking after Russell, and to an extent Arthur, now fell onto Aubrey.

Despite all the difficulties in his home life, Aubrey managed to do well at school, particularly in mathematics, sport and art.[81] Enrolling at Brynglas Central School from March 1936, Aubrey clearly enjoyed his later school years, although not to the same extent as some pupils who deliberately failed their exams so that they could prolong their time there.[82] In an environment where sport, music and drama were encouraged, Aubrey played for the school rugby, football and baseball teams, captaining the rugby team in the 1936/37 season.[83] Representing the town rugby team in this season, he helped them reach the semi-final of the Welsh Schools National Rugby competition, the Dewar Shield (and a round further than when I played in the same competition over 40 years later). Here, they lost their only match of the season to Cardiff.[84] Aubrey's abilities on the rugby pitch also led to an unsuccessful trial for Welsh Schoolboys, which he admitted to me in the 1980s went dreadfully.

It was on his return to Newport that the first known signs of his political activity emerged. On 9th March 1938, at the age of 15, he was appointed draw secretary of the Malpas Labour Party and later that year he attended the count for the selection of a councillor for the Malpas Ward in the local elections.[85,86] As in Griffithstown, he was in the right place at the right time for a future politician with socialist ideals. Newport Labour Party was one of the largest in the UK at this time, and in his walk to school he passed the houses of two prominent Malpas Labour councillors, Mary Dunn and Thomas Mooney.[87] Both future mayors, and later as aldermen, they sat with Aubrey on the council when he started his political career in the 1950s.

Aubrey attended Brynglas Central School until shortly after his 16th birthday in January 1939, having stayed on past the school leaving age of 14 to further

---

[81] Davies, T. Aubrey Hames reference from Brynglas School headmaster. 20 October, 1938.

[82] Hobbs, A. *The Story of Bryn-Glas House.* Newport. Brynglas Community Education Centre, 1989.

[83] This comes from a job application of Aubrey's in the 1980s, where he states he went to Swakeleys School in Hillingdon in the 1930s.

[84] "Newport boys draw, but Cardiff backs were superior." *South Wales Argus.* 28 April, 1937.

[85] Malpas Ward Labour Party. Minutes of Malpas Labour Party meeting. 9 March, 1938.

[86] Hames, D. Personal diary for 1938 of Aubrey Hames.

[87] Tanner, D., Thane, P. and Tiratsoo, N. eds., *Labour's first century.* Cambridge University Press, 2000.

his education.[88] Applying to join the RAF, he passed the entrance exam, but later failed the medical, although he later successfully managed to join the army; with war with Germany imminent, like many other pupils at Brynglas Central School, he signed up as a boy solider on 24th January 1939.[89]

Newport Boys Rugby Team 1936/7. Aubrey is standing in the back row, 2nd from left. On his left is Herbie Andrews, his best friend from Brynglas School.

---

[88] Until the Education Act 1944, you could leave school at 14.

[89] Army personnel centre. A.E. Hanes army service records. Army No. 889196.

CHAPTER 2

THE WAR YEARS

Boy soldier

With the annexation of Austria and the Sudetenland into Nazi Germany over the previous nine months, by the start of 1939, Europe was slowly but inevitably slipping into another world war. Today, joining one of the armed forces at a time like this may not seem like an obvious choice for a 16-year-old boy with his whole life ahead of him. However, with the depression of the 1930s not yet at an end, it seemed for many like a better choice than unemployment, and a more attractive option than a potential career in the mines or on the railways.[1] Driven by a rapid recruitment drive due to Germany's activities at this time, many of Aubrey's contemporaries admitted that they joined the armed forces because they saw no prospect of work elsewhere; the army offered a solid career, with three (basic) meals a day, accommodation, and free clothing.[2,3] And for Aubrey, like many others, he would also have seen it as a bit of an adventure and an opportunity to leave behind a difficult childhood, particularly now that his brother Russell had reached an age where he could provide for himself.

---

[1] This was a career followed effectively by default by Michael Touhig and Ronald Murphy, both fellow Pontypool boys a few years older than Aubrey. They are the fathers of Paul Murphy and Don Touhig, both former colleagues of Aubrey in the Labour Party, and now members of the House of Lords.

[2] Chandler, D. and Beckett, I. *The Oxford history of the British Army*. Oxford University Press, 1994.

[3] Cloughley, B. Trumpeters: T*he story of the Royal Artillery's boy trumpeters*. Bognor Regis. Woodfield, 2008.

With many students from Aubrey's year at Brynglas Central School looking to join one of the armed forces, Aubrey and his best friend Owen "Herbie" Andrews therefore decided to apply to join the Air Force together. With aviation only a generation old, and memories of Amy Johnson's and others' aviation feats still fresh in the memory, it would not have been surprising that adventurous boys like Aubrey and Herbie would have seen it as the service of choice. With a clutch of aviation films in the 1930s, including Test Pilot (the second highest grossing film of 1938) it would have offered a far greater appeal than the army or navy.[4] When thinking of joining the army, the stories of First-World-War mud, trenches, lice and bayonets would clearly have made it a less attractive option. However, for Aubrey, it was perhaps still a more attractive option than the Navy; his father had served on HMS Britannia for most of the First World War before being transferred to another post in August 1918.[5] He had undoubtedly told Aubrey stories of his lucky escape from a vessel that just three months later was torpedoed and sunk, with the loss of 50 men, the last British vessel sunk in the First World War.

Aubrey though, was deaf in his right ear – a consequence of contracting measles as a child and the reason that he failed his Air Force medical. However, any disappointment he had was not noted in his diary, and soon after he successfully applied to join the army as a member of the Royal Artillery, somehow managing to hide this defect.[6] His friend, Herbie, had little trouble with his Air Force medical, passing to take his place as an Airman Apprentice.[7] Aubrey set off for the Royal Artillery Depot at Woolwich just five days after his 16th birthday on 24th January 1939 to become a Boy Trumpeter.[8] As a full-time solider, he signed on for 9 years, although his service would not start until after his 18th birthday. Aubrey therefore committed himself to the army until January 1950 when he would be 27 – and his father was requested to sign a certificate agreeing that he could receive physical punishment as a boy soldier if he was charged with any misdemeanours. The principal crime was smoking which was strictly forbidden. This would merit several whacks on your bare backside with a bamboo stick if caught, and the eating of any

---

[4] Entries in Aubrey's diaries in the early 1940s confirm that he had a fascination and great interest in flying.

[5] Hames A.C. *Letters of recommendation from the wardroom messman and the fleet paymaster.* 1 August, 1918.

[6] Personal communication with Annette Hames, Aubrey's eldest surviving daughter.

[7] Hames, D. Email correspondence with Garry Stuart, Owen Andrew's nephew. 31 May, 2022.

[8] Hames, D. Personal diary for 1939 of Aubrey Hames.

cigarettes caught on you [9,10]

On arrival at the Royal Artillery Depot, Aubrey together with 60 other boys of the January intake, reported to the guard room where he was given his regimental number, and was allocated to Ross section in the 2nd Boys Battery.[11] Here, he started a one-year training course that aimed to produce 360 boy trumpeters each year for the Royal Artillery and the Royal Horse Artillery.[12] These were to act as the timekeepers of the day in an era where watches were rare and there were no other means of informing large numbers of soldiers of the various tasks and duties for which they had to be called.

Starting with "reveille" at 6:30am, blasted out by one of the trumpeters, Aubrey began a very regimented daily routine of foot drill, sounding practice, physical education, and education at the military school until tea at 5:00pm. With boys not allowed to leave the barracks during the week, the period after tea was often spent on homework, or bugle or trumpet practice before lights out – sounded by one of the trumpeters at 10:30pm.[13] All these routines were kept to by the trumpeter's call, delivered from the square, with the ultimate aim of making sure that all boys passed the Army 3rd and 2nd class certificates of education and the sounding exams set by the Director of Music.[14]

Despite being hospitalised for a month only two weeks into his training, (probably due to the relatively common allergic reactions to one or more of the vaccine injections given), Aubrey seemed quite at home in this environment[15,16] Although pay was low at one shilling (5p) a day, of which two thirds was kept back for periods of leave, the strong emphasis on sport would have been something he enjoyed. This was very near the top of army priorities, keeping him fit and giving him the chance to try new sports such as cricket. However, rugby his real love, did not appear to be

---

[9] Imperial War Museum. Interview with Cyril Thompson Mount. 1993. Catalogue number 13123. Available at: http://m.iwm.org.uk/collections/item/object/80012845. Date accessed 15/07/13.

[10] Timbers, K. *The Royal Artillery Woolwich: A celebration*. London. Third Millennium Publishing Limited, 2008.

[11] Hames, D. Personal diary for 1939 of Aubrey Hames.

[12] The operational use of horses at this time was being phased out, a process that was completed before Aubrey finished his training as a trumpeter.

[13] Imperial War Museum. Interview with R. Smith, 2001/02. Catalogue number 21081. Available at: http://m.iwm.org.uk/collections/item/object/80025406. Date accessed 16/07/13.

[14] Hames, D. Personal diary for 1939 of Aubrey Hames.

[15] Ibid.

[16] Allergic reactions amongst soldiers in the British Army to vaccine injections were common, with soldiers often hospitalised for several days with high fevers.

played at Woolwich. Others probably enjoyed the sporting activities less so – especially those who struggled to swim, and who were chucked into the water and poked with a stick if they tried to get out.

Early Swimming photograph at Woolwich taken in 1939 (2nd Boys Battery, Ross Section). Aubrey is in the back row, fourth from the left.

Weekends were allowed off – but you could only leave the barracks on weekend afternoons to visit friends and relatives in the area, and church attendance on Sundays was compulsory. Leaving the barracks was allowed on the proviso that permission from your parents had been given, and the soldiers were "taught to walk about smartly." Aubrey regularly visited his maternal grandfather in Lambeth, and the 2 shillings and sixpence a week wages (about £6.00 now accounting for inflation) gave him the opportunity to visit the cinema across the road from the Royal Artillery Depot as well as his first taste of dance halls.[17] This provided Aubrey with the most embarrassing moment in his army career, recalled in an undated mayoral speech given in the late 1970s. Recalling his first dance, where he was too shy to approach the most attractive girl in the hall who was a similar age to him, he instead chose a much older girl standing a little further away. Asking her for the next dance she replied with distain "I don't dance with a child." Quite innocently,

---

[17] It was not uncommon for people to visit the cinema three or more times a week during the Second World War, with weekly attendances of 19 million in 1939, rising to 30 million by 1945 (see Street, S. British national cinema.)

Aubrey replied, "Oh I am sorry, I didn't know you were pregnant." It was some time before Aubrey had any idea why she then slapped him.

Although these recreational activities would have taken at least a third of his allowance for the week, he could always borrow from, or lend money to, his fellow trumpeters – a regular occurrence on payday on Friday afternoons.[18] He was probably less happy with the money that he had to spend on Dubbin for his boots which cost 4 old pence in 1939, and the Silvo for his bugle which probably cost a similar amount.

The highlights of Aubrey's time at Woolwich came in July 1939. On the 18th, he was dispatched to the Park Lane Hotel in Central London to blow two fanfares for David Lloyd George MP, who was Prime Minister during the First World War, and Leslie Hore-Belisha, the Minister of War. Four days later, he sounded a general salute for Queen Mary. However, with Germany preparing to invade Poland in the summer of 1939, training of the trumpeters ceased, and on 27th August 1939, Aubrey together with all other members of the Royal Artillery, relocated from their vulnerable Woolwich home to Ascot Racecourse, 30 miles further west.[19]

War and desertion

With the whole of the Royal Artillery re-located to Ascot Racecourse, there was little time to get used to their new surroundings when on 1st September 1939, Germany invaded Poland. This brought an end to the slow and inevitable descent of Europe into war, and two days later on 3rd September, Britain together with France declared war on Germany.

Although war with Germany had been inevitable for some time, this clearly was a shock to Aubrey and the other boy trumpeters. On the day war was declared, Aubrey noted this twice in his diary, with "WAR" spelt out in capitals. Three days later, he wrote in capitals "WHY?", followed by "everyone else in the same state." Tensions were running high, and this was obviously getting to Aubrey, who at one point, punched one of his fellow trumpeters, putting it down to a loss of memory.[20] For some of the boy trumpeters, the prospect of war was clearly too much to take. Many boys saw the army as a kind of apprenticeship, others as an opportunity to

---

[18] Aubrey's diaries regularly showed who owed money to whom, always recorded on a Friday.

[19] Hames, D. Personal diary for 1939 of Aubrey Hames.

[20] Ibid.

escape home/or the depression, or an opportunity to travel or play sport.[21] Some were also under the impression from the recruiting office that once in the army it would be relatively easy to leave if it wasn't for them. They did not join the army to go to war. For those who had signed up underage, a not uncommon occurrence, the rapid retrieval of a previously lost birth certificate or contact with the parents unaware where they were was all that was needed. For others, terrified at the prospect of war, there was only one option, and that was desertion.

Over the next eight weeks, Aubrey noted in his diary that seventeen boy soldiers from his section deserted – some more than once. Based on surviving photographs and known intake numbers, this amounted to at least 10% of boy trumpeters. This was a significant number and was approximately twenty times the official desertion rate over the first year of the war – and in a sixth of the time-period. Even though soldiers under the age of eighteen were more than twice as likely to desert, this was still a large percentage.[22] Aubrey would not have been aware of all the attempted desertions, and official figures would only relate to reported desertion rates. Most officers were sympathetic to the soldiers under them, particularly those officers who had gone through the horrors and fears of the First World War. From personal diaries and interviews carried out after the war, most cases of desertion were hushed up, or kept within the company. For a boy's regiment, with officers specially picked for their ability to deal with young, immature soldiers, levels of understanding of the fear they were going through would have been greater still. This seems to have been the case, as only two of the boy soldiers mentioned by Aubrey seemed to have been punished. These were the last two boy soldiers who deserted, both of whom had deserted more than once. They were confined to barracks for fourteen days, the same minor punishment as given to eight boys for raiding the stores a few weeks earlier. Attitudes had moved on from the First World War when desertion had been a capital offense although no solider would have been sentenced to death if they were known to be under the age of eighteen and then only in the rare case of the desertion being reported.[23]

---

[21] Ahrenfeldt, R.H. *Psychiatry in the British Army in the Second World War.* London. Routledge and Kegan Paul, 1958.

[22] Ibid.

[23] Herbert Burden was sentenced to death and executed during the First World War when he was 17 years old. However, having given his age as 18 instead of 16 when he enlisted, and having not given his true age at his court martial, there was no reason to question his age. He is believed to have been the only British soldier under the age of 18 executed for desertion in the First World War.

However, despite the initial shock and probable fear of war, life at Ascot soon settled down. Apart from the training and the arrival of approximately 3000 reservists by the start of September, and many more arriving over the following month, there was little sign of the war. Indeed, for Aubrey and his fellow boy trumpeters, life probably became more pleasurable. The long days of lectures and bugle practice at Woolwich, with little time for social activities in the evening, were modified. They now had regular route marches supplemented with regular concerts and shows in the evenings. Britain was also now entering the period known as the "Phoney War" that was to last until May 1940, and life at Ascot also appeared to be relatively sedate. This gave Aubrey plenty of time to indulge in his love of murder mysteries from Collins Crime Club, as well as political books published by the Left Book Club, while he waited for his first posting.[24] This arrived on 17th November 1939 when together with three others he was posted as a trumpeter to the newly formed 23rd Medium and Heavy Training Unit in Devonport, Plymouth.

Training

The 23rd Medium and Heavy Training Unit was one of five Medium and Heavy Training Units formed as a need to train the large number of soldiers now entering the war.[25] As a training unit, they required the best soldiers, and these were either handpicked based on their performance, or chosen as a result of an aptitude test.[26,27] This included Aubrey's new adjutant, John Durnford-Slater, who the following year raised and trained the first commando unit. Although life in a training unit during wartime later proved to be painfully dull, with little prospect for active service, Aubrey's initial impressions of his posting were favourable, noting in his diary that he was going to enjoy himself.[28,29,30] Aubrey, in common with many soldiers not

---

[24] The Left Book Club was one of the first book clubs in the UK that covered political and social events at the time from a left-wing perspective.

[25] Medium and Heavy referred to the type of weapons on which training was carried out.

[26] Interview with Mark Smith, curator of the Royal Artillery Museum, Woolwich, 31 August, 2013.

[27] Imperial War Museum. Interview with K Reynolds, 2004. Catalogue number 27319. Available at: http://m.iwm.org.uk/collections/item/object/80024754. Date accessed 04/08/13.

[28] Interview with Mark Smith, 2013.

[29] Imperial War Museum. Interview with K Reynolds, 2004.

[30] David Niven a famous Hollywood actor also commented on the "deadening boredom" of a training unit and joined the commandos to get away from it. Niven, D. (1971) The moon's a balloon. London. Hamish Hamilton.

required for military action in Europe, continued his apparently sedate, yet cold lifestyle in what was at that time, the coldest winter of the 20th century. His diary entries noted daily letter writing, visits to the pictures and the Royal Sailor's Rest, commonly known as Aggie Weston's, as well as regular games of rugby.[31] The early days of war seemed to be treating Aubrey favourably, and apart from the time when he accidently fired the regimental sergeant major's revolver (with fortunately no adverse circumstances), was relatively uneventful.

However, by May 1940 with the start of the Battle of France, events in Europe were about to take a dramatic turn for the worse, with significant consequences for Plymouth. On 10th May, the same day as Winston Churchill became Prime Minister, German units moved through the Ardennes region of France, cutting off and surrounding allied forces in Belgium. Within 10 days, they had swept north through France, cutting off allied forces near Dunkirk, including Stewart Watson, later to serve with distinction on the council in Newport. With many including Aubrey speculating an invasion of Britain within six weeks, over 300,000 soldiers were evacuated from Dunkirk between 27th May and 4th June – a significant number of them landing in Plymouth. This included many French troops, with Aubrey noting thousands of them pouring into Plymouth over the first six days of June 1940. In total, approximately 80,000 French troops passed through Plymouth over this period, with most being shipped back to Western France to continue the fight against the German forces.[32] Within a week of the last troops returning to France, many returned, this time supplemented with British and Belgium refugees as the situation in France became untenable. On 22nd June, France surrendered, and consequently Plymouth was now exposed to front-line danger with little armed defence against enemy air attack.[33] With its naval dockyard, and the presence of a number of armed personnel in the city, Plymouth was much too important a target to remain immune from enemy attack, and targets had already been identified from German civilian flights over the city in the 1930s, including some as late as June 1939.[34,35]

---

[31] Royal Sailors' Rests at Plymouth and later Portsmouth were the inspiration of an Agnes Weston who raised the funds to provide a place to provide baths, food, and lodgings as well as recreational facilities for sailors. Hence these affectionately came to be known as "Aggie Weston's."

[32] Gill, C. Plymouth: *A New History.* Devon Books, 1993.

[33] Wasley, G. *Plymouth a Shattered City: the story of Hitler's attack on Plymouth and its people 1939-1945.* Wellington. Halsgrove, 2004.

[34] Wintle, F. *The Plymouth Blitz.* Bodmin. Bossiney Books, 1981.

[35] Wasley, G. *Plymouth a Shattered City,* 2004.

Consequently, within a week of the fall of France, the first of Plymouth's 602 aid raid warnings during the Second World War were heard.[36] These early warnings were recorded in Aubrey's diary, as was the first bombing of Plymouth on 6th July in which a lone aircraft dropped a number of bombs killing three people. [37]

Plymouth B 05

Abb. 8   Blick von SW über **Devonport**, im SW Plymouths an der Biegung des H a m o a z e noch N gelegen
Linker Anschluß nächstes Bild, rechter Anschluß Abb. 12

One of a number of aerial photographs issued to Luftwaffe pilots during the Second World War to enable them to identify their targets. This photograph shows Raglan Barracks where Aubrey was stationed during the initial raids on Plymouth in late 1940. Courtesy Michael Cole, The Clique.

Further raids took place the following day, and these were stepped up throughout July and into August, with some of these lasting all night. This included one, believed to be on 22nd July, when Aubrey and his best friend Fred Brawn were stranded on a ferry returning from Torpoint.[38] On 8th July, Aubrey noted air raid warnings "by the dozen" with four bombs dropped

---

[36] Clamp, A.L. *The blitz of Plymouth 1940-44.* Plymouth. P.D.S. Printers, 1984.

[37] Bombing dates and locations are recorded in the "*Bomb Book*" held by Plymouth and West Devon Record Office.

[38] Interview with Chris Brawn (née Jones), Mrs Jones daughter and later wife of Aubrey's best friend in the Royal Artillery, Fred Brawn, 17 November, 2013.

within the vicinity of Raglan Barracks, where Aubrey was stationed.[39] On 13th August he noted in his diary "8 buggers in succession. Boy! Did they give us the shots."[40] Unknown to Aubrey, these bombs landed about ½ mile away in the Stonehouse region of Plymouth, killing four people. By coincidence, these bombs landed within a few metres of the house where Reginald Silas Tyack and his family lived around the time of the First World War. Together, although for different reasons and mainly over different periods, these two men were later to dominate Newport politics over the second half of the 20th century (as will be outlined in Chapter 6). A month later on 11th September, the bombs dropped even closer to Raglan Barracks with significant loss of life, although at this time Aubrey was on leave in Newport. On 6th November ten more bombs were dropped on Plymouth, four of which landed either on or very near Raglan Barracks. With the inevitable loss of life following a raid, Aubrey was often called on, together with another trumpeter, to play a salute at a funeral. This included one on 9th July after the initial raids, as well as one on 16th August (which mean that he missed a visit to the training units of Raglan Barracks by Anthony Eden, Secretary of State for War).[41] This salute was almost certainly for three naval ratings killed during the raids of 13th August and buried within a few yards of each other in Plymouth Weston Mill Cemetery.[42] The last salute noted in his dairy was on 5th September, the same day as fourteen RAF airmen and one airwoman were buried from a bombing of an unknown date.[43]

Plymouth was clearly not a safe place for the military, nor for civilians for that matter. With 21 raids by the end of October alone, in mid-November 1940, the 23rd Medium and Heavy Training Unit packed their bags and, as was the norm at this time, travelled overnight to Newtown in mid-Wales.[44] As for Plymouth, the heaviest raids arrived in March and April 1941, with almost 1,000 enemy aircraft dropping over 200,000 incendiary devices and bombs with further raids continuing throughout the war.[45] By the time of the last bombing raid in May 1944, Plymouth was considered the worst blitzed city in the country, although the extent of damage at the time was

---

[39] Hames, D. Personal diary for 1940 of Aubrey Hames..

[40] The 13th August 1940 was the start of significant bombing raids by the Luftwaffe in the UK with the aim of destroying the British Royal Air Force. This was known as "Adlertag" or "Eagle Day".

[41] "War Minister at Plymouth." *Western Morning News.* 19 August, 1940.

[42] "Raid victims buried." *Western Morning News.* 17 August, 1940.

[43] "Raids interrupt funeral of RAF victims." *Western Morning News.* 6 September, 1940.

[44] Gill, C. *Plymouth: A New History.* Devon Books, 1993.

[45] Wasley, G. *Plymouth a Shattered City,* 2004.

given little publicity due to the importance of the dockyard. In total, at least 1,172 civilians were killed, with 4,448 civilian casualties.[46] There were also significant casualties among service personnel, although official figures have never been released.[47] Practically every street in Plymouth had been bombed with more than 70,000 incidences of damage to housing – interestingly far more than the number of houses in Plymouth. This indicated that a number of properties had been damaged several times, including Aubrey's favourite haunt during his time in Plymouth, Aggie Weston's. Thirty years after the war finished, reports from the government's regional advisor and director of home intelligence were released, advising that "Plymouth should have been made an evacuation area on the fall of France" and "the pre-blitz preprations of the Plymouth local authority appear to have envisaged nothing on the scale of what actually happened."[48]

[46] There was a huge shifting population in Plymouth at this time. It is likely that many more may have been killed or injured during the war, including many who were moved to hospitals out of the city and who later died.

[47] Clamp, A.L. *The blitz of Plymouth 1940-44*. Plymouth. P.D.S. Printers, 1984.

[48] Wintle, F. *The Plymouth Blitz*. Bodmin. Bossiney Books, 1981.

Fire at Turnchapel oil depot 27 November 1940, following a bombing raid. Although this raid took place two weeks after Aubrey left Plymouth, it demonstrates the damage inflicted on Plymouth during his time there. By coincidence, on the day this bombing took place, Plymouth's own paper the Western Morning News was given permission by the Ministry of Information to report on the most seriously bombed locations in Britain, except Plymouth. The bombing of Plymouth was therefore reported in the following day's paper as bombing of a "south-west town." However, in the same story, it quoted the German News Agency as saying this south-west town was Plymouth. Wartime reporting restrictions meant it was quite common to not be able to report on what was happening on your doorstep, although it was acceptable to report the story by quoting what German reports were saying had happened. Photograph courtesy Derek Tait.

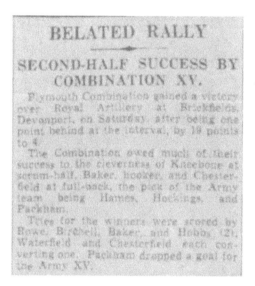

It wasn't all about bombing raids in Plymouth towards the end of 1940. The clipping to the left from the front page of the Western Morning News of 7th October 1940 is a report on the Rugby match played two days earlier, between Plymouth Combination and the Royal Artillery, in which Aubrey was highlighted as being one of the picks of the Army team, despite noting in his diary that he was "crocked" before the end of the first half.

Connie

Considered safe from the bombing raids that afflicted many towns and cities in the UK, the arrival of over four thousand military personnel brought a significant boost to the fortunes of Newtown in Wales.[49,50] Competition in the woollen industry had led to a gradual decline in the town since the latter half

---

[49] It is believed that no bombs were dropped on Newtown during the Second World War, although several bombs were dropped nearby, probably from German bombers returning from bombing raids on Liverpool55.

[50] Stott, L. "Looking back." *The Newtonian.* Volume 24. Spring, 2006.

of the 19th century. However, now many of the redundant woollen mills acted as ideal army accommodation, later supplemented on completion of the army barracks on Dolfor Road the following spring.[51] With hundreds of munitions workers also brought in to make aircraft components and submarine gun barrels in one of the government's "shadow factories," as well as over a thousand children evacuated from Merseyside, Newtown changed from being a sleepy little market town into a lively military establishment bringing with it a significant economic boost to the area.[52,53,54]

With so many members of the Royal Artillery arriving in Newtown, there was also a dramatic increase in the number of dances and other entertainments. Dances at the Church House doubled to twice a week, later supplemented by dances at the Drill Hall, where Aubrey's party trick of standing on his head to encourage people to dance always seemed to work.[55] Programmes at the Regent Cinema changed twice-weekly, and the approximately 30 licensed premises in Newtown undoubtedly witnessed a significant increase in trade. For Aubrey, the life of daily letter-writing, dances, and visits to the pictures changed little, although unsurprisingly for a Welsh town, there was a noticeable increase in the number of rugby matches he played.

There was no Aggie Weston's in Newtown, with army meals taken in the County Pavilion, an old aircraft hangar brought from Lincolnshire between the wars.[56] However, within a couple of months, Aubrey soon found the perfect alternative to Aggie Weston's: Mrs Jones' Fish & Chip Shop on Frolic Street. This very quickly became a firm favourite with Aubrey and his friends. Although thrown out once and told to never come back, they all soon became very close to Mrs Jones and her two daughters Chris and Cassie, who were later to marry two of Aubrey's best friends, Fred Brawn and Bill Ladd.[57] Games of monopoly were a particular favourite, and recalling these games

---

[51] Transcript of a recording by J.L. Jennings made for the local history department of the county library, Newtown ("Memories of Newtown whilst with the 23rd Field Training Regiment, Royal Artillery during the war." The Newtonian. Volume 10. Autumn, 2002.).

[52] Shadow factories were developed to implement additional manufacturing capacity for the British aircraft industry in the Second World War. The factory in Newtown employed a largely female workforce of up to 1,600.

[53] Pugh, D. "The Second World War in Newtown." *The Newtonian.* Volume 22. Autumn, 2005.

[54] Wilson, D. (2005) "The day war broke out." *The Newtonian.* Volume 22. Autumn.

[55] Interview with Ray Jones, Ruth Lewis, Mair Jones, and David Lewis, nephews and nieces of Connie Williams, 31 August, 2013.

[56] Wilson, D. "The day war broke out." *The Newtonian.* Volume 22. Autumn, 2005.

[57] Interview with Chris Brawn (née Jones), Mrs Jones daughter and later wife of Aubrey's best friend in the Royal Artillery, Fred Brawn, 17 November, 2013.

70 years later, Chris, Fred Brawn's widow, giggled when remembering the problems these caused as someone was always trying to cheat. Mrs Jones' Fish and Chip Shop was also a few yards from 38 Park Street, the home of a Connie Williams, who was a friend of Chris and Cassie. Although not mentioned in Aubrey's diary until October 1941, over eight months after getting to know Chris and Cassie, it is unlikely that Aubrey was unaware of the young woman who three years later he would marry.

A rare photograph of the Royal Artillery marching through Newtown on Armistice Day 1940. Although it was an offence to go out with a camera at this time, one exception in Newtown was the Montgomeryshire Express photographer Geoff Charles. This photograph shows one of about 65 surviving photographs taken by him in Newtown during the Second World War, and now held in the National Library of Wales in Aberystwyth.

As for the 23rd Medium and Heavy Training Unit, the first signs of Aubrey's frustration and boredom as a drill and small arms instructor was starting to show. Occasional military exercises and learning to drive in a Bren Gun Carrier could not overcome his desire for action.[58] In March 1942, he put in

---

[58] Aubrey learnt to drive in a tank in 1941. This would almost certainly have been a Bren Gun Carrier, a light armoured tracked vehicle, which was commonly used by the Royal Artillery in Newtown at this time.

for the newly formed Airborne Division. This was followed over the next three months by several requests for postings into action, all turned down by his Commanding Officer (CO). Whether for his own protection, or considered too valuable for his regiment, the reasons given by his CO were that he was too young. Both Aubrey and his CO would have known that this was not true, and that he could have been posted abroad any time three months past his eighteenth birthday.[59] However, whilst this was going on, Aubrey's new-found relationship with Connie was blossoming, and a week after putting in for the Airborne Division they had decided on an unofficial engagement. On 30th June 1942 his diary entry read "I don't think I could ever live without her now!! She's everything to me." This was a rather apt entry coming at a time when as a result of his constant requests to be posted into action, he was doing his upmost to increase her chances of living without him.

However, in August 1942 Aubrey finally got his wish and he succeeded in getting a posting to the 180 Field Regiment stationed in Grantham in Lincolnshire. His diary entry on hearing the news read "Hurrah!!! Whoopee!"

Of the other surviving photographs taken by Geoff Charles, four feature a game played between a team from Newtown and Towyn on 4th April 1942.

---

[59] Interview with Mark Smith, curator of the Royal Artillery Museum, Woolwich, 31 August, 2013.

Aubrey played in this game, which the Newtown team lost 11 points to nil. He is shown in the team photo taken by Geoff Charles before this game, kneeling in the front row, second from the right. He described this game in his diary as fair, with some good hard tackling.[60]

Grantham

Housing a large percentage of the British airfields, Lincolnshire was a major target for German bombing raids during the early stages of the war. Grantham in particular was heavily bombed due to the manufacture of armaments in the town.[61] Although it claimed to be the 2nd most bombed town in England at this time, it did not suffer anywhere near the same extent that Plymouth had during Aubrey's time there two years earlier.[62]

By the time Aubrey arrived though, no bombs had dropped on Grantham for a year. With Germany's attention diverted by the invasion of Russia, as well as a greater focus on the strategic bombing of larger cities, Grantham was probably considered a safe place to be in 1942. With significant members of the armed services, and the usual dances and visits to the cinema, Aubrey would have found life little different from what was on offer in Newtown. Combined with a strong economy, and a busy place that required traffic to be regulated by staggering working hours, it was certainly a place undeserving of the title "the most boring town in England," a dubious honour it was to later receive from several different sources in the 1980s.[63,64]

Grantham was also home to several personalities who would have been of great interest to Aubrey. A statue of Isaac Newton, Britain's greatest ever mathematician who had been born near Grantham 300 years earlier stood outside the Grantham Museum. This may well have inspired Aubrey who was a keen mathematician and had excelled in maths throughout his school career.[65] Less inspiring would have been the presence in Grantham of Alf

---

[60] Photo supplied by Llyfrgell Genedlaethol Cymru / National Library of Wales.

[61] This was a shadow factory, similar to the one situated in Newtown.

[62] Knapp, M.G. Grantham: The war years 1939-1945. A pictorial history. Lincolnshire books, 1995.

[63] Moore, C. *Margaret Thatcher, the authorised biography, Volume One: Not For Turning.* London. Penguin Books, 2013.

[64] In the 1980's, Grantham won the "Golden yawn award" in a Radio 1 poll for the most boring town in Britain. It has also been claimed that it was awarded the same title from several other sources, including both the Sun and Guardian newspapers.

[65] Aubrey's one surviving school report from Brynglas Central School in July 1937 had exam performances in the top 2 in all 3 different maths subjects, and top in drawing. He was also top of the class in Geography and 2nd in Gardening, but noticeably near the bottom in

Roberts, local conservative councillor of St Wulfram, where Aubrey spent much of his time, as well as Alf Roberts' daughter Margaret.[66] Aubrey would almost certainly have taken an interest in the local politics of Grantham and may well have known about Alf Roberts. He probably did not know his daughter, who of course later became better known as Margaret Thatcher. Although history will never tell us if Aubrey met the young woman destined to become the longest-serving Prime Minister of the 20th century, and the scourge of the Labour Party some forty years later, it does tell us of Margaret Thatcher's possible first disagreement with a socialist. In an interview in 1995, Margaret Thatcher tells of her love of the cinema in Grantham as a teenager during the war, naming Jeanette MacDonald as one of her favourite film stars.[67] On 26th August 1942, fellow teenager Aubrey made the first of several visits to the cinema in Grantham to watch *Smilin' Through* at the Picture House, Margaret Thatcher's favourite cinema.[68] Aubrey's only comment on the film was "don't like Jeanette MacDonald."[69]

Whether Aubrey met any members of the Roberts family or not, he certainly couldn't fail to meet members of the RAF who had four air bases locally, or the Airborne Division whom he had also tried to join.[63] He probably also met members of the newly formed Glider Pilot Regiment with whom he would finally succeed in achieving his wartime flying ambitions over three years later. Although no record of the Glider Pilot Regiment in Grantham has been identified, the Horsa gliders that they flew needed pilots, and these gliders were a common sight in the skies over Grantham. They were identified in photographs in Walter Lee's (an air-raid warden in Grantham) diary, and clearly Aubrey could not have failed to notice them.[70] Combined with possible meetings with members of this regiment, it was possibly during Aubrey's short four-month stay in Grantham that his interest in this regiment was ignited. The strategic importance of Grantham was also something that the Germans were reminded of in the autumn of 1942, with tragic consequences. During this period, there were several press reports that referred either directly or indirectly to the manufacture of arms in the town. This came to a head on 9th October, with two major reports relating to the production of

---

English and French.

[66] Campbell, J. *Margaret Thatcher, Volume One: The Grocer's Daughter.* London. Jonathan Cape, 2000.

[67] Jim Allen interview with Margaret Thatcher. 1995. Available at: http://www2. granthamtoday.co.uk/gj/site/news/thatcher/grantham.htm. Date accessed 24/02/14.

[68] Ibid.

[69] Hames, D. Personal diary for 1942 of Aubrey Hames.

[70] Grantham Library. W Lee diary titled Grantham Day by Day.

arms. This included a disagreement between the town's MP William Kendall and the Auditor General regarding the price of goods supplied by the arms factory, of which William Kendall was the Managing Director.[71] With news heavily censored, it was unusual that stories identifying the location of the manufacture of arms were reported, and this wisdom was questioned by Walter Lee, as well by a W.H. Howard in the letters page of the Grantham Journal the following week.[72,73] Both Lee and Howard speculated that this might bring the town to the attention of the Germans – and this proved prophetic. On the 24th October, Grantham was subjected to its last, and by far its worst, bombing raid. Thirty-two people were killed. This amounted to one third of all those killed in all the raids on Grantham during the war, and more than twice as many victims from any bombing raid in Plymouth during Aubrey's time there. No mention of this raid was made in the Grantham Journal, and no more reports referring to the manufacture of arms in the town were to appear in future editions. William Kendall still received several mentions in most editions, but the Grantham Journal, perhaps too late, learnt the reason for press censorship during wartime. Members of the 180th Field Regiment assisted in the clearance and recovery of bodies and although Aubrey was not involved, it was not long before he too was to personally witness a similar tragedy – his first war death.[74]

At approximately 1:45am on November 13th, returning to Newport from a visit to his grandfather in London, the train he was travelling in collided with a derailed freight train that had passed through a red danger light near Appleford, just outside of Didcot.[75] As a result the three carriages, containing approximately 200 passengers, overturned with Aubrey smashing into a window.[76,77] Recounting this story to me in 1986 after the death of my

---

[71] William Kendall was a highly controversial figure in the 1940s, and the leading figure in Grantham certainly in terms of press coverage. Elected as an Independent MP for Grantham in March 1942, he was considered to have controversial views on the production of arms during wartime. He was also a figure of interest to MI5 who kept a file on him, expressing concern that he was carelessly revealing wartime production figures in his election speeches, as well as suspecting him of gun-running and smuggling (files held on William Kendall at the National Archives, catalogue number KV 2/2779-2781. Available at: http://www. nationalarchives.gov.uk/releases/2008/march/rightwing.htm. Date accessed 30/06/15).

[72] "Helping the enemy" (letter from W.H. Howard). *Grantham Journal*. 16 October, 1942.

[73] Interestingly, William Kendall also raised this issue in the original newspaper article on 9th October 1942.

[74] National Archives. 180th Field Regiment war diary, 1942. Ref: WO 166/7063.

[75] National Archives. 180th Ministry of War Transport enquiry by Major G.R.S. Wilson. 10 February, 1943. Ref: RAIL 1053/128/5.

[76] Ibid.

[77] Hames, D. Personal diary for 1942 of Aubrey Hames.

grandfather, Aubrey's father-in-law, he told me that he had to crawl over passengers who had been killed in the crash and smash what was left of a window before climbing out under the overturned carriage. Three people were reported to be killed on the scene, including the driver of the freight train who by coincidence was from Newport. The apparent discrepancy between this, and Aubrey's account, which suggested that more people were killed, can probably be explained by the wartime reporting restrictions that may have resulted in the details of certain casualties being omitted. In addition, fourteen people were reported to be injured, nearly all of whom were army personnel.[78] With the main impact taken by the mail carriage, no passengers were reported to have been directly killed, although three RAF men were reported to be seriously injured and trapped under the wreckage. The most serious of these was a John Pritchard who lived a few miles away in Benson and who suffered several broken ribs as well as two broken legs.

With the help of fellow passengers, Aubrey used the splintered coachwork to light fires that provided light and to assist in the rescue of these RAF men. This was strictly illegal and against stringent wartime blackout regulations, but imperative in the circumstances. Although all three RAF men were rescued up to eight hours after the crash, John Pritchard died of his injuries a week later. Like the crash, his death was widely reported in several newspaper articles, including a small article on the front page of the Gloucestershire Echo on 21st November 1942. Also on the same page was news of the first operation carried out by members of the Glider Pilot Regiment and the Airborne Division; a raid of two gliders into Norway. This resulted in the death of all thirty-four crew members of the gliders, as well as all seven members of one of the tugs. German wireless announced at the time that they had all been killed in action. The truth was that although half of the crew members had been killed on landing, the remainder, most of whom were injured, had been captured by the German's without offering any resistance. They were later murdered under Adolf Hitler's Commando Order although these details did not emerge until after the war had finished.[79]

In Grantham, it would have been unlikely that Aubrey would have failed to be aware of both of these events – particularly with the concentration

---

[78] "Troops hurt in express crash." *Derby Daily Telegraph.* 13 November, 1942.

[79] The Commando Order was a secret order issued by Adolf Hitler on 18th October 1942 stating that all Allied commandos encountered by German troops were to be killed immediately without trial, even if they had surrendered. Even though this was a contravention of the Geneva Convention, any German commander or officer who did not carry out this order was considered to have committed an act of negligence, punishable under German military law.

of Airborne troops in the town – despite the fact that neither event was mentioned in the Grantham Journal. There also appears to be no mention of the Norway raid in any local Lincolnshire paper. Attending a wedding in Newport the day the news broke may have initially helped distract him, particularly news of the death of John Pritchard whose life he had played a small part in trying to save. His forthcoming marriage to Connie would also have acted as a distraction, as well as his regiment's imminent move a week later up the road to Alford.

The move to Alford had coincided with a notable change in the war for the allies. The second battle of El Alamein, won by the British Army under the leadership of Lieutenant General Bernard Montgomery (see also Chapter 10), was the first major offensive for the allies since the start of the war. Famously described by Winston Churchill as the "end of the beginning" it resulted in many divisions being posted abroad and others gutted to make up for lost troops in places such as Libya and elsewhere.[80] This included the 180th Field Regiment who had lost 70% of its strength to the Middle East by the end of 1942.[81] With the future of the regiment uncertain, and further postings out of the regiment before the end of March, Aubrey was devastated when on his 20th birthday on 19th January, it was announced that the remaining members of the 180th Field Regiment were to become a reserve. Supplemented with young members from other disbanded regiments, the 180th became one of four regiments responsible for completing the entire training of soldiers for operations both at home and abroad.[82] Aubrey's desperate desire to get abroad and see some action now seemed to have dissolved, particularly as reserve divisions could not be utilised in any operational role apart from an emergency that required all training to stop. Having finally managed to escape a training unit in Newtown, just five months later he now found himself back where he started, but this time with Connie an overnight journey away rather than just a short walk down the road. The uncertainty of the regiment's future was noted in their war diary, with the comment "had the original regiment been kept together (as was first promised), we would now have been ready for absolutely everything," further commenting "even greater horrors greet us." As for Aubrey, despite bemoaning his luck, he was sure it would change. It would, but he still had a long wait.

Aubrey now settled back into a familiar life of training raw recruits, with 260

---

[80] Winston Churchill speech at the Lord Mayor's luncheon in Mansion House London on 10th November 1942.
[81] National Archives. (1943) 180th Field Regiment war diary. Ref: WO 166/11312.
[82] Ibid.

new young soldiers joining the regiment every fortnight to undertake their initial eight-week course. Missing Connie, and unhappy in Alford which was described by a friend of his as an "uncivilised, undulating and desolate" place, Aubrey settled down to what appeared to be a relatively uneventful, yet frustrating time over the next two years.[83] His diary for 1943 records few events of note apart from his developing relationship and impending marriage to Connie the following February. There are few known details of Aubrey's personal life after 1943, with none of his diaries covering the period 1944 to 1950 having survived. In addition, as a training unit, war diaries for the 180th Field Regiment stopped in January 1943, and no war diaries exist for the 120th Field Regiment after he transferred to them in September 1944. With no local history society, and little published material on Alford during the war, there are few facts known about army life in Alford over this two-year period. Newspaper reports are also very limited. In fact, the only mention of Alford during the first six months of the war, was the fining of a local man for riding his bike without lights.[84] Despite this, the material that is available, including peripheral related material, does give some insight into many of the experiences Aubrey would have been through at this time, particularly the actions of the RAF in the bombing raids over Germany.

Aubrey and Connie married in Newtown on Aubrey's 21st birthday on 19th February 1944. Although members of Connie's family were present, including Connie's sister's family from the Rhondda in South Wales, there is no evidence, and no personal recollections, from any of Aubrey's family being at the wedding. The photograph above was supplied by Margaret Crewe (née Walters), Connie's niece who was a bridesmaid. It shows Aubrey and Connie on honeymoon in Trafalgar Square in London.

---

[83] Dunk, D. Undated letter from Bombardier Doug Dunk to Aubrey, circa. 1944.

[84] Haythorne, I. "A study based on the Arthur Marwich model of the effect of the Second World War on the Alford district of Lincolnshire." MSc. Sheffield Polytechnic. June, 1989. Alford Library and Focal Point.

Aubrey's move to Alford coincided with the Casablanca Conference held in January 1943, which laid out the Allied strategy for the next phase of the war. On 4th February, as a result of this conference, a directive was issued that laid out a series of priorities for the strategic bombing of Germany. The primary objective of this directive was the progressive destruction of the German military, industrial and economic system, with the consequent undermining of the morale of the German people. The direct result for much of Lincolnshire, including Alford, was a significant increase in the number of bombers flying overhead as they headed off for bombing raids.

Leading up to these raids, there would often be an increase in night-time activities in Alford. For example, prior to the Battle of Arnhem in September 1944, airborne troops went on a "spree" in Alford suspecting that an operation was close.[85] This was also probably repeated approaching D-Day (although not for the week or so leading up to it because from the 27th May 1944 troops were confined to camp). For Aubrey and others of the 180th Regiment, this was probably the lowest point of their time in Alford. They would have known the invasion was imminent, and when the first aircraft flew over Alford, they would have realised what it meant. Ena Hardwick, a resident of Alford, and a year younger than Aubrey, noted that when bombers took off for Germany, they started to drone overhead at about seven in the evening. This went on all night, with further bombers taking off as the first bombers reached their targets.[86] She noted that sleep was almost impossible on these nights, of which there were many. On D-Day, the first gliders and bombers took off about 10:30pm the night before, and as George Ritchie, a member of US Eighth Air Force noted, the drone of airplanes "filled the sky."[87] One of the largest airborne operations in history flying overhead a few hours later than normal, with no troops other than the 180th Field Regiment on the ground, meant that Aubrey would have known the invasion of German-occupied Western Europe had started, and he had no part in it. Three months later, he would have stood and watched the start of the largest airborne operation in history, Operation Market Garden, while his new colleagues of the 120th Field Regiment recounted their experiences in France on D-Day, and future colleagues of the Glider Pilot Regiment flew overhead. The war seemed to be drifting towards an end, and Aubrey probably felt he had played no part in it. However, convinced at the start of 1943 that his luck would change, as 1944

---

[85] Taylor and Bogg. *Children's memories of Alford 1920s-1950s*, 2007.

[86] Ibid.

[87] Darlow, S. *D-Day bombers: The Veteran's Story*. Bounty Books, 2004.

drew to a close it finally did.[88] On 15th December he boarded a troop ship for an unknown destination after volunteering for service overseas. Over the next $2^1/_2$ years he was to see no action in the Second World War but was to witness first-hand the conclusion of two of the most significant historical events of the post-war period. Inevitable as they may have seemed later, neither of them was on his or the army's agenda in December 1944.

Gone "Deolali"

Contemporary evidence indicates that boarding a troop ship in wartime was an exciting yet nervous event for army troops, and was tinged with disappointment for those leaving wives and children behind. For most, they would have been the first of their families to go abroad and something – growing up in the depression of the 1930s – they could have only dreamt about. Typically travelling as a convoy of about forty over-crowded vessels protected by destroyers, the normal route was to set off north, before swinging south into the North Atlantic to avoid detection by German submarines. By this time, the excitement of the journey would have started to wane, replaced by boredom if you were lucky, and continual seasickness if you weren't. In the first part of his war memoirs, *Adolf Hitler: My part in his downfall*, Spike Milligan noted that 80% of those on board suffered seasickness when he was posted to Algiers in 1943, with a notable increase in availability of food for those who weren't.[89] The smell of stale cigarettes, sweat, and sick, exacerbated by the swinging of the hammocks in rough seas are a common theme in almost all contemporary accounts. Many resorted to sleeping on deck as a result, particularly as they moved into warmer waters. Leaving the UK as Typhoon Cobra was wrecking devastation on the United States Pacific Fleet in the region of his eventual destination, it is likely that Aubrey had a similar journey to Spike Milligan.[90] The length of his journey suggests a trip in the rougher seas around the southern tip of Africa, reducing the risk of an unwanted encounter with a German U-boat in the Mediterranean. Spending Christmas probably off the west coast of Africa, Aubrey would have got his first idea of his eventual destination from the constant rumours that would have swept the ship. Undoubtedly, these would have been greeted with great excitement as he realised he was being posted to India – although undoubtedly also tinged with some trepidation at the thought of fighting the

---

[88] Hames, D. Personal diary for 1943 of Aubrey Hames.

[89] Troop ships were commonly referred to as "vomit-buckets" during the Second World War

[90] Typhoon Cobra in the Philippine Sea sank three US destroyers, killing at least 790 people on 17th December 1944.

uncompromising Japanese in the heat and humidity of the Burmese jungle.

Arriving in Bombay, Aubrey's initial experience would have been of bumboat men travelling alongside the vessels trying to sell them fruit and other wares.[91] This would have been quickly followed by young Indian boys introducing soldiers to their first experience of "Baksheesh" – the art of tipping or charitable giving in Asian and Middle Eastern countries, that was (and is now) for youngsters a common way of relieving foreign visitors of as much money as possible, as soon as possible. Onshore however, their experiences would have been significantly different. Less than two years earlier, the Bengal famine of 1943 had resulted in upwards of four million deaths due to starvation, malnutrition and disease. This was greater than the number of Indians killed in both world wars, as well as its ongoing independence struggle and the consequent holocaust that accompanied the partition of British India into the separate dominions of India and Pakistan. Many contemporary accounts mention the squalid conditions and the general degradation of many of the people of India at this time, including a Captain PW Kingsford who shuddered at the sight of the "poor, skinny, spindle-shanked, emancipated, filthy, and diseased," who "would be everywhere."[92] Marching to the railway station at Victoria Terminus, it would have been difficult to miss the beggars that lined the route. Some blind, some deformed, others without limbs, and a further world away from Aubrey's experiences of the depression of the 1930s. This would have been a consistent sight throughout Aubrey's time in India. He would also have noticed the growing hostility towards the British as India moved towards independence which was at that time just three years away. Observing this hostility and the slogans scrawled on the walls, many soldiers in the army, particularly those with socialist tendencies, sympathised with the Indian cause.[93] This included Roy Hughes who was in India at the same time as Aubrey. Later to represent Newport and Newport East for more than 30 years as its MP, he noted seeing "Jai Hind" (Quit India) written on trains, and observed many noisy political meetings held in various towns and villages.[94]

Aubrey's destination from Bombay was Deolali, a vast sprawling transit camp and the largest in India. This was the initial destination for nearly all troops proceeding to and from Bombay and Britain. Housing a military

---

[91] A small boat used to ferry supplies to ships moored away from the shore.

[92] Imperial War Museum. Private papers of Dr P W Kingsford. Available at: https://www.iwm.org.uk/collections/item/object/1030003952.

[93] James, L. Raj. *The Making and Unmaking of British India*. London. Abacus, 1998.

[94] Hughes, R. *Seek fairer skies*. Spennymoor. The Memoir Club, 2003.

hospital where soldiers with mental health difficulties were sent prior to being returned to the UK, it had become famous for the origin of the slang word "doolally", a phrase used to describe someone who is "out of one's mind" or "crazy". In the 1970s Deolali also became well-known as the setting for the first four series of the well-known sitcom *It Ain't Half Hot Mum*, based on Jimmy Perry's experiences there with the Royal Artillery Concert Party in the Second World War. Later to become a big fan of *Dad's Army*, Jimmy Perry's most famous creation, Aubrey gave himself little time to enjoy any of the Royal Artillery concert party shows. Within a few days of arriving, an opportunity arose to join the newly formed Glider Pilot Regiment in what is now modern-day Pakistan. With no medical required, and no chance of the deafness in his right ear being discovered, Aubrey was one of several army personnel who applied. This time, his superiors were not allowed to block or hold back his application, unlike as happened with all his previous known requests for transfers.[95]

Glider Pilot Regiment: India

By late 1943, it had been decided that a glider pilot force would be formed in India to be operational by November 1944. It would be used for operations against Japanese forces in South Asia.[96,97] However, the forming of this division proved to be difficult. At this time, the regiment was fully committed to preparations for the Normandy invasion and only thirty pilots, out of a planned force of eighty, could be obtained from operations in the Mediterranean. This became even more difficult when Vice Admiral Lord Louis Mountbatten, the Supreme Allied Commander of South East Asia Command (SEAC), requested a greater force of a minimum of 517 pilots for forthcoming operations. Further reinforcements were eventually obtained from glider pilot operations in Europe. However, on 5th December 1944, one of two RAF Dakotas ferrying members of the Glider Pilot Regiment to India from RAF Northolt, crashed near the village of Mijanes in France, killing fifteen of the eighteen Glider Pilots onboard.[98]

---

[95] Glider Pilot's Notes. "The making of a total soldier - part one: glider pilot selection." *The Glider Pilot Regiment Society Magazine*. Summer 2018.

[96] Much of the history of the Glider Pilot Regiment in India has been taken from Smith, C. History of the Glider Pilot Regiment.

[97] Six glider squadrons were formed in India between November 1944 and January 1945, including the squadron which Aubrey was later to join, 670th Squadron, formed at Fatehjang on 14 December 1944.

[98] Mathevet, J.C. Flying drama in the Pyrenees. 5 December, 1944. Available at: https://the24sec.files.wordpress.com/2009/06/flying-drama-dakota-fl-588.pdf. Accessed 09/03/18.

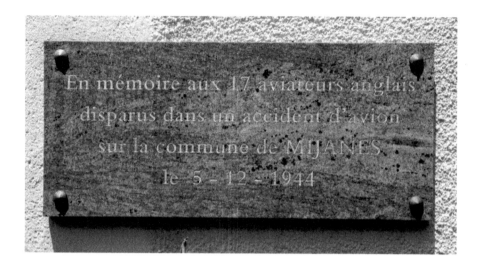

Plaque on the side of the Town Hall in Mijanes, France, in memory of the 15 glider pilots and 2 RAF Dakota pilots killed on route to India on 5th December 1944. This crash resulted in the call for more glider pilots from service personnel already in India, which led to Aubrey successfully applying to joining the Glider Pilot Regiment a few weeks later. Photograph courtesy Jon Etkins.

With a significant shortfall in glider pilots, volunteers were requested from existing army personnel already in India, probably a few days before Aubrey arrived in Deolali. The interviews were conducted by staff sergeants from original glider pilot forces which were operational in the Mediterranean, who were looking for individuals of exceptional intelligence and physical fitness. Consequently, only about a quarter of those who applied were interviewed, with many more possibly withdrawing when it was explained to them that not only would they be required to fly troops and vehicles into enemy-held territory on what possibly could be a "one-way ticket," but they had to do this as the only members of the aircraft without a parachute. Ultimately, only about 10-15 % of those interviewed were successful, including Aubrey.[99] Aubrey therefore joined No. 1 Elementary Flying Training School at

---

[99] Only about 4% of troops who initially applied to join the Glider Pilot Regiment finally achieved their wings. ("The Eagle." *The Glider Pilot Regiment Magazine*. Volume 13. Number 6. December, 2013).

Begumpet airport near Hyderabad less than two weeks after arriving in India as a member of the Royal Artillery.[100]

The gliders initially used in India were the Horsa gliders that Aubrey would have seen from a distance during his time in Lincolnshire. Weighing 20 tonnes, with a 67-foot wooden fuselage, a larger wingspan, and no engine, they did not seem the safest means by which to propel yourself headlong into enemy territory, landing almost vertically to get under anti-aircraft fire. This was particularly the case when closer inspection would have revealed a plywood body and a Perspex screen for the cockpit, and a potential loading of a jeep, a trailer, and several crew. However, regardless of any apparent shortcomings, these gliders had proved to be very successful in operations in Europe. They had led the first operation of the allied invasion of France on 6th June 1944, flying in armoured divisions to capture two bridges on the eastern flank of the Normandy landings area. The approach of the gliders into Normandy was later portrayed in silence in the 1962 war epic *The Longest Day*, highlighting the reason for the success of glider operations – the ability to bring in large numbers of troops and equipment quickly, efficiently, and without the knowledge of the enemy. However, the dangers for a glider pilot were clear. Over half of 1,378 glider pilots (fully 90% of the entire regiment at the time) had been killed, wounded or captured during the Battle of Arnhem, just four months previously, and even the Germans had abandoned their use after the Battle of Crete in 1941 because they considered them too dangerous. In addition, apart from Adolf Hitler's commando order, there was also a 20,000-franc bounty on offer in France for the capture of a glider pilot, dead or alive.[101]

However, the dangers of flying a glider would have been quickly removed from Aubrey's mind as he initially faced the months of rigorous army training that were designed to make glider pilots "Total Soldiers." This would have been far more demanding than anything he had been previously exposed to in the regular army.[102] The aim was to train a soldier to fly large numbers of troops and vehicles into battle, and then for that soldier to fight alongside these men as infantrymen, gunners or sappers – proficient in the handling of

---

[100] Aubrey Hames flying logbook.

[101] Ultimately the Glider Pilot Regiment trained 2700 pilots in the Second World War. Of these, 553 were killed in action, the highest ratio of any unit in the army. In addition, a further 763 were wounded or made prisoners of war, and the overall number of Glider Pilots who were withdrawn from service for all reasons reached 49.9% ("The Eagle." The Glider Pilot Regiment Magazine. Volume 13. Number 6. December, 2013).

[102] The training was so tough in the early days of the Glider Pilot Regiment that Winston Churchill demanded a report into its disciplinary regime.

all airborne weapons and vehicles.

Despite the extreme temperatures and high humidity levels, organised sport was played most afternoons at Begumpet. Usually this was football, cricket, hockey or volleyball although occasional games of rugby were also played.[103] There were weekly discussion groups in which the current situation in India was the main topic, and in which Aubrey took an active part (see Chapter 3) – although he missed what he would have found a most enjoyable discussion on the British Parliamentary System in the March of 1946.[104,105]

While stationed at Begumpet, Aubrey experienced temperatures in excess of 46°C during the summer of 1945, including twenty-two days when the temperature exceeded 42°C. However, moving to the Punjab area in July of that year, gave him the opportunity to enjoy cooler temperatures in the skiing resort of Gulmarg in the Himalayas. This photograph taken in January 1945

---

[103] National Archives. Operations records book of No. 1 Elementary Flying Training School, 01/02/41 to 30/06/45. Ref: AIR 29/616/1.

[104] Army education was compulsory for at least one hour per week in the form of group discussions. Addison, P. Now the war is over. London. British Broadcasting Corporation, 1985.

[105] National Archives. Operations records book of No. 1 Elementary Flying Training School, 01/02/41 to 30/06/45. Ref: AIR 29/616/1.

shows him third from the right.[106]

Many pupils struggled with this initial training; the operation's record book regularly noted what they termed the "wastage of pupils," and many had their training suspended. These soldiers were returned to their units and had the unfair indignity of RTU ("Returned to Unit") and LMF ("Lack of Moral Fibre") stamped forever on their record. [107] For those who passed the initial training period, flying was introduced after two months. All the glider pilots who completed this part of the training were promoted to sergeant.[108] This was undertaken on a De Havilland DH82A Tiger Moth which was used as it was considered an easy plane to fly.[109] Aubrey had clearly enjoyed his two previous flying experiences which were described in his 1943 diary. However, this would have been new and exciting, described for example by Ken Kirkham, who later became a good friend of Aubrey, as "the most thrilling thing I have ever done."[110]

Clocking up 90 hours of flying time, Aubrey finally qualified as a light aircraft pilot on 25th July 1945, at which point he was posted to Fatehjang in the Punjab to undertaking jungle survival training.[111] By this time, the war in Europe had ended, and Britain had had its first general election since 1935. However, despite the Labour victory, helped by the enormous proxy vote from those troops stationed abroad, the war in the East continued with little sign of the Japanese surrendering. However, with Aubrey waiting for his next posting, events in Japan started to overtake him. An atomic bomb was dropped on Hiroshima on 6th August 1945. On 9th August, the Soviet Union invaded Manchukuo, and later the same day, an atomic bomb was dropped on Nagasaki. By the time Aubrey was posted to 344 Wing on 27th August 1945, in anticipation of likely fatal airborne operations in Singapore, Bangkok and Sumatra, Japan was on the verge of surrendering. Six days later on 2nd September 1945, Japan surrendered.

---

[106] TuTiempo. Historical weather records for Hyderabad Airport. Available at: http://www.tutiempo.net/en/. Date accessed 14/06/14.

[107] The wastage rate of glider pilot soldiers was probably best emphasised on 10th June 1945 when twenty-four of the thirty-six pupils failed to complete their passing out course. Glider Pilot's Notes. "The making of a total soldier - part two: Tilshead and Fargo." The Glider Pilot Regiment Society Magazine. Winter 2018/19.

[108] The Glider Pilot Regiment was unique in its composition where no member had a rank lower than Sergeant. As such, it was commonly known as the "Regiment of Officers".

[109] Interview with Ken Kirkham, member of the Glider Pilot Regiment and friend of Aubrey. 9 September, 2012.

[110] Ibid.

[111] Aubrey Hames flying logbook.

With the surrender of the Japanese, and the ending of the Second World War, there was suddenly no obvious use for the Glider Pilot Regiment. So the instructors were posted away from the school leaving a skeleton staff who were tasked with closing the school down.[112] With training and activities reduced and little to do, Aubrey found more time for sport and other activities. This included devouring books on Russian politics and mathematics (which were plentiful in India) over the period September 1945 to the following April.[113] This time also gave him the opportunity to explore socialism, with a leaning towards finance, in practice – something that was to remain with him throughout his political career.

Elementary Flying Training Squad, no 1, in the sergeant's mess in Secunderabad 8th May 1945 receiving news of VE day. Talking to the South Wales Argus in 1995, Aubrey said this only caused muted celebrations in

---

[112] National Archives. Operations records book of No. 1 Elementary Flying Training School, 01/02/41 to 30/06/45. Ref: AIR 29/616/1.

[113] Many people with a leaning towards the left studied the Soviet Union in the 1930s and 1940s, including Sir Stafford Cripps, who served in several positions in the wartime coalition. Addison, P. (1985) Now the war is over. London. British Broadcasting Corporation.

India at the time. Even VJ day did not result in a great deal of celebration as all the soldiers wanted to do was come home and be demobbed.[114]

As for the future of the pilots, members of the RAF who had been recruited as an interim measure to make up for the shortfall in glider pilots after Arnhem, were returned to the RAF. The remainder of the glider pilots (of whom there were approximately 80) were dispersed all over India, and to their disappointment grounded to become involved in the task of repatriating ex-prisoners-of-war and tour-expired servicemen.[115,116] As for Aubrey, apart from a move a short distance to Chaklala in the Punjab in April 1946, his movements at this time are unknown, and there are few records to indicate any specific details of 344 Wing, or 670 Squadron (part of 343 Wing) to whom Aubrey had transferred in December 1945. His flying record shows that having passed as a light aircraft pilot, it was to be nine months until he flew again, and ultimately almost a year-and-half until he flew a glider for the first time. By this time, Aubrey together with about seven or eight other members of the Glider Pilot Regiment, had been posted to D Squadron at RAF Aqir in Palestine.[117] He transferred to Cochin Transit Camp in India on the very day of the first major terrorist attack of the 20th century in Jerusalem and entered Palestine on RMS Strathnaver at probably the tensest time in its history.[118] His experiences in Palestine ultimately had a significant effect on his life, resulting in a return 30 years later which indirectly led to the spurious accusations of fraud and corruption that destroyed his professional career and almost landed him a jail sentence (see Chapter 8).

Glider Pilot Regiment: Palestine

By the start of the First World War, Palestine had been part of the Ottoman Empire for 400 years. However, with the entry of Turkey on the side of Germany and Austro-Hungary in the First World War, Britain sought allies among those Arabs wanting independence from Turkish rule in Palestine. Supported by these Arabs, Britain conquered Palestine in 1917, and with the dismantling of the Ottoman Empire after the war, certain Arab-inhabited areas were put under mandate by the newly formed League of Nations. This

---

[114] "Singing, dancing and street parties." *South Wales Argus*. 11 January, 1995.

[115] "The Eagle." *The Glider Pilot Regiment Magazine*. Volume 1. Number 1. July, 1946.

[116] Seth, R. *Lions with Blue Wings: The story of the Glider Pilot Regiment 1942-1945*. London. Victor Gollancz Ltd, 1955.

[117] Interview with Bill Brunskill, colleague of Aubrey's in the Glider Pilot Regiment. 8 August, 2011.

[118] Now known as Kochi.

included Palestine, which came under British control. However, at the same time as courting the Arabs, Britain had also been looking to support from the Jews who they felt could greatly support its (WWI) war effort. This had resulted in the famous Balfour Declaration of 1917 that supported the establishment in Palestine of a national home for the Jewish people while also preserving the rights of "existing non-Jewish communities."

The promises made by Britain, to both the Arabs and the Jews, were not clear; nor was the settlement of Jerusalem with its shrines of such importance to both the Jewish and Muslim religions. The interpretation of the Balfour Declaration as containing the go ahead for the establishment of a Jewish state in Palestine, did not sit easily with the promise of supporting the "existing non-Jewish communities" who had owned and cultivated the land since the time of Mohammed the Prophet. The resulting conflict was almost inevitable.

Over the next ten years, many Jewish people relocated to Palestine which was now seen as their homeland. The Jewish population doubled during this time, and with rising anti-Semitism throughout Central Europe, and Hitler's rise to power in 1933, many more made the move. The increasing pressure to create a separate Jewish state within Palestine, as well as growing anger in the Arab population at being excluded from their homeland, resulted in a growth in terrorism from both sides against the British. This subsided during the Second World War, but by 1942, with news of the extermination of the Jews in Eastern Europe starting to filter through, tensions started to re-surface. In February 1942, these tensions culminated in the declaration of war against Britain by Menachem Begin, leader of the Irgun Tsva'i-Leumi (a Zionist paramilitary organization), for what he perceived to be Britain's anti-Zionist policies.[119] With the increase in attacks against British troops, and the end of the war in 1945, British troops were stationed in Palestine to act as a civilian defence force.

Palestine autumn 1945 to summer 1947

The main body of troops who arrived in Palestine were the 6th Airborne Division in the autumn of 1945 into which various members of the Army Air Corps, including the Glider Pilot Regime, were attached.[120,121] Most

---

[119] The Irgun Tsva'i Leumi were one of three many terrorist groups in Palestine at this time and generally posed the greatest threat to the British. The other two were the Haganah and the Lehi, also commonly referred to as the Stern Gang

[120] Wilson, D. *With 6th Airborne Division in Palestine 1945-1948.* Barnsley. Pen and Sword, 2008.

[121] Seth, R. *Lions with Blue Wings*, 1955.

troops who entered Palestine were generally ignorant of the situation in the region, although many had witnessed at first hand the sufferings of Jews in Europe. This included those who had been involved in the liberation of Belsen concentration camp just a few months earlier. Initially, these troops were to act in support of the local police, but they soon found themselves acting instead of them as the police became increasingly overwhelmed and recruitment stalled.

One of the tasks that remained uppermost in the memories of the stationed troops, including Ken Kirkham and Bill Brunskill who served with Aubrey in Palestine, was the cordon and search of mainly Jewish areas either in the hunt for weapons or for wanted individuals.[122] During these operations, they often faced intense hostility and hatred, being spat on and the subject of fierce abuse – and for many who were sympathetic to the plight of the Jews this would have been mystifying. The Arab populations were generally more quiescent, however, it was well-known that any who did not strongly support the Arab rebellion faced violence or death. The soldiers would therefore have felt under constant threat from the vast majority of the Palestinian population.

Acting against civilian units that were indistinguishable from the rest of the population, troops felt constantly at risk, identified as they were by their uniform, and their status in many eyes as an illegal occupying power. When interviewed in 2012, Ken Kirkham described how they were hated by the populous and under constant threat of terrorist action. For someone who had taken part in both the Normandy landings and the Battle of Arnhem, and who had seen underage boys die in battle, he described Palestine as his worst human experience of the war. Almost seventy years later, he visibly shook with emotion when recounting his hostile reaction to an act of kindness shown him by a terrified young Arab woman with a small child during one of these searches, a memory that he said he did not enjoy. The feeling of being traumatised by the up-close human experience of suspicion and fear was echoed in a number of other published accounts of British troops in Palestine. This included the commander of the 6th Airborne Division at the time, James Cassels who described his time in Palestine as "ten hellish months," as well as General Sir Evelyn Hugh Barker, General Officer Commanding of the British Forces in Palestine, who developed a deep hatred towards Zionism and the Jewish people as a result of his experiences in Palestine.[123,124]

---

[122] Interview with Bill Brunskill, colleague of Aubrey's in the Glider Pilot Regiment. 8 August, 2011.

[123] Bethell, N. *The Palestine Triangle: The struggle between the British, the Jews and the Arabs 1935-1948*. London. Futura Publications Limited, 1980.

[124] This is based on letters written to Katy Antonius, with whom he had a relationship with

Coming at a time when 50,000 Jews lined the route of the funeral of three members of the Haganah (Zionist paramilitary group) killed in a failed terrorist attack, the tensions felt by Ken Kirkham, Bill Brunskill and other British soldiers were understandable. These tensions came to a head on 25th April 1946, when the Lehi (another Zionist paramilitary group) killed seven soldiers in Tel Aviv, six of whom were unarmed. Deliberate attacks on British personnel were unexpected, and unlike in wartime the soldiers were not allowed to fight back. The situation brought British troops to the point of mutiny that was only averted when (while regiments held secret meetings) quick-thinking officers locked up weapons. Troops then instead enacted reprisals by breaking windows in Jewish areas.

In an attempt to deal a serious blow to the Jewish insurgents after recent kidnappings of British soldiers, a major operation known as "Agatha" was carried out in late June 1946 during which British troops flooded into Jerusalem and detained over 2,700 Jewish people. As a result of Operation Agatha, Menachem Begin started to make plans for reprisals. On 22nd July the Irgun Tsva'i-Leumi perpetrated what was to turn Palestine from a political problem into a serious terrorist issue; part of the King David Hotel in Jerusalem was blown up resulting in the deaths of ninety-one people including twenty-eight Britons.

This unprecedented attack brought widespread condemnation across the world, including from Jewish political leaders. The Haganah distanced themselves from the event. Even some of those involved were privately shocked by the deaths, including Adina Hay who had sent the telephone warnings to the hotel. Interviewed for a television documentary in 2004, she said, "It did not mean to kill anyone."[125] This attack ramped up the conflict between the Jewish militants and the mandatory government. On 30th July, in an operation called "Shark", the entire city of Tel Aviv was cordoned-off by approximately twenty thousand soldiers and police including 200 members of the Glider Pilot Regiment (which records suggest would have been its entire force in Palestine at this time).[126,127] Over a period of four days, the city was sealed, every house searched, and each of the approximately 170,000 inhabitants screened in the most comprehensive search of a city ever carried out. Although nearly eight hundred people were detained, this included none of those involved in the attack on the King David Hotel, even though several

whilst in Palestine.

[125] "Palestine: The Jewish war", Episode 4 of *Empire Warriors*. TV mini-series, 2004.

[126] Wilson, D., 2008.

[127] National Archives. Quarterly historical reports. Glider Pilot Regiment. No. 1 Wing, 01/07/1946 to 30/09/1946. Ref: WO 261/391.

of those involved in the attack including Menachem Begin were inside the cordon.

Arriving in Palestine on 6th August, four days after Operation Shark had finished, Aubrey entered a tense, uncomfortable and restrictive environment in which curfews, roadblocks, searches, and identity checks were commonplace. The first kidnapping of British troops had taken place just six weeks previously in June, and as a consequence, troops could not leave camp without permission. If they did, they had to be armed, and in groups of at least two during the day, and three at night.[128] With many places, including Tel Aviv, out of bounds and Aubrey probably confined to barracks as soon as he arrived, it is likely that this would not have been a comfortable experience.[129] Problems of theft, mainly from members of the Arab community, meant that camps were basic.[130] The possibility of being shot did not deter many would-be thieves from entering tents occupied by sleeping soldiers, and many contemporary accounts highlight the killing of a thief in these or similar circumstances. Although recreational trips were organised to places of historical interest, including those in nearby countries, opportunities were limited (unlike in India), and for most of the time troops were, by necessity, imprisoned by their own security.[131]

---

[128] Wilson, D., 2008.

[129] National Archives. Ref: WO 261/392.

[130] Ken Kirkham noted that most weeks articles would go missing from his washing (from interview with Ken Kirkham, 2012).

[131] Wilson, D., 2008

Arms and ammunition found during a search of the Jewish settlement of Dorot during Operation Bream, 28th August to 2nd September 1946. This was probably the first cordon and search operation that Aubrey took part in after arriving in Palestine. This search, together with a parallel search at Ruhama, Operation Eel, were unparalleled in terms of the deliberate damage and destruction of property caused by many troops highlighting the intense anti-Jewish feeling among many ranks at this time.[132]

As for training and potential future operations, the Quarterly Historical Reports of the Glider Pilot Regiment (available up to March 1947) record training and exercises as "aims" rather than targets which had to be snatched as opportunities arose. Consequently, little progress was made with plans for staging airborne exercises in the Middle East.[133] This is confirmed by Aubrey's flying logbook, which notes that during his first eleven months in Palestine, he flew only four times. This compares to the almost 400 flights that Aubrey carried out during his $3^1/_2$ years in the Glider Pilot Regiment in India. Few clues are given to Aubrey's activities during his time in Palestine because written orders were kept to a minimum to prevent them falling into the wrong hands. But we know, from personal accounts, that he organized several impromptu rugby matches.

---

[132] Hoffman, B. *Anonymous soldiers: The struggle for Palestine, 1917-1947*. New York. Alfred A. Knopf, 2015.
[133] Wilson, D., 2008.

Despite limited opportunities outside of camp, and the basic conditions within, sport played a major part of the Glider Pilot Regiment's time in Palestine, encouraged by their Commanding Officer, Lt-Col FAS Murray. This photograph, the only known photograph in Palestine of Aubrey, shows him captaining the D Squadron rugby team in the 1946/47 season.[134]

Of greatest concern to the troops, was the threat and potential of kidnap; the Irgun Tsva'i-Leumi threatened reprisals against British troops for any Jewish insurgent given the death penalty. Partly as a consequence, no Jewish insurgent had been hung since 1938, and troops kidnapped in June were only released after the death sentences on two members of the Irgun Tsva'i-Leumi had been commuted to imprisonment. This certainly saved lives, but with British sympathies hardening against Jewish insurgents, it was inevitable that the troops' greatest fears would soon be realized.

On April 23 1946, an Irgun Tsva'i-Leumi raid on a Police station in Ramat Gan resulted in a gun battle in which an Arab policeman and a member of the Irgun Tsva'i-Leumi were killed. Another Irgun Tsva'i-Leumi member, Dov Gruner was seriously wounded and captured. Too severely wounded to initially be put on trial, Dov Gruner was subsequentially found guilty and sentenced to death in January 1947. As a former member of the British Army who had fought against the Nazis in the Second World War, it was anticipated that his death sentence would be commuted to imprisonment. However, despite his case gaining worldwide coverage, and with significant pressure for clemency, Dov Gruner refused to accept the legality of the court. While this trial was ongoing, members of the Irgun Tsva'i-Leumi robbed a bank in Jaffa. Three of the perpetrators were caught and tried, and one was later flogged as part of his sentence.[135] Enraged by the latter, the Irgun Tsva'i-Leumi sought revenge against British troops. Returning from a Christmas Eve trip to Bethlehem amid great festivities, Aubrey was to experience the troops' greatest fear when on 29th December six British soldiers were kidnapped and flogged in retaliation – an operation known as "the Night of the Floggings."[136] In turn, this led to several cordon-and-search operations involving Aubrey's regiment, including one in the city of Netanya – the heart of support for the Irgun Tsva'i-Leumi and the place at the centre of the later Sergeants affair (see below) – on 31st December. Five of Irgun Tsva'i-

---

[134] "The Eagle." *The Glider Pilot Regiment Magazine.* Volume 1, Number 4. June, 1947.

[135] This sentence caused outrage in the Palestinian Government. As a result, this sentence was never used again in Mandatory Palestine.

[136] "The Eagle." *The Glider Pilot Regiment Magazine*, Volume 1, Number 4. June, 1947.

Leumi's armed men were caught at a roadblock carrying a whip. One was killed when the troops opened fire and three others were arrested and later sentenced to death.

With four executions imminent, tensions among both the British and Jewish populations were running high. Non-essential British civilians had already been evacuated from the country, and the Irgun Tsva'i-Leumi announced that they would kill six British soldiers for every death sentence carried out. On April 16th, the four Jewish insurgents were hung in Acre Prison. No announcement of their impending executions was made, and the prisoners were not told until the evening before. Five days later, two other prisoners blew themselves up in their cell with a hand grenade smuggled in with an orange, the day before they too were due to be hung for terrorist actions. Unable to carry out their threat of kidnap against British soldiers due to the security measures in place, the Irgun Tsva'i-Leumi turned their attentions to other targets. On 21st April they bombed a train, killing five British soldiers and three Arab civilians. On 24th April, they kidnapped a British businessman, who almost certainly avoided being hung only after he convinced them that he was Jewish.

On 16th June, three further Jewish insurgents who had participated in a prison breakout from Acre prison the previous month were sentenced to death. Again, the Irgun Tsva'i-Leumi stepped up their efforts to find hostages although it was becoming increasingly difficult with the British protected in guarded compounds. For Aubrey however, the personal risk of kidnap came to an end when his squadron was broken up and several members, including Aubrey, were sent back to the UK on the 24th June.[137] During his time in Palestine, approximately 100 members of the security forces, army and/or police were killed (although no members of the Glider Pilot Regiment).[138,139] With no threat of being torpedoed by German submarines, he returned to the UK via the much shorter route of the Mediterranean, arriving in the UK less than two weeks later on 6th July. However, memories of Palestine could not be allowed to fade, and less than a week later, the Irgun Tsva'i-Leumi kidnapped two British Sergeants. Held as hostages in retaliation for the capture of the Jewish insurgents, they were hung on 29th July – the same

[137] "The Eagle." *The Glider Pilot Regiment Magazine*. Volume 1, Number 5. December, 1947.

[138] Between May 45 and April 47, British intelligence sources estimated that casualties suffered by the security forces, the army and the police, as a result of terrorist's activities stood at 103 killed and 391 wounded (Rose, N. A senseless squalid war, 2010.)

[139] Osborn, B. and Pasley, D. *I just wanted to fly: The story of WWII Glider Pilot Bernard Osborn*. Baverstock and Pasley Memoirs Book II, 2019.

fate that was imposed on the Jewish insurgents on the same day. They were the last to be hung under the British Mandate. In a deliberate attempt to make the executions as public as possible, the two sergeants' bodies were taken to a eucalyptus grove where they were booby-trapped and hung from two adjacent trees.

The discovery of these bodies dominated news stories across the world, with widespread condemnation, including from other insurgent groups within Palestine. The Jewish Agency described it as a "crime against humanity and against the Jewish people" and issued a joint statement with the Jewish National Council stating that it was "a dastardly murder of two innocent men by a set of criminals."[140,141]

This picture, taken from the front cover of the Daily Express on 1st August 1947, shows the two sergeants, Clifford Martin and Mervyn Paice, hung in retaliation for the hanging of three members of the Irgun Tsva'i-Leumi. This one act probably had the greatest personal impact on the troops in Palestine. Even under the guise of a valid terrorist war, many, including Koestler 1983 (page 252) argued that this was the one act against the British in Palestine

---

[140] Also known as the Vaad Leumi.

[141] "Jewish agency condemns deed." *Palestine Post*. 1 August 1947. Available at: https://www.nli.org.il/en/newspapers/pls.

that went beyond the narrow limits of acceptability.

On the 1st August 1947, *The Daily Express* published, on the front cover, a photo of the bodies of the two sergeant's hung in the eucalyptus grove. Largely as a result, this image garnered a far greater reaction – both among the troops and the British population – than had the King David Hotel bombing a year previously in which ninety-one people had been killed. The act largely dispelled any remaining vestige of sympathy that many had for the Jewish insurgents in Palestine.[142] For some of the more volatile troops and policemen, these murders were one atrocity too many and they wanted revenge; in Palestine, five Jews were killed, Jewish shop windows were smashed, and vehicles overturned in subsequent reprisals. In Britain, anti-Semitic riots broke out in many cities including Manchester, Liverpool and Glasgow.

With much parliamentary debate, Harold Lever, MP for Manchester Exchange expressed the view of several MPs, and spoke for many troops in Palestine, when he said that the British were detested "by both the Arab and the Jew." Urging Britain to withdraw from Palestine, he was strongly criticised by, among others, Major Tufton Beamish MP for Lewes who had served in Palestine in 1938. Beamish dismissed Lever's comments based on what he perceived to be both his military knowledge and personal knowledge of Palestine.[143] If ever Aubrey was best qualified for a commons debate that he would seek twenty years later, it was probably now.

The subsequent history of both India and Palestine are well documented. The separate dominions of India and Pakistan came into being just six weeks after Aubrey arrived back in the UK, and the partition of Palestine to create the new state of Israel occurred less than a year later. Both events have subsequently led to several religious wars, including a mini war between Israel and Palestine in July 2014, which is dominating the news as this sentence is written. Although Aubrey's feelings and opinions on the events in both countries are not known, his experiences would have certainly been useful in later years when as a local councillor he represented the ethnically diverse area of Pill. Unlike many troops in Palestine, he held no animosity towards any members of the Jewish population. Indeed, in later life his best friends outside of politics were Leo and Hana Ichilov who were both Jewish.

---

[142] Lowe, E. *Forgotten conscripts: Prelude to Palestine's Struggle for Survival.* Trafford Publications, 2007.

[143] Hansard HC. Parliamentary debate on Palestine. Series 5. Volume 441. 12 August, 1947. Available at: https://hansard.parliament.uk/.

Carole

Aubrey returned to the UK to an uncertain future.[144] Having joined the army as a sixteen-year-old in January 1939, he had found himself involved in the deadliest conflict in human history involving most of the world's nations. He had got married, served in India and Palestine for more than $2^1/_2$ years, and become a member of a regiment whose existence, and vehicles for existence, did not exist at the start of the war. However, with the end of the war and the advent of the jet age, glider landings were now obsolete and he found himself in a regiment that now had no obvious purpose.[145] With most operational aircraft engaged in the Berlin airlift, Aubrey flew a glider for the last time on 21st July 1948 and trained as a parachutist with several other colleagues at Upper Heyford in Oxfordshire. Glider pilot stations started to close, and all potential pilots were confined to RAF Booker, where Aubrey became an instructor with No. 21 Elementary Training School. With the natural life of the Glider Pilot Regiment nearing its end, and with RAF Booker later to close in March 1950, Aubrey was starting to find life in the army tedious and dull.[146,147]

Connie was now pregnant, and he was keen to pursue his political ambitions in a world that had changed significantly since the recession-hit 1930s. However, having signed up to the army until at least January 1950, there was only one way that he could leave early, and that was to buy himself out. To the surprise of no one, he paid his £50 on 31st January 1949 and bought himself out of the smallest, most short-lived, and deadliest regiment in the history of the British Army and became an adult civilian for the first time at the age of twenty-six.[148,149,150]

Leaving the army was a significant time in the lives of both Aubrey and Connie; since marrying five years previously, they had seen very little of each other. For most of this time, Aubrey had served abroad, only seeing Connie once during a short period of home leave. Returning to the UK

[144] Much of the information in this section is based on stories related to friends of Aubrey and Connie, or younger relatives of Connie by others such as their parents. These include Chris Brawn, Ray Jones (Connie's nephew), Ruth Lewis and Margaret Crew (Connie's nieces) and Marion Marsh and Hana Ichilov (friends of Aubrey).

[145] Cooper, A. *Wot! No engines? Military gliders, RAF pilots and Operation Varsity, 1945.* Bognor Regis. Woodfield, 2002.

[146] "The Eagle." *The Glider Pilot Regiment Magazine.* Volume 2. Number 2. June, 1950.

[147] "Singing, dancing and street parties." *South Wales Argus,* 11 January, 1995.

[148] "Aubrey steps out of the hot seat." *South Wales Argus,* 29 April, 1987.

[149] Aubrey Hames Freedom of Newport ceremony, 19/02/98.

[150] Smith, C. *History of the Glider Pilot Regiment,* 1992.

from Palestine, he was then stationed at Syerston and Wycombe, returning to Connie at weekends and on leave. Since leaving Newtown in August 1942, their relationship had mainly existed via letters. Aubrey's letters were brought to an excited Connie by her father who was the local postman and who used to meet her on her way to work whenever there was a letter from Aubrey.[151] Aubrey returned to Newtown and obtained a job as a clerk in a local shop. For the first time in his working life, there was no expectation that he would have to move elsewhere with no notice and against his will. Aubrey also returned to a family who adored him, despite their many political differences, and a family that was soon to increase with the birth of his first child.[152] Connie gave birth to their daughter Carole at Montgomery County Infirmary in Newtown, the day after Aubrey left the army. In the bed next to her was Chris Brawn, wife of Aubrey's best friend Fred, whose son Richard was born the following day.

This should have been a happy occasion for Aubrey and Connie, made all the more special by close friends having a baby at the same time. However, it soon became clear that there was a problem with Carole. Two days after she was born, a Dr Clark came to see Chris Brawn believing she was Connie. Talking to Dr Clark, Chris Brawn realised that something was wrong, and she then watched as he talked to a bemused Connie. Carole would not feed and was having trouble keeping food down. Although Carole's medical records no longer exist, the events described by Chris Brawn suggest that Carole had a congenital medical condition known as Esophageal atresia.[153] In addition, it appears that she may also have had a physical and mental disability, common for children born with this condition (although her mental condition may not have been known about at this time).[154] Connie returned home without Carole, who stayed in hospital for some time.

Both Aubrey and Connie were devastated by the circumstances of Carole's birth. Anger followed their grief, some of it directed at each other – a common

---

[151] Interview with Connie and Clive Evans. Aubrey's ex-wife and her husband, 21 July, 2010.

[152] Connie's brother-in-law Hughie Walters often used to stay with Connie's parents for work. Returning home he often commented that Connie's parents thought the world of Aubrey, jokingly adding that "I don't think they liked me that much." Connie's father was a Conservative, and he and Aubrey often used to have "vigorous" political discussions."

[153] An obstruction of the oesophagus.

[154] Brunner, H.G. and Winter, R.M. "Autosomal dominant inheritance of abnormalities of the hands and feet with short palpebral fissures, variable microcephaly with learning disability, and oesophageal/duodenal atresia." *Journal of Medical Genetics*. Volume 28, 1991. pp 389-394.

process for parents who give birth to a disabled child.[155] With time though, Aubrey and Connie became more accepting of Carole's condition which was greatly helped by Connie's parents George and Fanny. Having lost their only son Ivor at Dunkirk, they perhaps found it easier to cope with the shock of having a disabled granddaughter, particularly George who idolised his granddaughter. However, with Carole home, life still had to go on and within a year of her being born, Aubrey took a three-month business course at the Birmingham College of Commerce. He was taking advantage of special bursaries that were available for soldiers after the war. Connie therefore took on most of the responsibility for looking after Carole during the week when Aubrey was in Birmingham, and she understandably found this time difficult. Spending a lot of time with Chris Brawn, Connie would often comment on how active her son was in comparison with Carole who never moved. With the strain telling, and perhaps missing Aubrey, Connie started to spend time in the Sergeants' Mess in Newtown with two or three friends.[156] She struck up a friendship with the young barman there, Clive Evans, and they started a relationship. At some point after 25th November 1950, when he returned to Newtown to work as a trainee with Pryce Jones (a mail order business and department store) Aubrey found out about Connie and Clive and was devastated.[157] Unable to be in the same house as Connie, he left and returned to live with his father in Newport, leaving his beloved Carole behind.

Carole's condition made her vulnerable to illness, particularly respiratory problems, and sometime before the end of 1950 she developed bronchitis. After a short illness she died on the 30th December 1950 just before her second birthday, having never walked nor talked. Returning for her funeral with Fred Brawn, Aubrey left straight after without talking to Connie. After saying goodbye to George and Fanny, he packed all his remaining belongings in Carole's pram before going to talk to the doctor and then Fred Brawn in the Cross Guns Inn (up the road from Connie's parents' house). After pouring his heart out to Fred Brawn, he then returned to Newport a few hours after arriving, never to see Connie again. However, he did get to return to Carole's grave on many occasions, helped to a great extent by the All-Wales Labour Rallies held annually at Newtown in the County Pavilion, with the

---

[155] Kandel, I. and Merrick, J. "The birth of a child with disability. Coping by parents and siblings." *The Scientific World Journal*. Volume 3, 2003, pp.741-750.

[156] Several interviews carried out for this book suggest that Aubrey and Connie never recovered from the circumstances surrounding Carole's birth, and it was this that ultimately drove them apart.

[157] Based on register of electors (Gwent Archives) which shows Aubrey living at 38 Park Street in Newtown on 25th November 1950.

first opportunity occurring seven months after Carole died in July 1951.

Moustache

In about 1990, when passing through Newtown, I went to find Carole's grave. With no idea where she was buried, or when she had died, I went to Newtown Cemetery on Pool Road which I considered her most likely burial place. Approaching a man in a small building which just happened to contain the burial records, he pointed me towards a large pile of burial books. Handwritten, and covering what appeared to be a few thousand entries, this presented a daunting task in the search for her burial place, in a cemetery or town where I wasn't even sure she was buried. Guessing her earliest date of death as 1952, I picked up an earlier burial book by mistake – the book that covered burials from the end of 1950. Unable to read the first entry because of poor handwriting and no idea where to start or finish, I asked a friend to read it instead. However, the task suddenly became very easy when remarkably the first entry looked at was for Carole's burial. Although this event has little relevance to Aubrey's biography, the fresh flowers on Carole's grave on this date unexpectedly led to a meeting with Connie at a time when she was still a relatively young woman. This gave me the chance to find out more about Aubrey's life with Connie. Although I remember little about this meeting, one thing that became clear was Connie's continued fondness for Aubrey. Connie was well aware of his political career after leaving Newtown, noting that whenever he appeared on the television, someone would always ring her up to tell her, "Your Aub is on the telly." Twenty years later when I started to write this book, I returned to talk to Connie and her husband Clive, the young barman from the Sergeants' Mess. Although this time I was more prepared, and armed with a series of questions, Connie was now in her late 80s and suffering from advanced dementia. Unable to answer many questions, Connie did though give a clue to a very important question, which was when did he grow his famous moustache? Giggling when remembering her mother's reaction to his moustache, the story told by Connie and memories from Ken Kirkham in 1949, suggest that he grew his moustache sometime after leaving Connie in 1950.

Connie died on 28th August 2013, a couple of years after I last saw her. She is now buried next to Carole, with a photograph of Carole in her top pocket. Carole was never forgotten by Aubrey or Connie. The flowers on Carole's grave when I originally visited were not an irregular occurrence, despite her death forty years earlier. Aubrey never talked about Carole to his family – almost certainly because his wife Mary found it difficult. However, he did talk to his friends about her, including Lihu and Hana Ichilov and John and Marion Marsh. He had found it deeply upsetting that he could not see Carole after leaving Newtown, as this would also have meant seeing Connie. Although it is not known what effect losing Carole had on his life, it is known that any sadness was greatly eased by the birth of Annette, his eldest surviving child just over six years later. Talking to me about her earliest memories of our father, the first thing Annette mentioned was teaching her to stand on her head; the same party trick performed by Aubrey as a young drill sergeant at the Drill Hall in Newtown.

Carole's grave in Newtown

CHAPTER 3

THE "YOUNG TURK"

"Young turk": A young progressive or insurgent member of an institution, movement, or political party.

From service to politics

Although army protocol barred soldiers from being signed-up members of political parties, it was inevitable that a conscripted army would contain a vast number of men interested in discussing, and as much as possible, engaging in, political activity. With memories of what they had left behind, the main discussion points invariably revolved around the home that they would return to, and crucially, what sort of life they would be expected to lead when the war ended.

After the First World War, these men would have observed their fathers, the first generation of conscripted men from the United Kingdom, coming home only to realise that finding employment was difficult after all the lost years of learning a trade. The jobs that they previously carried out, or aspired to, were now filled by those who had stayed behind and who had acquired the skills and experience that they now lacked. As with Aubrey's father, many would have had to leave the areas where they had been born and brought up in pursuit of work elsewhere.

Consequently, unemployment among those who had served in the First World War was disproportionately higher than among those who had not gone to war. By 1924, six years after the end of the First World War, over 600,000 ex-servicemen were unemployed out of a total unemployment figure of nearly 2 million.[1] Moreover, many lived in properties that were considered unfit

---

[1] Reese, P. *Homecoming Heroes*. London. Leo Cooper, 1992.

for human habitation. The famous pledge of David Lloyd George (Prime Minister over the period 1916 to 1922) to make "homes fit for heroes," had proved to be a worthless promise, and by the start of the Second World War there was a greater shortage of houses than at the end of the First.[2,3] Multiple occupancy of houses was commonplace, with the war veterans and their families the most likely to be affected – including the types of homes that Aubrey and Russell lived in as children during the 1930s. Throughout their childhood, they had to share their family home with at least one other family or other non-family individuals.[4] The social failures of the inter-war years, as well as the 1930s' policy of appeasement (the policy that allowed the expansion of Hitler's Germany), were therefore mainly blamed on the Conservatives who dominated UK government during this period, despite two short periods of minority Labour rule. The Liberals, the party of David Lloyd George, had by this time ceased to be a party of potential leadership.

It is therefore unsurprising that a large majority of servicemen were against the idea of a future Conservative government. This was borne out following the instigation of compulsory army lectures on current affairs that were introduced to members of the armed forces in 1941. While the aim was to educate and relieve boredom among servicemen, these debates proved to be a breeding ground for left-wing discussion. Indeed, David Niven the famous Oscar-winning movie actor and a major in the commandos at the time commented:

> One thing stuck out a mile in these debates - the vast majority of men who had been called up to fight for their country held the Conservative Party entirely responsible for the disruption to their lives and in no circumstances would they vote for it next time there was an election – Churchill or no Churchill.[5]

In some places, these debates became formalised with "Parliaments" established, motions introduced and debated, and votes cast. The most famous of these was the Cairo Forces Parliament of 1944 which was ultimately disbanded when Leo Abse, later MP for Pontypool, was arrested

---

[2] This relates to a speech made by David Lloyd-George on 12th November 1918, where his exact words were, "Habitations fit for the heroes who have won the war," although this is commonly abbreviated to "homes fit for heroes."

[3] Labour Party Conference. Homes for the future. Labour's policy for housing, 1956.

[4] Occupancy of Aubrey's childhood homes can be traced every six or twelve months by a variety of street directories and polling books for most years.

[5] Niven, D. *The moon's a balloon*. London. Hamish Hamilton, 1971, p 226.

for introducing a motion supporting nationalization of the Bank of England.[6] Other parliaments were formed in India and probably elsewhere, although these were generally short-lived. Due to a chance discovery of a speech used as a bookmark in the Labour Party headquarters in Stow Hill before it was closed in the 1980s, it is known that Aubrey took an active part in these debates. Speaking in January 1946 when he was stationed in Begumpet, Aubrey gave a strong argument against British rule in India. Referring to a country "subjected to the harsh English Rule" and accusing the East India Company of setting up an industrial system that "completely terrorised and eventually demoralised subject people," this speech was far more inflammatory than the content Leo Abse was arrested for. However, with the war over and India on the verge of independence, senior officers probably worried little about any possible implications, and many would have agreed with him. There was little doubt about what the "subject people" wished for, and they were to achieve it with independence a year later. A future government led by Jawaharlal Nehru, based on Fabian principles, may have inspired Aubrey; a year later when based in Palestine, he joined the Fabian Society.[7,8]

By this time, Labour had won the first post-war General Election securing its first absolute majority and its highest ever share of the vote. This occurred despite the fact that Winston Churchill was probably the most popular Prime Minister ever, with an approval rating in the opinion polls of 83% just prior to the General Election.[9] Although there was a belief at the time that the Conservatives had been defeated by the votes of the servicemen at war, this was not true.[10] While the vast majority of servicemen voted for Labour, they contributed just 7% of the votes cast – partly because most servicemen were unable to vote as they were otherwise engaged.[11] However, many of their parents, bothers, sisters, wives or girlfriends had probably voted with the welfare of the servicemen in mind, and opinion polls showed that the

---

[6] Leo Abse was later to become a good friend of Aubrey and represented him in his court case against the British Transport Docks Board in the 1970s (see Chapter 8). It is not known when they first met, however, his diary entries suggest they knew each other from at least January 1951.

[7] The concept of a gradual rather than revolutionary means of spreading socialist principles.

[8] London School of Economics and Political Science. Aubrey Hames membership card. 14 February, 1947.

[9] Addison, P. "Why Churchill lost in 1945." BBC website, 2011. Available at: http://www. bbc.co.uk/history/worldwars/wwtwo/election_01.shtml. Date accessed: 08/11/15.

[10] Ibid.

[11] Crang, J.A. "Politics on parade: army education and the 1945 general election." *History.* Volume 81. Number 262, 1996. pp.215-227.

civilian vote was strongly pro-Labour.[12] However, even though the forces may not have changed this result, the war politicized many servicemen from whose ranks many future politicians emerged. These numbers included all three future leaders of Newport Borough Council who served in the Second World War, as well as Roy Hughes who served as MP for Newport and later Newport East for over 30 years from 1966.[13] Roy Hughes actively followed political events during his time in the army, particularly while in India.[14] Stewart Watson, Aubrey's predecessor as leader of the council, had also been very forthright in his political ideals while in the army and had previously tried to sign up for the Spanish Civil War in support of the Republican government against the rise of fascism (he was unsuccessful because the recruiting officer knew he was underage).[15] The politicisation of the forces was not just restricted to future Labour politicians. Trevor Warren, the Conservative leader of Newport Borough Council for a short time in the mid-1970s, was not that interested in politics at the start of the war but after joining the RAF his interest grew. During his time in service, he had been surrounded by people more fortunate than him, many from public schools, and he believed that observing their lives and standards of living is what swayed him towards Conservative views – even though it would be twenty before he entered politics.[16] The Fabian Society and the Labour victory in the 1945 General Election had whetted Aubrey's desire for political office and he was the first of these ex-servicemen to seek political office in Newport.[17,18] But he was not the first of the main post-war Newport politicians to engage in political activity at the conclusion of the war. That particular honour probably goes to Paul Flynn, who as a precocious 10-year-old worked at the 1945 General Election.[19] Although Paul Flynn did not enter local politics in Newport until 1972, he was later to become Newport's longest ever serving MP, representing Newport West for 32 years from 1987 until his death in

---

[12] Addison, P. "Why Churchill lost in 1945"

[13] Conservative council leaders Leo Driscoll (1950) and Sidney Teece Miller (1967-1971) who both served in the First World War, carried out civilian roles during the Second World War.

[14] Hughes, R. *Seek Fairer Skies*. Spennymoor. The Memoir Club, 2003.

[15] Interview with Mary Evans. Stewart Watson's daughter. 9 September, 2014.

[16] Interview with Trevor Warren. Former leader of the Conservative Group on Newport Borough Council. 31 October, 2014.

[17] "Aubrey steps out of the hot seat." *South Wales Argus*. 29 April, 1987.

[18] Roy Hughes, Stewart Watson and Trevor Warren all signed up for the duration of the war, so returned to civilian life after peace was declared in 1945.

[19] Flynn, P. My vote. 13 August, 2015. Available at: http://paulflynnmp.typepad.com/my_weblog/2015/08/my-vote.html. Date accessed 22/11/15.

2019.

Political life in Newtown

Aubrey joined the Newtown Labour Party shortly after returning to civilian life in 1949 – and it was here that he started his post-war political career. Support for Labour in Newtown was growing rapidly at this time, and a threefold increase in the number of Labour Party branches and members in the County of Montgomeryshire occurred in the years that followed the 1945 General Election.[20,21] Aubrey was elected Social Secretary of the Newtown Labour Party at the Annual General Meeting of 10th January 1950 at which there was record attendance.[22] The future for Labour and Aubrey in Newtown, on the surface at least, looked bright.

However, despite the surge of interest in the Labour Party itself in Newtown, support among the general population of Newtown was not strong despite the fact that it was the birth and resting place of the man generally considered to be the father of the cooperative movement, Robert Owen.[23] The rise in the number of members after 1945 was from a baseline of the lowest Labour party membership in Wales, and few Labour members were willing to give more than token support to the Labour cause.[24] Consequently, the Labour Party in Newtown struggled to get willing candidates for either local or county council elections. However, this was not something solely restricted to the local Labour Party, as both the Liberals and the Conservative parties had similar problems, with the result that as many as 20-25% of council seats were returned unopposed, or not even filled.[25] This lack of interest caused significant consternation in the local press with , for example, several articles in *The Montgomery Express and Radnor Times* on May 7th 1949 expressing frustration at the lack of people willing to come forward for political office.

---

[20] "Montgomeryshire Labour Party." *The Montgomery County Times and Shropshire and Mid-Wales Advertiser.* 26 March, 1949. Newtown Library.

[21] Tanner, D., Williams, C. and Hopkin, D. *The Labour Party in Wales 1900-2000.* Cardiff. University of Wales Press, 2000.

[22] "Montgomeryshire Labour Party annual general meeting." *The Montgomery County Times and Shropshire and Mid-Wales Advertiser.* 14 January, 1950. Newtown Library.

[23] Although Robert Owen died in 1858, he was a key influence on many during the growth of the Labour Party in the first half of the twentieth century. This included Stewart Watson, whose socialist ideals were strongly influenced by the classic novel The Ragged Trousered Philanthropists by Robert Tressell. The central character Frank Owen is named in homage to Robert Owen.

[24] Tanner, D., Williams, C. and Hopkin, D, 2000.

[25] Rallings, C. and Thrasher, M. *Local elections in Britain.* London. Routledge, 2013.

Seats that were filled tended to go to independents, not members of the main three political parties, although these were probably Liberal or Conservative candidates working together against any Labour challenge.

This general apathy towards active politics in Newtown in the late 1940s suggests that Aubrey would probably have gained some political office in either local or county elections if he had stayed there – although it is unlikely that it would have occurred with the Labour Party in any sort of power. Aubrey's influence over Labour in Newtown at this time is also difficult to fathom as few contemporary records of political activity in Newtown exist, including no records at all of the Newtown Labour Party. However, *The Montgomery Express and Radnor Times* is littered with correspondence from Aubrey during his short time as a civilian there. Constantly defending the Labour Party and their principles, and similarly attacking the Conservative Party for the same reason, his unyielding approach to correspondence often led to lengthy debates with fellow correspondents. This included one debate of eleven extensive letters written over a period of three months. Not for the first time in his early letter-writing career, the debate ended only when the paper's editor closed the discussion down. However, any influence Aubrey may have had on Newtown politics may ultimately have been dictated by a declining support for Labour, which peaked in 1949 and was to fall steadily to about half this level over the next 40 years.[26] Just staying in any political office may therefore have been difficult, although as noted, such was the extent of local apathy toward political office that he may have been returned unopposed in many elections – as occurred with many politicians across both Newtown and Powys as a whole.[27] To have entered national politics would have been a significantly greater challenge and was something that Aubrey probably would not have achieved in Newtown. With little competition for the Labour candidacy in most general elections, Aubrey could have had several attempts as the Labour Party candidate for Montgomeryshire, but he would have faced stiff competition from the long-standing leader of the Liberal Party, and MP for Montgomeryshire, Clement Davies. Clement Davies was a hugely popular figure within the constituency, and even after his death in office in 1962, Montgomeryshire was to remain strongly Liberal for the rest of Aubrey's life, apart from a brief period from 1979 to 1983 when it was held by the Conservative Party. Labour by contrast, consistently finished a distant third in all general elections over the next 50 years, apart

---

[26] Based on newspaper accounts of local election and general election results since 1949.

[27] In 1952 for example, there were no contests in over half the seats across the UK for county elections (Smellie, B. A history of local government. London. George Allen & Unwin, 1957. Third edition.).

from in 1951 and 1955 when the party finished second, or alternatively last in a two-horse race.

Returning home to Newport in 1950, where Labour was beginning to thrive, was to prove a fortunate political move for Aubrey despite the unhappy circumstances of a ruined marriage and the loss of a much-loved daughter.

Arrival of the turk

When Aubrey left Newport to join the army in 1939, it had never had a Labour-controlled council despite Labour attaining half the council seats at the 1933 borough elections.[28] He therefore returned in 1950 to the familiar scene of a joint Conservative- and Liberal-controlled council, known as the "anti-Labour" vote, with the Labour Party in opposition as it had been in 1939.[29] But the wider political landscape in post-war Newport bore little resemblance to that which Aubrey had left behind. In 1945, in the first municipal elections since 1938, Labour had gained control of the council for the first time. The General Election of the same year resulted in a Labour MP being elected for only the second time in Newport, Peter Freeman.[30] Moreover, Labour was to remain in power in Newport for the rest of the 1940s and although losing control of the council in the year that Aubrey returned, this was to prove only a minor blip; they returned to power in 1951 and this was a position they didn't relinquish until 1967.[31]

So when Aubrey re-joined the Labour Party in Newport, in about June 1950, it was in a fairly healthy position. In contrast to the Labour party in Newtown, it was a massive organisation that had grown during the inter-war period to be the largest in Wales and one of the largest in the UK.[32] Although by

---

[28] Labour was denied power in 1933 by the ten anti-Labour Alderman.

[29] It was common practice until 1952 for the Conservatives and Liberals to join forces as an "anti-Labour" party, with only one candidate nominated in each ward to stand against the Labour candidate. Typically, about 70% of the candidates were Conservatives, and 30% of the candidates Liberals. This was also repeated at general elections where, prior to the 1945 General Election, 1923 was the only general election in Newport where both a Conservative and Liberal candidate had stood. This practice stopped after 1952, as the Conservatives no longer considered the Liberals of any importance in Newport politics.

[30] Newport's first Labour MP was James Walker, who represented Newport for the period 1929-1931. Following Peter Freeman's election in 1945, Newport (and the subsequent east and west constituencies) was represented by a Labour MP apart from 1983-1987, when the Conservatives were in power in Newport West.

[31] Newport was the only county borough in England or Wales to pass from Conservative to Labour control in 1951.

[32] Tanner, D., Williams, C. and Hopkin, D., 2000.

1950 support had started to wane slightly, membership still stood at just shy of 3,300, about two thirds of whom were women.[33] Leading the party was Reginald Silas Tyack who had been elected leader in 1941. Tyack was one of seven aldermen, three of whom were women.[34] Together with the twelve male councillors, these were Labour's representatives on the council. Typical of Labour council members nationally at the time, these were a rather elderly bunch, with an average age of 60, or 66 amongst the aldermen.[35]

All the Labour aldermen had first been elected to the council before the early 1930s, and three of them had been first elected in the early 1920s. Most of the Labour councillors had been elected in 1945, some of whom had been co-opted during wartime, and all had been elected since 1947.[36] None of them had been in any of the armed forces during the war on account of a combination of their age, or working in reserved occupations, or both.[37] It is therefore likely that they had all been active locally in the Labour Party since at least the 1930s. Nearly all the successful Labour nominees for the council from 1945 worked in traditional white-collar industries, many as trade union officials, and they all appeared to follow the traditional route – from a long apprenticeship within the party, to nomination, and ultimately to election.[38] Although young people were encouraged to join the Labour Party, a fear of Marxist views in the youth, as well as a fear of communist infiltration, meant that they were treated as naive and inexperienced youngsters who should

---

[33] Historic Labour constituency membership figures are notoriously inaccurate, although membership figures for Newport are a fair representation of actual numbers (based on unpublished research by Jim Criddle).

[34] Aldermen were members of the council elected by fellow council members, not the electorate, for a period of six years. Within Newport, there was generally a gentleman's agreement that the most senior councillors on the council were elected as aldermen. However, on occasion, the election of aldermen would be utilized by a political party to gain or maintain power on the council.

[35] Haydn Davis noted that "one only had to give a cursory inspection to photographs that appeared in the press at local election times to gain the impression that for the most part the town was in the not overly deft hands of rather elderly ladies and gentlemen." (Davis, H. The history of the Borough of Newport, 1998).

[36] With local elections prohibited during wartime, any councillors who left the council for whatever reason were replaced by invitation of the existing members. Generally, these were of the same political persuasion of those councillors who they replaced.

[37] War records for candidates were routinely noted in the South Wales Argus, as it was, for example, for Kenneth Baker, the Conservative councillor elected in 1951.

[38] Labour councillors were dominated by employees of the Great Western Railway, probably because they were recompensed for lost time for public duties by their union (South Wales Argus. "Council candidate," letter from Alderman Frank Humphries. 21 October, 1946).

quietly accept adult advice and majority decisions without question.[39],[40] By default, this included returning servicemen, particularly young upstarts like Aubrey returning to Newport from a Labour backwater such as Newtown. Consequently, it was of no surprise that by 1950 the Labour Party in Newport had not selected a single local election candidate who had seen service in the war. The Conservative Party were generally more prone to treating ex-servicemen as equals, even though they had only fielded one ex-serviceman at this time.[41] This was Derrek Whyalt-John who was elected to the council at his first attempt in 1949 at the age of 25.[42] His selection and ultimate election however, was almost certainly because he was the only candidate available, and he appeared to be a fairly anonymous figure during his one period as a councillor.[43]

Birth of the turk

The stability enjoyed by seniority had resulted in many Labour aldermen and councillors, as well as those from the Conservative and Liberal parties, having a laissez-faire attitude towards their responsibilities on the council and within their party. This was not an unusual problem on Monmouthshire councils, as had been expressed by Aneurin Bevan during his time as a councillor in Tredegar in the 1920s when he accused some Labour councils of stewing in their own juice for so long that they became "rancid".[44] In Newport, this was probably best demonstrated by sitting Labour councillors who, when faced with a re-election contest, often did not feel that it was necessary to appear before the panel that interviewed prospective candidates.[45] With councillors

---

[39] Layton-Henry, Z. "Labour's lost youth," *Journal of Contemporary History*. Volume 11, 1976, pp 275-308.

[40] This was also confirmed by Clive Shaksheff. Although he only joined the Newport Labour Party in 1963 when he was 19, he confirmed that the older members of the party treated younger members with an element of contempt (Interview with Clive Shaksheff, former member of Newport Labour Party. 1 April, 2022).

[41] Jarvis, D. "The Conservative Party's Recruitment of Youth," in Orsina, G. and Quagliariello, G. eds., *La formazione della classe politica in Europa: 1945-1956*. Volume 3, 2000.

[42] The average age of the Conservative candidates in Newport in 1945 for example was just over 40 ("Politics out of place in town government," *South Wales Argus*. 27 October, 1945), which was a common theme for Conservative candidates in municipal elections in the immediate post-war era. However, most of the youngest of these candidates stood in unwinnable seats.

[43] Newport Conservative Party executive committee. Executive committee minutes. 16 March, 1970. National Library of Wales.

[44] Foot, M. *Aneurin Bevan 1897-1945*. Volume 1. Harper Collins, 1962.

[45] Newport Labour Party general committee. *General committee meeting minutes*. 2 October,

assuming that past records should suffice, compromises had to be found by the different wards in the face of these refusals.[46] Attendance for some Labour councillors at committee and ward meetings had fallen to less than 25% and those who did attend often treated them as social events, where you "went to see your mates," as you would in the local pub.[47,48] It is of no surprise therefore that by June 1950 there had not been a proposal of any substance from any ward for at least five years, and no noted ward activity since 1947.

With the lack of attendance of councillors and aldermen at meetings, and little consideration given towards the needs of their constituents, it is not surprising that dissatisfaction among many Labour Party members had been growing for several years.[49] Almost without exception during the early 1950s, annual reports of the constituency Labour Party paid fulsome tribute to the efforts of the women's sections in providing money for the running of the party by arranging and running bazaars and fetes, and almost as frequently complained about the lack of support from male council members, particularly at election time.

However, with Aubrey joining the Newport Labour Party in late 1950, things started to change noticeably. Within a few months, more correspondence had flowed out of the Malpas Ward than from all other wards combined in Newport since the end of the war. Initially these were identified as from the Malpas Ward, but later from Aubrey himself. The first proposal identified as from Aubrey was to try and force aldermen and councillors to take a more active part in their respective ward meetings by calling for open monthly interviews of the ward councillors. This was endorsed by the executive committee.[50] In the first proposal of any substance since the end of the war, Aubrey made it clear what he felt was the responsibility of socialist council members.

1953.

[46] Based on unpublished research by Jim Criddle.

[47] Newport Labour Party executive committee. *Executive committee meeting minutes*. 2 October, 1950.

[48] See for example Shaw, E. Discipline and discord in the Labour Party: the politics of managerial control in the Labour Party, 1951-87. Manchester. Manchester University Press, 1988.

[49] A letter described as being from the "Newport Labour Party" was read out at the Labour group meeting of 11/09/1950 regarding the lack of attendance of aldermen and councillors at meetings of the party general committee (Newport Labour group. Labour group meeting minutes. 11 September, 1950).

[50] Newport Labour Party executive committee. *Executive committee meeting minutes*. 4 September, 1950.

With no motions proposed from any ward since the end of the war, by mid-1951 they were coming from the Malpas Ward every couple of months. The first concerned the accommodation needs of the chronically sick – and this was later raised in Parliament by Newport's MP, Peter Freeman.[51] By July 1951, with Aubrey now a member of the general committee, he proposed several resolutions on various topics such as housing, and the NHS. This was the only means by which an individual member of a constituency party could influence Labour Party policy, and therefore its manifesto. Unbelievably, these were the first resolutions proposed by the Labour Party in Newport since 1934.

By now, Aubrey had established himself as one of the main figures in the Newport Labour Party, and at the age of 28 the "young turk" leading the new breed of young socialists, mainly ex-servicemen and women, entering the political scene in Newport. Unafraid to force his point, and not interested in acquiescing to the political dinosaurs of the day, less than a year after joining the Labour Party in Newport he had started the process of transforming it.

Mary

The radical changes that Aubrey was driving through the Labour Party in Newport in the early 1950s left little time for anything else in his life and so he withdrew from beginning an economics degree at the University of London that had been due to start in the autumn of 1951.[52] He did however join the Cardiff Flying Club so that he could continue flying two-seater biplanes.[53] In November 1951 he was chosen as a prospective candidate for the Caerau Ward in the 1952 Municipal Elections.[54] Standing against the popular previous Caerau councillor and Newport Labour Party agent, Reginald Ley, Aubrey probably stood little chance of securing the nomination, and at best, an evens chance of winning the seat. However, with work pressures growing due to imminent promotion and the likelihood of more regular travel as a result, he was finding it impossible to devote as much time to the Labour Party as he would like. He therefore withdrew his candidacy from the municipal panels

---

[51] Hansard HC. Parliamentary question from Peter Freemen MP to Arthur Blenkinsop, Minister of Health. Series 5. Volume 491. 26 July, 1947. Available at: https://hansard.parliament.uk/.

[52] From a letter from the University of London dated 29/05/51, Aubrey had been accepted as an economics student based on a special university exam that he had taken in January 1951.

[53] Article about prominent Catholics in Society. *St. Marys Church Magazine.* Easter, 1966.

[54] Newport Labour Party General Committee. *Newport general committee meeting minutes*, 30 November, 1951.

list two weeks after being chosen as a potential candidate.[55]

Aubrey's withdrawal from the municipal panels list caused quite a stir among the Labour Party members in Newport. It coincided with the arrival of a new girlfriend in his life, Mary, who he had met at the Palm Court Dancing Hall, probably in the summer of 1951.[56] The reason for their concern wasn't the distraction of a new girlfriend, but more the fact that Mary was a member of the Young Conservatives.[57] But the fear that Aubrey's political beliefs could be turned were groundless; Mary had little interest in politics let alone the Conservative Party. As possibly the largest political youth organisation in the world in the 1950s, and with little to do in the immediate post-war period, Mary was one of about two-thirds of people who joined the Young Conservatives for its social activities rather than for any political affiliation.[58,59]

This dilapidated building shows the old Palm Court Dancing Hall as it was in 2016, 65 years after Aubrey first met Mary here in 1951. Apart from Mary and Aubrey, a large number of people from Newport seem to have met their

[55] Letter from Aubrey withdrawing from the municipal panel, Newport Labour Party general committee, *Newport general committee meeting minutes*. 14 December, 1951.

[56] The first mention of Mary in Aubrey's diary is on 13th October 1951 with a note to ring her. Aubrey's sister-in-law Nell Hames, who was there when Aubrey met Mary, believes it was in the summer of 1951 when they first met.

[57] Interview with Marion Marsh, friend of Aubrey and wife of John Marsh, 19 June, 2022.

[58] Lamb, M. "Young Conservatives, young Socialists and the great youth abstention: Youth participation and nonparticipation in political parties." Doctoral dissertation. University of Birmingham, 2002.

[59] Abrams, F. and Little, A. "The young activist in British politics." *British Journal of Sociology*. Volume 16. Number 4, 1965.

future partners here in the 1940s and 1950s, including about half the people from Newport interviewed for this book.

A vivacious, fun loving 24-year-old with a sense of mischief, Mary was clearly a good match for Aubrey and they were soon to form a close and loving relationship. This was despite Russell turning up for their first date to tell Mary that Aubrey would be late as he was delayed in a meeting, and Mary ending Aubrey's flying career by refusing to accompany him in two-seater biplanes. About six months after Carole's death, and a year since Aubrey had left Connie, this appears to have been Aubrey's first relationship since these events. As for Mary, she had recently gone through a traumatic and enforced breakup of an engagement to an interesting character, and Aubrey was probably also her first boyfriend since this significant breakup.

Mary had been engaged to a German aristocrat by the name of Bernhard Von Werminghausen – a Luftwaffe pilot who had been a prisoner of war based in St Brides, a small hamlet to the south-west of Newport. One of 123,000 German prisoners of war shipped to the UK from America in 1946, he was in the UK until the end of 1947, working on the estate at Tredegar Park before being repatriated back to Germany.[60] Mary got to know Bernhard while he was working at Tredegar Park near where she lived with her parents and her sister June. This friendship happened despite fraternization with German prisoners-of-war being discouraged and it having been a criminal offence to even talk to them until December 1946.[61] However, with hostile attitudes towards Germans diminishing drastically in the early post-war years, prisoners of war were free to marry their British girlfriends from July 1947 onward.[62,63] Mary and Bernhard therefore became engaged soon after and hoped to get married after Bernhard had been repatriated back to Germany.[64]

However, Bernhard was no ordinary German prisoner of war. His uncle, Franz Von Papen, was Chancellor of Germany in 1932 and Ambassador to

---

[60] Weber-Newth, I. and Steinert, J. *German migrants in post-war Britain: an enemy embrace*. London. Routledge, 2006.

[61] War Office, memorandum, 12.12.1946. Wolff, Die deutschen Kriegsgefangenen, p 42. H. Faulk, Die deutschen Kriegsgefangenen in Grobbritannien. Re-education, Bielefeld: Gieseking, 1970, p 627. Ref. PRO WO 32/11686.

[62] Harvester, file report (No. 2565). "Attitudes to the German people: Review of attitude changes among British public during the war." February, 1948.

[63] Weber-Newth, I. and Steinert, J. *German migrants in post-war Britain: an enemy embrace*. London. Routledge, 2006.

[64] Various letters between Mary and Bernhard indicate that they were engaged by the summer of 1948.

Turkey during the Second World War.[65] As Chancellor, Franz Von Papen was the man who was primarily responsible for persuading the German President, Paul von Hindenburg, to appoint Adolf Hitler as Chancellor in 1933. Von Papen convinced Hindenburg that he could control Hitler; arguably the most disastrous misjudgement in history which helped to expedite a chain of events that ultimately led to the outbreak of the war. Although Bernhard could not help who he was related to, his relationship to such a prominent leader within Nazi Germany would have meant that under a secret rule in place at the time, he almost certainly would have been considered "politically undesirable" for marriage by the British authorities.[66] This was confirmed by his date of repatriation which was reserved for the most committed members of the Nazi Party – even though Bernhard himself was not a member and hated their regime. In some of his surviving letters to Mary from Germany, he described being treated (by both the British and the Americans) as a Nazi sympathiser. He was probably aware that his treatment was the result of his relationship to Franz Von Papen, although it appears that he never let Mary know this. He lost his house, and with hyper-inflation, his savings were now worthless. He became one of about half a million Germans banned from all but the most menial jobs.[67] He subsequentially worked as an apprentice gardener where this wasn't deliberately thwarted, and he was reduced to sleeping in cellars and under any shelter that he could find. With widespread food shortages across Germany, he was always hungry and any money he saved went on his fees for studying.[68] Mary did manage to travel to Germany and get work there in the summer of 1948, but there were frequent reprisals against British women seen with German men, especially from the Russians. It is likely therefore, that she returned to the UK without seeing Bernhard. Bernhard would almost certainly have been refused permission to return to the UK, and with an uncertain future, his letters clearly indicated that there was little prospect of a life for them together in Germany. Marriage, and the consequent form-filling, would have brought renewed attention to himself and who he was related to; he knew that life for Mary in Germany would

---

[65] It is not clear how Bernhard was related to Franz Von Papen. Although they were both aristocratic Catholic families from Westphalia in Germany, and the families would have known each other well, Bernhard is not related to Franz Von Papen by any of his aunts or uncles, even by marriage. It is most likely that Franz Von Papen was a more informal uncle such as a Godfather or old family friend.

[66] Hames, D. Email from Dr Christopher Knowles, Research Fellow, Kings College London. 18 March, 2016.

[67] Biddiscombe, P. *DeNazification of Germany 1945-1950*. Tempus, 2007.

[68] Collingham, L. *The taste of war: World War Two and the battle for food*. London. Penguin Books, 2012.

have been difficult if not impossible.[69]

They continued to write to each other two to three times a week, but this seems to have stopped by the end of 1949 when it is likely that Mary accepted that there was no future in their relationship. Despite this, they were to remain friends for the rest of their lives. By 1956, Bernhard had finished his studies with a PhD in agriculture. A year later he was married and went on to have four children. Aubrey and Mary visited Bernhard in later life, and Bernhard wrote to Mary to express his condolences after Aubrey died in 1998. Despite an operation for cancer of the intestine in 1998, he lived for another 17 years, dying in his hometown of Limburgerhof, 60 miles south of Frankfurt, aged 95. Unfortunately, with a mistaken belief that Bernhard had died of cancer in the 1950s, and no immediate rush to uncover the details of his life, it wasn't until about 6 months after he died that I managed to track down his last address. The opportunity to discover more details about his time with my mother was therefore lost, as well as his relationship to Franz Von Papen. However, unable to ask Bernhard how he was related to Franz Von Papen did uncover one unexpected surprise in the subsequent search to discover their relationship. In Franz Von Papen's memoirs published in 1952, he talks about his first experience of coming to England in about 1903 to sample hunting in the shires.[70] His overriding memory of that visit was being supplied with what he called the best horses that he had ridden in his life, and probably the single biggest reason that he then became a keen advocate of what he called the vitality and strength of the British Empire. He believed that this advocacy was the reason that he was offered the post of military attaché in Washington in 1913. This in turn led to him following a political career, and it ultimately led to the role of Vice Chancellor to Adolf Hitler. By chance, the name of the horse trader that supplied these horses was a Mr Hames, a rare surname then as it is now. Although no relation to Aubrey, a check on the 1911 census reveals that this was a Mr Samuel Hames, the same name as my son, and Aubrey's youngest grandson.

For the sake of one more vote

Although Aubrey had withdrawn from the municipal elections in 1952, these elections were the first public sign of the post-war rise of the youth in the Newport Labour Party. Chosen to represent Labour for the first time in the relatively safe Conservative seat of Maindee, Lorna Kennedy, at the age of 22, was by quite some distance Labour's youngest candidate since

---

[69] Von Werminghausen, B. Letter to Mary Hames. 20 May, 1948.

[70] Von Papen, F. *Franz Von Papen Memoirs*. London. Andre Deutsch Limited, 1952.

the war. Having been active in the Labour Party for some time, Kennedy's nomination was indicative of the increased ambitions of, and opportunities for, young women after the war.[71] Lorna Kennedy also stood again a year later, as did John Marsh, who was aged just 23, in Alt-yr-ryn. This injection of youth within the Newport Labour Party was led by Aubrey who was by then a relative veteran at the age of 30 when he was again chosen to represent Caerau.[72] Of the three, Aubrey was the only one fighting a ward with a reasonable chance of success, while John Marsh took the traditional route for new or young members of the party – that of representing Labour in the ultra-safe Conservative ward of Alt-yr-ryn.

Campaigning in the Caerau Ward for the first time on his own behalf, Aubrey introduced the system of door-to-door canvassing that is now standard within all parties in both local and national elections even though it was to remain rare in most elections for at least another 20 years.[73] Up until this point, all parties campaigned by holding public meetings where the candidate for that particular ward would address any electors who turned up and respond to any questions they wished to ask. Although this method had been in operation for many years, with the meetings usually reported on in the *South Wales Argus*, it had become very inefficient. Attendances were poor, rarely attracting more than 10-15 people including the journalist and one or two members of the opposition. Aubrey could see that this was an ineffective means of harnessing votes and preferred something known as the "Reading" or "Mikardo" system. Developed by the Reading Constituency Labour Party and Ian Mikardo (their candidate for the 1945 General Election) this system involved a process of door-to-door canvasing to identify likely Labour voters, and then concentrating efforts on getting these voters out to the voting booths on election day. The concept of not canvassing potential supporters of the opposition was a process that Aubrey referred to as "not waking up the opposition." On the day of the election, poll numbers of voters were collected from their polling cards, and Labour voters' names crossed off the list so that it was possible to see who had voted. Efforts were then concentrated on getting the remaining Labour voters out. This was a process that became more streamlined in time with the Labour Party gaining more vehicles to match those of the Conservatives, and with their typically younger members tending to work harder on election day than their older

---

[71] Lorna Kennedy is regularly referred to in the various Newport Labour Party minutes prior to 1952, with the earliest reference from at least November 1948 when she was 19 years old.

[72] Newport Labour Party. *Executive committee meeting minutes*. 2 February, 1953.

[73] This method of canvassing was unheard of in other elections in Gwent until at least the mid 1970s (see interviews with Lord Don Touhig and Lord Paul Murphy).

Conservative counterparts. In 1953 in Caerau, this process was managed from the front room of Will and Ada Brown's house at 63 St. Mary Street in Baneswell where Aubrey organised a team of helpers to knock on the doors of Labour voters. This team, which included the Brown's 10-year-old daughter Dianne, as well as many other excited children, worked right up to the closing of the booths at 10pm in the evening to get the Labour supporters out.[74] Aubrey leading the voters to the polls with his team of young helpers was to become a familiar and legendary sight in Baneswell over the next 30 years, with many residents calling out "here comes the pied piper" as he led lines of voters off to cast their votes. At the end of a hot day, Aubrey returned to the Brown's house in the evening, dripping with sweat. After a clean-up, and a freshly washed and ironed shirt courtesy of Mrs Brown, Aubrey set off for the count in the Civic Centre for what he hoped to be a successful result.[75]

Aubrey had a tough fight to win a seat in Caerau. Despite Reginald Ley's success for Labour the previous year, this was the only time Labour had won a seat in this ward since Reginald Ley's win in 1945. Aubrey was therefore trying to overturn a Conservative majority. However, due to the Conservative Arthur Dolman's elevation to the Aldermanic Bench, Aubrey was now standing against a new Conservative candidate, William Huckle. The early signs for Aubrey and his use of the Reading System in 1953 were good. Turnout in Caerau was 5% greater than any turnout since the war, and the only ward that year where the percentage of people voting increased from the previous year. With many of these additional votes down to Aubrey's new technique of canvassing, which later research suggests probably increased his share of the vote by the order of about 5%, this indicated a close result, although not as close as anybody could have predicted.[76]

When the count finished there were no celebrations by either the Labour or Conservative supporters, but a deadly hush.[77] The result was close, and the thoughts of those present were probably the same as the presiding officer, a Mr Roy McLeod who thought "Oh no, not one vote!". William Huckle had apparently won, but with a winning margin of one vote, Aubrey unsurprisingly called for a re-count. The re-count gave the same result, a margin doubly frustrating because if it had been a tie, the casting vote would

---

[74] Hames, D. Email from Dianna Huntley (nee Brown), Will and Ada Brown's daughter. 5 January, 2015.

[75] Ibid.

[76] Bochel, J.M. and Denver, D.T. "The impact of the campaign on the results of local government elections." *British Journal of Political Science*. Volume 2. Number 2, 1972. pp.239-244.

[77] "Report of council election results." *South Wales Argus*. 8 May, 1953.

have gone to the returning officer, Alderman William Pinnell, a socialist, who would have voted for Aubrey. Aubrey lost his first election by the slenderest of margins, and the first time that any political contest in Newport had been won or lost by a single vote.[78]

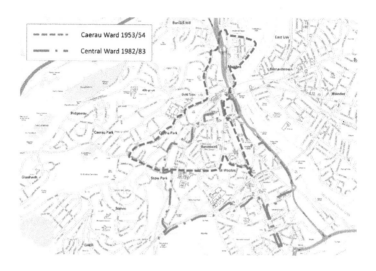

Aubrey was to represent Caerau Ward from 1954/55 to 1961/62; Central Ward, which replaced Caerau Ward from 1969/70 to 1982/83; and Stow Hill Ward (which in general covered the same area as Central Ward) from 1983/84 to 1986/87. The figure above shows the areas covered by Caerau Ward as it was in 1953/54 and Central Ward as it was in 1982/83.

Success

Aubrey was determined to stay with the Caerau Ward and fight the seat again – an opportunity that was to arise the following year when he was once again adopted as the Labour candidate for the same ward.[79] With Lorna Kennedy and John Marsh standing again, they were also joined by 22-year-old David Turnball whose turn it was to take the Labour graveyard seat of Alt-yr-ryn. Stewart Watson, a year older than Aubrey at 32, was also selected as a candidate and given the winnable seat of St. Woolos.[80]

---

[78] Ibid.

[79] Interview with Shirley Newnham. Newport Labour Party member, 23 February, 2013.

[80] It was standard policy for all political parties in Newport to give their most able candidates the best chances of winning at the municipal elections. Hence Aubrey and Stewart Watson were given the best available winnable seats in Newport, even though neither of them lived in the constituencies they were contesting.

This time Aubrey was intent on making sure that he did everything possible to win. With the experience of 1953 behind him, and knowledge of the voting patterns from his successful application of the Reading system (which was not adopted across the party until 1958, with some wards still not using it as late as 1967), he spent a considerable period of time working in the Caerau Ward over the next year.[81,82] This helped to strengthen support for Labour and to convert Conservative votes into Labour ones. It seemed to work; the turnout in 1954 yet again increased by 5% resulting in one of the largest turnouts in a ward for a council election since the war. More importantly, his one vote loss turned into a 343 majority and Aubrey was elected to the council in Newport on 14th May 1954. Despite the presence of several Labour candidates in their twenties in the last three elections, none were elected. As such, he was the youngest Labour candidate elected to the council since before the war (Richard Davies had been elected at the age of 23 in 1925).[83] Also elected for the first time was Stewart Watson.

The loss by one vote was to stay with Aubrey for the rest of his political career and he vowed never to lose by such a margin again. In the one other election that he lost – in 1969 – he lost by three votes.

Marriage

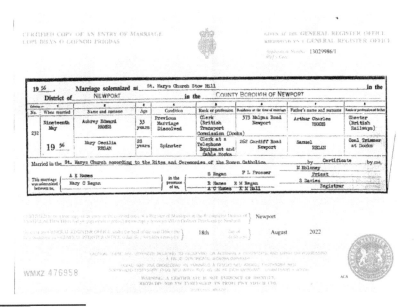

---

[81] Newport Labour Party. *General committee meeting minutes.* 6 June, 1958.

[82] Newport Labour Party. *Executive committee meeting minutes.* 24 July, 1967.

[83] "He was Newport's youngest mayor." *South Wales Argus.* 4 March, 1963.

There are few things in life that are certain beyond the quote made famous by Benjamin Franklin about death and taxes. But one other certainty often quoted regarding marriage, is that divorcees cannot marry in a Catholic Church. Yet Aubrey did; he was married to Mary in a Catholic Church, and his condition for marriage, as quoted on the wedding certificate, was "previous marriage dissolved."

The apparent mystery about how Aubrey and Mary married in a Catholic Church was contained on a small newspaper clipping that fell out of Aubrey's wallet when I picked it up several years after he had died, titled the "Pauline Privilege." Together with something called the "Petrine Privilege," these are the two circumstances in which a divorcee can marry in a Catholic Church Under the Pauline Privilege, a marriage can be dissolved if it occurs between two non-baptized persons and one of them (but not both) gets baptised and converts to Christianity while the other leaves the marriage. As neither Aubrey nor Connie was baptised when they were married, and Connie had clearly left the marriage, being now re-married, this gave Aubrey the circumstances under which he could marry as a divorcee in a Catholic Church.

Aubrey and Mary at their reception on their Wedding Day, 19th May 1956.

Aubrey and Mary were therefore married as Catholics in St. Mary's Church on Stow Hill on 19th May 1956. This was after a long engagement that was almost certainly due to the time it took for the church to investigate the conditions of the Pauline Privilege – probably in the order of a year.[84,85] Interestingly, 65 years later almost to the day, a marriage took place under similar circumstances when the then Prime Minister Boris Johnson married his third wife, Carrie Symonds, in Westminster Cathedral. As Boris Johnson was a baptised Catholic, but his previous marriages had not taken place in a Catholic Church, it is likely that this marriage took place under the Petrine Privilege (or perhaps it was because he was the Prime Minister).

The turk's evolution

By the time Aubrey was elected leader of the Council in 1974, the culture of the Labour Party in Newport had changed completely – most of it driven by Aubrey in the 1950s. After Dame Rosemary Butler was elected as a councillor in 1973, she described the debates within the Labour Group as "sensational" because as the leader, Aubrey kept the discussion within the relevant parameters and did not allow debates to go off on tangents. She also mentioned how indulgent Aubrey was with her, always ready to try out new ideas that she was interested in, including the setting up of the Friends of Tredegar House.[86] Similar comments about Aubrey were made by others who were elected as Labour councillors in the 1970s, including Ron Jones.[87] Aubrey's style of leadership was still in complete contrast to other Labour Groups within Gwent which became apparent with the creation of Gwent County Council in 1974. These groups had still not evolved from the typical Labour Group of the 1950s, and as it had been in Newport before Aubrey arrived, seniority dominated the decision-making process, debates were not allowed, and new councillors had no say in the running of the party.[88,89] The radical changes that Aubrey initiated in the Newport Labour Group were to inherently change the way that Labour groups operated throughout Gwent –

---

[84] A letter from Aubrey to Mary dated 30/01/55 clearly indicates that Mary was getting frustrated by their long engagement.

[85] Hames, D. Email from Father Michael Doyle, parish priest of All Saints Church Newport. 2 May, 2022.

[86] Interview with Dame Rosemary Butler, 2012.

[87] Interview with Ron Jones. Former Newport Labour Party councillor. 25 May, 2013.

[88] Interview with Lord Don Touhig. Member of the House of Lords, and former MP for Islwyn and Gwent County Councillor. 12 May, 2021.

[89] Interview with Lord Paul Murphy Member of the House of Lords, and former Secretary of State for Wales and Northern Ireland and former MP for Torfaen. 12 May, 2021.

and to the way that the Gwent County Council would operate when it was formed. It is difficult to quantify the exact effect that Aubrey had on politics outside of Newport, but it is likely that many politicians who entered the political scene from the mid-1970s onwards, including future government ministers, had a more successful political career as a direct result of Aubrey's influence and style of leadership.

CHAPTER 4

"PILLED" DOWN

Housing shortages

At the outbreak of war in 1939, Britain had approximately twelve and a half million houses.[1] Over the next six years, because of bomb damage, lack of maintenance, and other factors such as the requisition of properties, this had reduced by approximately 600,000 even though 160,000 houses had been built during this period.[2] And the increase in the population of 1.5 million people (despite the 450,000 people who were killed during the war), meant that Britain had a significant housing shortage. The housing issues were at their greatest in the most severely bombed parts of the UK – especially in places such as Plymouth where pre-war housing shortages were already chronic.[3]

Unsurprisingly, every opinion poll showed that repairing and replacing war-damaged housing came at the top of people's concerns – even more than having employment.[4] But there was also a labour shortage. There was now a building force of less than 350,000 compared to over a million before the war. Many young men had been killed in the war, and many other skilled labourers were still waiting to be repatriated. There was also a lack of basic building materials, so all of these factors combined meant that progress was

---

[1] Foot, M. *Aneurin Bevan - 1945-1960*. Volume 2. Granada Publishing Limited, 1975.

[2] Short, J.R. *Housing in Britain: The post-war experience*. London. Methuen, 1982, p. 42.

[3] Watson, J. "Some notes on post-war development at Plymouth." *Journal of the Royal Sanitary Institute* (Great Britain). Volume 69. Number 2, 1949, pp.71-78.

[4] Hollis, P. *Jennie Lee: A life*. Oxford University Press, 1998.

initially slow.[5]

What little resources there were, went to the most badly-damaged areas first, which meant that less badly affected areas like Newport suffered.[6] Relative to its population, Newport already had noticeably fewer houses compared to neighbouring authorities. And many of the houses that Newport did have, were built before the First World War and still lacked pavements and proper roads – so Newport suffered during this time more than most.[7,8] This was made worse by the migration of predominately young families into Newport.[9] Young families moved to Newport due to the establishment of industries such as the Monsanto chemical works and Uskmouth power station, as well as because of the growth of civic amenities and a significant increase in white-collar jobs. In the four years between 1946 and 1950, the population of Newport had therefore grown by 14%, with the waiting list for houses in Newport in 1951 being over 5000 and growing by approximately 500 people a year.[10,11] Yet by 1951, only 1,860 permanent houses (as opposed to prefabricated houses) had been built in Newport since the war, mostly under a Labour administration.[12] Labour's policy of generally refusing licences for private housing for sale in favour of social housing for let, resulted in a rate of house-building that was twice that of the Conservative administration, which had encouraged private house building. This was probably the main reason for the Conservatives' election defeat in 1951, just one year after regaining control of the council.[13,14] Newport was the only county borough in England or Wales to pass from Conservative to Labour control in 1951

---

[5] Foot, M. *Aneurin Bevan - 1945-1960*. Volume 2, 1975.

[6] Donnison, D.V. *Housing policy since the war.* Codicote Press, 1960.

[7] Relative to its population, Newport had about 40% of houses compared to the neighbouring boroughs of Bath, Bristol, Cardiff, Gloucester, and Swansea (Newport Labour group. Labour group meeting minutes, circa February 1970).

[8] Although Newport was subjected to several air raids in 1940 and 1941, Newport was not as badly affected as Cardiff or Swansea, although probably over 100 properties were damaged to varying degrees, including a number that were destroyed.

[9] Malpas Ward Labour Party. Letter to the Newport Labour Party general committee, probably instigated by Aubrey. 21 September, 1951.

[10] Davis, H. *The history of the Borough of Newport*. Pennyfarthing Press, 1998.

[11] Based on housing waiting figures published in the South Wales Argus between 1949 and 1951.

[12] "Newport eve-of-poll claims by parties." *South Wales Argus.* 9 May, 1951.

[13] Houses could only be built based on permits granted by the Welsh Board of Health. This meant that councils had little control over how many houses they could build, regardless of their resources.

[14] Articles in the *South Wales Argus* leading up to the 1951 Council Elections were dominated by housing issues.

against a general trend of Conservative gains across the rest of the UK. With a significant increase in marriages and births compared to pre-war figures, by the time Aubrey was elected to the council, many families had been on the waiting list for almost 10 years with many having lived in properties considered unfit for human habitation. Average occupation rates across Newport were also excessive, being over one person per house above the national average – and they were at their highest in Aubrey's ward of Caerau as well as Central and Alexandra wards. Long waiting lists and excessive occupancy rates were ultimately to remain a major housing issue in Newport until the 1960s when new housing estates such as those at Ringland, St. Julians and Bettws became substantially established.

Slum properties

When Aubrey was elected to the council in 1954, the housing situation was therefore dire. Partly to blame, was a claim made 16 years earlier by Newport's Chief Sanitary Inspector, that there had never been any slums in Newport.[15] Consequently, it was not until 1945 that Newport started to address the problem of poor-quality housing whereas across the rest of the UK, some 300,000 properties considered slums had been demolished or closed from the 1930s onward.[16,17] Exacerbated by the lack of materials and labour, slum landlords who did no repairs proliferated in Newport. The most notorious culprits were Nellie and Brice Duckham, and Nellie's daughter Kathleen Richards.[18] Multi-millionaires by today's standards, they owned in excess of 500 slum properties either side of the River Usk between what is now the location of the M4 motorway and the docks.[19,20] This was almost half the number of houses owned by the council at the end of the war, and it is believed that the total number of properties they owned in Newport (including

---

[15] "Rehousing the people." *South Wales Argus.* 19 October, 1938.

[16] "Newport and rehousing." *South Wales Argus.* 9 January, 1945.

[17] Yelling, J. "The incidence of slum clearance in England and Wales, 1955–85." *Urban History.* Volume 27. Number 2, 2000, pp.234-254.

[18] These houses were originally acquired by Nellie Duckham before passing over to her husband and her daughter when she died in 1948, and then solely to her daughter when Brice Duckham died in 1953.

[19] This is based on Brice Duckham's will who left almost £100,000 in his will when he died in 1953, five years after his wife Nellie, as well as the vast number of houses that they owned.

[20] This is based on various council housing minutes where properties and their owners are listed as having legal proceedings listed against them for nuisance. A such, it has only been possible to establish properties owned by the Duckham's, which at some point have been identified as a slum.

properties that were not slums) was of a similar number to the council.[21] The Duckhams and Richards, with their empire of houses supplemented by properties in Cwmbran and probably elsewhere, dominated the list of landlords who had legal proceedings issued against them for "nuisances" and were probably the type of landlords who were later to be described as "verminous" by Paul Flynn.[22,23,24]

Many of the housing shortages were glossed over by the building of temporary prefabricated houses that had a design life of around 15 years – although these proved to be very popular and many were still inhabited until the turn of the century.[25] New houses were also initially prioritised for key workers coming into Newport to work in the new factories that had been built. In some cases, companies would put pressure on the council claiming that they would only stay in Newport if they were provided with housing for their employees.[26] Consequentially, with a lack of houses for local families, it was common for married couples to live with two or three children in a single room with limited and often shared cooking and washing facilities with other families. A particularly bad case highlighted by Aubrey when he initially became a councillor, was of one couple in Caerau Ward who were living in two rooms with six children and another on the way.[27]

Aubrey had been opposed to the policy of prioritising new houses for key workers, even before he joined the council, and he was later to succeed in changing this policy within the Labour Group in favour of ensuring that houses went to the most deserving cases first.[28] With Labour holding the

---

[21] Interview with Gerald Davies. Former Newport Conservative councillor. 6 August, 2013.

[22] Nellie Duckham owned at least 25 properties houses in Cwmbran, having purchased them in 1935 (Western Mail. "Owners state houses were bought for re-conditioning." 17 October, 1935.

[23] "Councillor describes Pill landlords as 'verminous.'" *South Wales Argus.* 8 May, 1974.

[24] This is based on various council housing minutes where properties and their owners are listed as having legal proceedings listed against them for nuisance. As such, it has only been possible to establish properties owned by the Duckham's, which at some point have been identified as a slum.

[25] Many people who lived, or who had relatives living in prefabricated houses talked of their fondness of them. This was summed up well by a letter of thanks sent to Stewart Watson on 17/07/67 and addressed to "Mr Councillor" where the writer said, "I am in my little Prefab and very nice it is too."

[26] See for example, Newport county borough council Housing committee meeting minutes. 21 November, 1944, Minute 12, p 87.

[27] "Council storm over housing allocation for key workers." *South Wales Argus.* 14 June, 1955.

[28] Newport Labour Party. "Labour Party general committee meeting minutes." 27 November, 1953.

balance of power on the council, this also meant a change in council policy – much to the consternation of many Conservative councillors.[29] However, before this policy change, occupation was not nine tenths of the law in Newport – so if you were a key worker living in a council house and you left or lost your job, you also lost your home. The council also had no qualms in kicking families out of their council homes if their family circumstances changed.

With the housing shortage and the initial prioritising of new houses for key workers, this also meant that there were a disproportionate number of local people who had been on the council housing list for a considerable period of time. It is likely that many of these were families with young children because some landlords refused to rent out properties to families with children (although the aforementioned Duckhams did not have this policy). When slum clearance got underway, preference for new council housing was given to those whose homes had been demolished. But there was a view among some council housing officials that those on housing waiting lists had failed to provide for themselves, and so consequently did not deserve a choice about what type of house they were given, or where. Any refusal when accommodation was offered was also of little inconvenience to these officials as they were more concerned in finding accommodation for residents in properties identified to be demolished, as this could hold up the regeneration of an area.[30]

Slum clearance

Housing issues dominated Aubrey's activities over his first six years on the council, as they did for many new councillors across the country at the time. The earliest surviving correspondence, from his first week as a councillor, are letters from people across Newport, not just his own constituency, pleading for help to secure a property for them and their family. Two of these families had been on the council waiting list from the mid-late 1940s, and within two weeks of being elected, Aubrey had secured a property for them. However, the housing issue that truly defined Aubrey's first six years as a councillor was the slum clearance of an area known as the Marshes Estate and what were known as "problem families".

The Marshes Estate, an area of about six hectares enclosed by Shaftesbury

---

[29] "Council storm over housing allocation for key workers." *South Wales Argus.*

[30] Dunleavy, P. *The politics of mass housing in Britain: 1945-1975*. Oxford. Clarendon, 1981.

Park, Crindau Pill, the B4591, and the River Usk was the first place identified by the council in Newport as a potential clearance area. The houses were generally considered by the council as slums, and the whole site was identified as needing to be cleared and re-developed. Some of these properties had already been closed or demolished by the time Aubrey became a councillor. As promised, most tenants from these properties were re-housed in the area of their choice when suitable houses became available – and most of them wanted to be rehoused in Brynglas or Malpas. However, by around mid-1958, the council decided to mainly rehouse them in Ringland.[31] The tenants were not happy, and they complained to Aubrey.

Raising the various concerns of his constituents with the housing manager, Aubrey, as in most things he did, was meticulous in his arguments. Often not satisfied with the answers given, he would raise these issues again, and then often raised further issues as they arose. Proving to be a thorn in the side of the housing manager who was not used to having to justify his decisions, many of Aubrey's letters were deliberately ignored. But Aubrey did not relent, and just like Andy Dufresne in the Shawshank Redemption, the more his letters were ignored, the more he wrote.[32] And just like in the Shawshank Redemption, it was 6 years before the housing manager was to react. His reaction triggered a complaint brought up by the leader of the Conservative Group on the council, Arthur Dolman, Aubrey's most regular combatant during his first stint on the council.[33] Reported in the *South Wales Argus* under the headline "Too many Questions," Aubrey must have been one of the few councillors in history criticised in a council meeting for working too hard for his constituents.[31] The residents of the Marshes Estate were also concerned about a proposal to house what were known as "problem families" (because it was felt that this would make those families "easier to manage") in a block of streets in this area.[34] Unsurprisingly, this was met with considerable opposition from residents, with most saying they would leave, or want to leave the area if this happened.[35] Equally unsurprisingly, Aubrey opposed this proposal, and despite a lengthy debate, only four council members voted for it; two of whom were the leaders of the Labour and Conservative groups,

---

[31] "Newport Councillor's Reply to 'too many questions' Comment." *South Wales Argus.* 13 January, 1960.

[32] Ibid.

[33] The Dolman Theatre is named after Arthur Dolman, who owned property where the Kingsway Shopping Centre was built.

[34] Watson S. *Memorandum on problem families.* 24 February, 1964.

[35] Caerau Ward councillors. *Memorandum on problem families.* 9 May, 1963.

Reg Tyack and Arthur Dolman.[36]

It wasn't just the householders whose corner Aubrey fought. Proposals to increase near-expired leases tenfold, affecting both householders and businesses, led to an ugly argument between Aubrey and a Conservative councillor that was played out in the *South Wales Argus*. This simultaneously enhanced Aubrey's growing reputation as the key advocate for his constituents, and at the same time, the principal combatant of the Conservative group.[37,38,39,40]

But with the Marshes Estate being considered as the first area to be cleared in Newport, attention was to suddenly turn towards Pillgwenlly (commonly known as Pill) in March 1962. The early decisions taken in Pill did not involve Aubrey directly because by September 1961 he had resigned as a councillor due to the pressure of work. However, a later threat to the re-development of Baneswell was to draw him back into local politics in May 1970.

Pill clearance

In March 1962, the council made the decision to redevelop the Marshes Estate as soon as possible. However, while this decision was being discussed with the Ministry of Housing and Local Government (the Ministry), a house in Marion Street in Pill collapsed. As a result, a quick external survey of houses in the Pill area was undertaken in April 1962 which found that some parts of Pill were in a worse state than many houses in the Marshes Estate. With the Ministry now indicating that they would only agree to the early redevelopment of the Marshes Estate if it was the worst area in the town, priorities changed, and Pill now became the central focus for redevelopment.[41]

Following this survey, and with no notice to residents, the council put an immediate ban on further council mortgage loans and improvement grants on twenty-eight streets in Pill, with applications from a further five streets to be considered on their merits.[42] With 1800 houses affected, and council mortgages usually reserved for those people who struggled to

---

[36] Newport county borough council. *Council meeting minutes*. 10 March, 1964.

[37] "Marshes Estate meeting 'we were not invited' says Tory councillors." *South Wales Argus*. 9 March, 1956.

[38] "Councillor Hames explains why he called meeting." *South Wales Argus*. 12 March, 1956.

[39] "Leases dispute" (letter). *South Wales Argus*. 23 March, 1956.

[40] "Commercial rents" (letter). *South Wales Argus*. 5 April, 1956.

[41] Newport county borough council. Pill area survey. 10 July, 1964.

[42] Newport county borough council. *Housing committee meeting minutes*. 4 April, 1962.

obtain mortgages from building societies, this was a major hammer blow to an estimated 8000 to 10,000 residents in Pill who were amongst the most vulnerable in Newport.[43,44]

Houses in Pill became unsellable overnight, and those people who wanted to leave due to family, work or other reasons could not do so. All were essentially doomed to an area that would naturally degrade with time, with little incentive, or means (from improvement grants) of repairing or improving their properties. Understandably, residents in Pill were furious, and in a public meeting attended by 700 people in May 1962, many expressed their anger with the council's decision.[45] They then demanded a detailed survey of the Pill area which was agreed, and a report called "The Pill area survey" was finally delivered in July 1964.[46]

The survey was carried out on 1686 houses in an area south of Cardiff Road and George Street but excluding the mainly commercial areas of Commercial Road and Lower Dock Street.[47] The report only considered houses that were built before 1875 in an area referred to as the "main area" of Pill. In addition, a survey was carried out on 1 in 7 properties in Baneswell as well as a quick external inspection of the Marshes Estate.[48]

The report was of little comfort to residents. The conclusion of the survey was that 20% of the properties in the main area of Pill were unfit, with about 80% of the houses projected to become unfit within the next 15 years. Less than 1% of the properties were considered to have a life of more than 30 years, and in total, about 45% of these properties were owner-occupied.[49] The report recommended a complete embargo on council mortgage loans, improvement grants, and standard grants in respect of the 1686 houses, as well as an immediate start on the clearance of unfit houses.[50] The report on the Baneswell properties was little better. It was recommended that the same embargos as for Pill should be placed on 643 houses, with the clearance of the whole of the Baneswell area within about 5 years.[51] Although the

---

[43] "Angry protests by 'doomed' tenants." *Western Mail.* 1 June, 1962.

[44] "Pill and Banswell homes are reprieved – Council rejects plan for mass demolition." *South Wales Argus.* 31 August, 1964.

[45] "Angry protests by 'doomed' tenants." *Western Mail.* 1 June, 1962.

[46] Newport county borough council. Pill area survey. 10 July, 1964.

[47] Ibid.

[48] Ibid.

[49] Ibid.

[50] Ibid.

[51] Ibid.

final recommendations for Baneswell were to be based on a later more detailed survey, the results from the Pill survey suggested that the final recommendations were unlikely to be any more positive. The results for the Marshes Estate were a little less dire, and it was recommended that redevelopment was not necessary until after 1980. However, this conclusion was immediately rejected by the council who felt that the Marshes Estate should be redeveloped as soon as possible.[52]

In 1964, the day after the report was issued confirming the initial survey (carried out in April 1962) and the worst fears of the Pill residents, a mass meeting of residents was announced.[53] However, before this meeting could be arranged, and in front of a public gallery packed to overflowing, the council overwhelmingly rejected the recommendations from the Pill area survey.[54] They proposed to rehabilitate as many of the houses as possible and encouraged owners and landlords to apply for improvement grants.[55] But with costs to rehabilitate most houses proving to be excessive relative to the increased life expectancy of properties, it was later decided to look at a programme of phased redevelopment starting in the mid-1970s.[56]

The results of the survey of Pill in April 1962, confirmed by the later survey in July 1964 came as a shock not only to the residents of Pill, but also to the council itself. Having granted several mortgage loans and improvement grants to residents a short time before the initial report came out, they now faced the problem of compulsory purchasing these same houses, potentially based on a valuation less than the outstanding mortgage. With these valuations set by the district valuer, this also caused problems when householders felt the valuations given on their properties were too low or based on their blighted value.[57] With the ban on improvement loans and an active discouragement from the council to improve these houses, this also led to a natural decline in the state of these properties. As owner-occupiers moved out, many of their properties were taken over by landlords looking for a short-term profit. In common with many existing landlords in Pill, they had no interest in maintaining these houses in a fit state. This further dilapidation of the area was inadvertently exacerbated by the council themselves as they

---

[52] Ibid.

[53] "Clearance plan shocks residents." *Western Mail.* 25 July, 1964.

[54] Newport county borough council. *Council meeting minutes.* 31 August, 1964.

[55] "Pill and Banswell homes are reprieved – Council rejects plan for mass demolition." *South Wales Argus.* 31 August, 1964.

[56] Newport county borough council. Pill, Baneswell and Marshes committee – interim report. Circa 5 November, 1964.

[57] "Pill homes outmoded compensation." *South Wales Argus.* 29 March, 1972.

waited for more houses in an area to become unfit so that they could create clearance areas. There was also understandable dismay for those who kept their houses in a good state of repair, only to find them included in an area to be cleared as the adjacent properties became unfit. With many of these clearance areas not yet large enough for redevelopment on their own, they were temporarily used as grassland or children's playgrounds, and many years later current and former residents of Pill still complained that good quality houses were demolished and nothing was built to replace them over a period of several years.

Houses waiting to be demolished on Capel Crescent, Pill, 1976 (courtesy Robin Weaver)

Although Pill was designated a "twilight area" (as areas marked for demolition were commonly known), it wasn't until 1971 that the first clearance of houses took place on Francis Street and Williams Street (which no longer exist).[58,59] By now, residents had been living with the threat of re-development for nine years. Properties which under normal circumstances would have remained fit and in good condition, had become dilapidated and communities had been eroded. There was also no clear plan for when circumstances for residents

---

[58] An urban area in a state of dilapidation or economic decline.
[59] "Pill redevelopment begins." *South Wales Argus.* 6 October, 1971.

would return to some form of normality, and whether this would be in Pill or somewhere else (even though few wanted to leave the area). During this time, Aubrey had continued to play an active role in the Labour Party in Newport, but he had no tangible influence on the decision-making process for the redevelopment of Pill or the proposed future for Baneswell during this time. He was clearly not happy with how things were progressing, and in 1969 he decided to again take on a more active role in local politics.

A £1 a house

Aubrey's attempt to return to local politics occurred by standing for election in the Central Ward. Due to boundary changes, Central Ward had replaced Caerau Ward and now covered part of Pill. But local politics were significantly different in 1969 compared to when he left the council in 1961. The spectre of re-development had resulted in the rise of candidates for the Ratepayer's Association, who targeted Labour seats in certain wards in co-operation with the Conservative Party (who stood down in these wards).[60] The Ratepayer's Association had strong support and undertook aggressive and successful electioneering in the press. As a result they had won several seats off Labour in the mid-1960s. In 1969, one of these seats – in the key Central Ward – was held by their leader, Reg Dray, who would be Aubrey's opponent. Facing a strong candidate at a time when support for the Labour government was at its weakest, Aubrey lost for the second and last time at a local election in Newport – this time by three votes as opposed to one in 1953. In 1969, every Conservative candidate won the seat they were contesting (the first time this had happened in Newport's history), and across the country Labour were left with their lowest number of councillors for years.[61] Aubrey's loss was therefore likely in part due to Labour's performance in government rather than any of his, or Newport Labour's, failings. But when he stood in the same ward the following year, against another retiring Ratepayer's Association candidate, he won by over 600 votes.

Returning to the council, Aubrey argued for sensitive slum clearance, and where it was still possible, full-blooded, community-style consultations.[62] He recognized that this was something that had been absent from many

---

[60] Minutes of the Newport Conservative Party municipal elections committee indicate that the Ratepayers Association had regular meetings with the Conservative Party over various issues since at least the 1940s, including at the time of the Pill re-development, the allocation of seats to fight in council elections. National Library of Wales.

[61] "Crushing defeat for Labour at Newport." *South Wales Argus.* 9 May, 1969.

[62] "Aubrey steps out of the hot seat." *South Wales Argus.* 29 April, 1987.

decisions made since he had left the council. On 14th July 1970 he succeeded in persuading the council to remove properties on fifteen streets across Pill from redevelopment, therefore removing the blight on these properties that had been in place for eight years.[63] Later in January 1971, he argued against the Welsh Office's desire to increase the density of houses in Pill stating that it would "detract from the original concept" and expressing concern that it would "sacrifice what we are hoping to achieve in Pill."[64] But Aubrey's greatest intervention in Pill during the last few years of redevelopment was his idea of the £1 a house scheme.

Proposed by Aubrey in October 1971, this scheme was to sell houses that had been purchased in advance of slum clearance and were in a reasonable state of repair, for £1. Priority would be given to those most in need of somewhere to live, and preferably to those who were already living in Pill.[65] The aim of this scheme was so slow down the rate of deterioration in the development area by keeping properties occupied until they were needed for demolition. This plan would also help to keep the community together. When these houses were needed, they would be sold back to the council for the same sum that was paid for them.[66] Conditions were set to ensure that these schemes weren't abused such as a requirement to bring them up to a good state of repair, and renting or subletting was not allowed. People who were already on the housing list were prioritised, with their position on the waiting list unaffected when they eventually had to sell their house back to the council.[67] For the new homeowners, the benefits of this scheme were that the cost of bringing these houses up to a good state of repair and subsequent costs of rates before they sold them back to the council were less than they paid in rent for one or two rooms in a shared house. For the council, they benefited from rates paid on these properties, they promoted owner-occupation, and they reduced the deterioration of adjacent properties with less spread of damp, for example. Crucially, as houses were less likely to become rundown, this also helped to reduce discontent in the area.

Although several councillors opposed the £1 a house scheme it was approved, and in January 1972 Aubrey proposed a modification to include unfit houses,

---

[63] "'Blight' on Pill homes removed." *South Wales Argus.* 14 July, 1970.

[64] "Plan for higher density at Pill." *South Wales Argus.* 30 October, 1971.

[65] Newport county borough council. *Pill, Baneswell and Marshes committee meeting minutes.* 20 October, 1971.

[66] "£1 a house bargain plan for Newport families." *South Wales Argus.* 21 October, 1971.

[67] Ibid.

which was also approved.[68,69] The scheme was applauded by the residents of Pill with the first residents moving in in April 1972, six months after Aubrey's proposal.[70,71] The first family to move in, Winston and Margaret Berry, described their spacious centrally-heated three-bedroom house as a "bargain".[72] After this, the Ratepayers Association whose stated aim in standing had been to protect the residents of Pill, did not win another council seat in Newport again.

Baneswell

The recommendation in the Pill Survey of 1964, of an immediate embargo on mortgage loans, improvement and standard grants for certain properties in Baneswell, meant that just like Pill, all properties essentially became unsellable. Although the recommendations were due to be confirmed following a detailed survey at a later date, the experience from Pill gave the residents little hope that Baneswell would not be cleared within the next five years.

However relative to Pill, the initial reaction to the likely redevelopment of Baneswell was muted. Although one resident said that the council would have to "bulldoze their property with them in it," other residents had become resigned to their fate, particularly older residents (a third of the homeowners in Baneswell were of pensionable age).[73] Many of them had lived with the threat of demolition since 1945. This was when the post-war "grand plan" for Newport included a proposal to provide a link road between the Civic Centre and St. Woolos Cathedral that would have passed right through the middle of Baneswell.[74] In the intervening 20 years, the plan for the link road had been modified repeatedly but the threat still existed.

The initial fight to prevent the redevelopment of Baneswell was driven by Aubrey (despite not being a councillor or resident of Baneswell) and

---

[68] "£1 house plan gets go-ahead." *South Wales Argus.* 27 October, 1971.

[69] Newport county borough council. *Pill, Baneswell and Marshes committee meeting minutes.* 26 January, 1972.

[70] "Temporary homes in Pill." *South Wales Argus.* 9 February, 1972.

[71] "A three-bedroomed house for only £1." *South Wales Argus.* 7 April, 1972.

[72] Ibid.

[73] Baneswell housing questionnaire. Housing questionnaire of Baneswell organised by Aubrey. August, 1964. In author's private collection.

[74] There were big plans for the redevelopment of Newport centred around the Civic Centre in 1945 as highlighted in several issues of the *South Wales Argus* such as on 10th March, 19th April and 17th August.

supported by the three ward Labour councillors. A public meeting held in July or August 1964 was followed by a survey of residents in August 1964 which showed that few residents wanted to leave Baneswell. If they did, it was usually to move closer to other family members, and if they had to leave temporarily, most wanted to return, and return with the same neighbours.[75] The desire to stay in Baneswell, or to return if they had to leave temporarily, was strongest amongst the older residents. However, with no immediate threat to Baneswell, little appears to have happened over the next three years as the residents waited for the detailed survey. This was not helped by the fact that their main advocate, Aubrey, was not on the council, not a resident of Baneswell, and not in a position to directly influence the decision-making process.

The long-anticipated wait for the detailed survey of Baneswell came in November 1967 when a recommendation that it should be carried out was passed at a council meeting on the casting vote of the Deputy Mayor.[76,77] With the threat to Baneswell now obvious, this was likely the moment that Aubrey decided to return to politics.[78] The first task was to mobilise the residents of Baneswell; this began with a public meeting that was held three days later and attended by 280 residents.[79] At this meeting, the Baneswell Residents Association was formed based on proposals from the ward councillors. This now provided the residents with a formal means of lobbying the council on issues of concern to Baneswell and, at the invitation of the council, opportunities to sit on and address them at key council meetings.[80] With Aubrey returning to the council in May 1970, he started to lobby on their behalf from within the council rather than from the outside – an unwelcome prospect for many council officers. On 14th July 1970 (the same day he had persuaded the council to remove fifteen streets in Pill from redevelopment), he challenged the council officers on the redevelopment of Baneswell.[81] Presenting alternative proposals to redevelopment based on meetings with the residents, he asked the council officers to consider delaying the plans for

---

[75] Baneswell housing questionnaire. Housing questionnaire of Baneswell organised by Aubrey. August, 1964. Author's private collection.

[76] Newport county borough council. *Pill, Baneswell and Marshes committee meeting minutes*. 8 November, 1967.

[77] "Survey plan fought." *South Wales Argus*. 15 November, 1967.

[78] Interview with Paul Flynn, former Newport West MP 1987-2019. 22 September, 2012.

[79] "Baneswell residents unite." *South Wales Argus*. 18 November, 1967.

[80] Based on several discussions with John Bader, formally Newport's housing manager, August-October 2020.

[81] "'Blight' on Pill homes removed." *South Wales Argus*. 14 July, 1970.

Baneswell and to instead maintain Baneswell for the immediate future. This did not go down well and was dismissed by the council officers. They could see no alternative to the redevelopment of Baneswell and re-iterated their belief that they could no longer delay their plans.[82] However, the fight went on. Sometime in late 1970 or early 1971, an agreement was made in Baneswell to set up a housing association. Whether this was at a public meeting, a ward meeting, or a meeting between the ward councillors and residents from Baneswell is not known, but recollections from Paul Flynn suggest it was initiated by Aubrey.[83] This seems to be confirmed by a council meeting in early 1972 that was attended by Aubrey and five other councillors, together with two residents of Baneswell, one of whom was Peter Gotobed. At this meeting, the proposed Baneswell Housing Association (BHA) was agreed in principle. Its main aim was to provide houses to let, for local residents, prior to the redevelopment of the area. Although it was almost two years before the BHA was actually set-up, Peter Gotobed was its first shareholder and was to prove a key figure in driving the BHA forward over the next few years.

Baneswell Housing Association

Setting up a housing association then, as now, was not an easy task. The people forming the association had to have a formal written constitution. Some groups had to form themselves into charitable trusts, others a not-for profit company or, as the BHA was, a company limited by guarantee with charitable status. Shares were issued to the sum of £1 which limited personal liability if the association went bankrupt, and members of the association and their families could not benefit from the organisation or (only in exceptional circumstances) from a tenancy. This would have been daunting for those initial shareholders with little or no experience of setting up a company and dealing with the various logistical and political problems, but not for Aubrey. He had held a managerial post with the British Transport Docks Board for almost 10 years, and had helped turn the South Wales ports from regular loss makers into the most profitable ports in the British Transport Docks Board network. A few years earlier he had also played a key role in establishing St. Joseph's School, the first Roman Catholic High School in Newport, against considerable opposition from both the council and the church.[84] He was also an instrumental figure in bringing comprehensive education into Newport.[85]

---

[82] "Baneswell homes may get respite." *South Wales Argus.* 14 July, 1970.

[83] Based on several interviews with Paul Flynn MP and posts on his website.

[84] Interview with Alan Shewring, founding governor of St. Joesph's R.C. High School. 23 June, 2012.

[85] Newport is believed to be the first town in the UK that chose an all-comprehensive system

With Aubrey's help, the formation of BHA in November 1973 was therefore a relatively straightforward task. Having been formed it now needed houses, and what could have been considered the hardest part, was probably the easiest; Baneswell had a plentiful supply of them. Many were empty and in good, or relatively good, condition, they were owned by the council, and available to the BHA for £1.[86] Aubrey's £1 a house scheme brought in for Pill, was now to provide the BHA with their source of houses for less than the cost of a round of drinks in the local pub.

Over the next few years, the BHA was to buy, do up, and rent out properties throughout Baneswell. This stopped these houses from becoming run-down, provided accommodation for many residents in Baneswell, and kept the area alive. It did not remove the threat of re-development, but this threat was to gradually disappear following the election of a new Labour government in 1974, and their introduction of a new Housing Act.

The issue of whether to refurbish houses or demolish them, was a regular topic of debate in Parliament in the run-up to the new Housing Act of 1974. The main advocate for refurbishment in Wales was Sir Anthony Meyer, Conservative MP for West Flintshire, although many others raised similar issues, particularly Conservative MPs from constituencies in North Wales. Whether these debates influenced the wording of this new Act of Parliament or not, when it became law on 31st July, it provided financial assistance to housing associations to improve and repair accommodation, including in areas identified for clearance. With this Act of Parliament providing a means for improving the poor condition of houses, a housing renewal programme was set up in Newport in 1975 under the leadership of David Brightmore. Recognizing that grants for housing improvements were now available, and that the application process could prove a daunting task, it was decided to simplify and streamline the process by introducing something called a package deal.[87] Under these deals, everything required to apply and carry out improvements to a property was covered by payment of a subsidised fee of £25. For this fee, house surveys, building estimates, working drawings, and engagement and supervision of the building work, would be arranged and carried out by the council, with no hidden costs or paperwork for the residents.[88] Many residents at first saw the scheme as too good to be true. But

---

of education.

[86] Newport county borough council. *Housing committee meeting minutes.* 2 July, 1973.

[87] The package deal system was originally conceived following the 1969 Housing Act which created what were known as General Improvement Areas (based on discussions with John Bader).

[88] Interview with David Brightmore, manager of Newport's housing renewal scheme 1975-

it proved a masterstroke; it transformed the housing stock across Newport and provided many architects and builders with work that would not have existed without this scheme.

As properties started to be improved, and the benefits of Aubrey's £1 a house scheme became clear, the attitude towards redevelopment on the council started to change, and by the beginning of 1975 the topic of conversation in council meetings was improvement rather than development.[89] Officially, the threat of redevelopment for Baneswell remained until 1981. But in practice, it's fate was sealed toward the end of 1975. There had been a meeting attended by council officers in May of that year, where Aubrey had outlined a plan to improve 500 houses in the area based on discussions with the residents. The plan was approved at a council meeting on 7th June 1975, where it was stated that this was expected to regenerate and maintain most houses in Baneswell for 10-15 years. This led to the establishment of what was known as a Housing Action Area (HAA) in Baneswell in 1976 – something that had been introduced in the Housing Act 1974.[90] Houses in the HAA would be improved, and even though it was felt that these houses would eventually have to be replaced, this would not be for another 50 years as opposed to previous estimates of 5 years or less.[91] By the spring of 1978, the council had also started to talk about the likely lives of houses as opposed to their guaranteed lives, and with the second HAA established in Baneswell by the summer, the threat of redevelopment had been removed for many years. Talks also started about disbanding the BHA as many felt it had served its purpose.[92] Several HAAs were also introduced in Pill which went a long way to preventing the future threat of redevelopment there, although it sadly proved too late for most properties that had already been demolished.

Almost 50 years since the first HAAs were introduced in Baneswell and elsewhere in Newport, houses improved under these schemes should theoretically be near the end of their lives. But walking around the different areas where these HAAs were established, it no longer feels that any houses are unfit for habitation or should be demolished. If they are, it is probably for some other reason and nothing to do with a deterioration in the improvements

---

82. 30 July, 2022.

[89] Newport borough council. *Housing committee meeting minutes.* 10 December, 1974.

[90] Although the threat to Baneswell had probably been removed by the time the first HAA was set-up in 1976, it was to prove difficult to find buyers for houses until at least early 1978 (see: Newport borough council. Pill, Baneswell and Marshes committee meeting minutes. 10 February, 1978).

[91] "New plan for future of housing in Newport." *South Wales Argus.* 10 July, 1976.

[92] Newport borough council. *Housing committee meeting minutes.* 23 March, 1978.

made in the mid-1970s.

Success against the odds

In a speech made during his mayoral year in 1977/78, Aubrey noted that during his early years as a councillor "we tended to concentrate on bricks and mortar, and often I think paid insufficient attention to people." He also noted however, in the same speech, that the "popular cry at the time was more homes, more jobs and better education," and it is indeed these most basic of human needs that seemed to need the most attention at the time.

With Newport having made no attempt to address its housing problems before the war, by 1945 it had a disproportionate number of slum properties relative to neighbouring authorities, as well as a higher occupancy rate. This worsened yet further with the new industries that were established in the area, and the influx of young people and families that occurred as a result. It was also not helped by the significant rise in the population of the UK as a whole in the immediate post-war period. With the added strain of high costs and interest rates at the time, it is not surprising that the rate of house-building lagged behind the growth of the waiting lists for houses. And the solution of "just" building more houses was not as straightforward as it might have seemed; the shortage of materials and labour meant that one could only build a house if one had a permit from the Welsh Board of Health – whose priorities lay with bomb-damaged areas. By the end of 1946, Newport had therefore only built 14 permanent houses, although this was 6 more than the rest of the county put together.[93] By 1947, the rate of house-building had increased significantly – with almost 400 new houses in Newport – yet the average occupancy rate had also *increased* during this time by 0.2 residents per house.

Moreover, for every house built in Newport, there was probably at least one more that was unfit for human habitation with about 400 properties a year considered so bad that legal proceedings were issued against their landlords. Yet although the same landlords were taken to court every month, conditions did not change and there seemed little anyone could do to make them care more for their properties and tenants. By the early-mid 1960s, it is likely that more houses were being condemned than built – a situation that exasperated the council leader Stewart Watson.[94] His opposite number, Syd Miller, was

---

[93] The remaining 8 houses had all been built in Abergavenny.

[94] Over the period 1956-1967 approximately 9000 houses had been built by the council in Newport (based on by-election statement on behalf of the Labour Group, 6th July 1967 and undated note by Stewart Watson, circa March 1967).

more fatalistic about the condemned houses, feeling that the council could do nothing to stop "the ravages of time."[95] In reality, many of these houses probably needed little more than redecoration and modernisation, but in the 1950s and 1960s the universal solution to an unfit house was to demolish and rebuild, with some local authorities such as Bristol even advocating the demolition of any house over 100 years old.[96] Few saw the fallacy of this, even though throughout Britain and across other developed countries, subsequent housing literature suggests that slum clearance and housing renewal policies had the opposite effect on the poorest people in society who they were mainly aimed at supporting. Councillors such as Aubrey, Stewart Watson, and more famously Dan T Smith (leader of Newcastle City Council) who opposed widespread demolition faced a government system obsessed with the number of houses demolished and new homes built.[97] Faced with this governmental opposition, the redevelopment of Pill, the Marshes Estate, and elsewhere in Newport was almost certainly unavoidable. The council did however, at least, mainly refuse to go down the path of high-rise flats, a policy that was subsequentially proclaimed as one of the worst public policy failures in the field.[98,99] High-rise flats were to provide only 1% of Newport's accommodation needs which was a lot less than neighbouring authorities including, for example, the nearest cities of Cardiff at 3% and Bristol at 14%.[100]

As for Aubrey, there is little doubt that despite not being a councillor during the period when most re-development was taking place, he played the key role in pausing and ultimately preventing much of the re-development that in hindsight was seen as unnecessary. He, together with the other councillors representing the Central Ward, seemed to possess that rare ability of being

---

[95] "Council debate over Pill housing grants." *South Wales Argus*. 9 April, 1963.

[96] Dunleavy, P. *The politics of mass housing in Britain: 1945-1975*. Oxford. Clarendon, 1981.

[97] Dan T Smith was probably the best known and most effective post-war political leader in the UK. Although he was jailed for corruption in 1974 after he had left politics, he recognized that the renovation of traditional houses was cheaper than slum clearance, and that it helped keep communities together. Despite his plans to renovate homes in Newcastle rather than demolish them, the housing minister at the time Sir Keith Joseph refused to support it.

[98] A significant number of properties were improved in the Marshes in the md-1960s, so it was recognized that large scale clearance was no longer necessary (based on discussions with John Bader).

[99] Dunleavy, P. T*he politics of mass housing in Britain*, 1981.

[100] Newport had only 3 blocks of flats, all of one bedroom for childless couples or single persons – based on several discussions with John Bader, formally Newport's housing manager, August-October 2020.

able to consult and listen to residents on housing decisions affecting them, rather than imposing decisions based on what others perceived to be in their best interests. This was something that rarely happened across many local authorities at this time.[101] The £1 a house scheme brought in for Pill was revolutionary, and unique, and helped support the most vulnerable residents of Newport. It even drew in enquires from people all over the country with the forlorn hope that they might be eligible.[102] While similar schemes were brought in for Liverpool in the 1980s, and Newcastle in the 1990s, as well as possibly elsewhere, this appears to be the first time that this kind of scheme was proposed for houses due to be demolished under redevelopment plans.[103] Although initially brought in for Pill, it was also rolled out across Newport, and indeed the first house sold, to Winston and Margaret Berry, was not in Pill. This house is still standing and was later improved under a HAA, one of many that saved the ratepayers of Newport a fortune in demolition and subsequent rebuilding costs.[104] In many areas of Newport, it also achieved one of its aims of keeping areas alive and helping to support the shops, churches, and other services in the area. Unfortunately, it was ultimately too late for most of Pill whose population was to reduce by a third as a result of slum clearance.[105] For many of the younger residents who bought one of these houses, it provided them with their first house they could call their own and with little personal risk. But there were numerous ways in which people were helped and lives improved; one former owner told me how she was introduced to the scheme by a judge after her husband appeared in court. The first house she could call her own gave her the opportunity to escape her abusive husband and the confidence to rebuild her life.[106] I suspect others may have had similar experiences.

In Baneswell, there is little doubt that the £1 scheme was the major factor in preventing many houses being demolished and the area being redeveloped. Once the threat of development was removed, the BHA sold forty houses

---

[101] Dunleavy, P., 1981.

[102] "Pleas from all over country for £1 houses." *South Wales Argus.* 26 April, 1972.

[103] A £1 a house scheme existed in Windsor in the late 1950s, but this is believed to be for new as opposed to unfit houses (Sydenham, Forest Hill & Penge Gazette. "The £1 down house a spur to all councils." 4 July, 1980).

[104] It has not been possible to establish how many houses were sold under this scheme, however, based on the minimum number of houses known to be owned by Baneswell Housing Association when it sold them back to the council in 1979, as well as how many houses were believed to have been sold in Alma Street in Pill, it is likely to run into several hundreds.

[105] Interview with Bob Bright, former leader of Newport Borough Council. 17 August, 2013.

[106] The name of this person has been withheld.

back to the council for the £1 it had paid for them.[107] Many of these were then sold to the people living in them at below market rates, which enabled them to buy a house that they already lived in, at a cheap price, and with no moving costs.[108] Everybody I spoke with who lived in or bought one of these £1 houses thought it was a wonderful scheme; and even if they did not later take up the offer to buy their house, they said it gave them the confidence in the future to buy rather than rent.

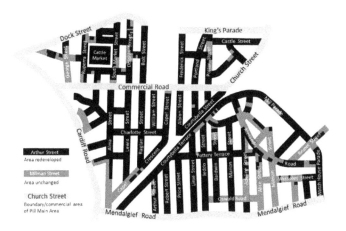

Areas redeveloped in the Pill main area since the 1960s. This schematic indicates that Pill is almost unrecognizable from the immediate post-war period, with in general, only houses built in the 1930s remaining.

With the HAAs brought in from the mid-1970s, at the same time as Aubrey became leader of the council, many of these houses also became eligible for improvement grants. Newport's enthusiastic approach to housing renewal, although not completely unique, was generally considered one of the most enlightened across the UK.[109,110] Over the period 1975 to 1982, it was to transform the housing stock across Newport; 8000 houses received home improvement grants, typically in the order of £6500-£7000. In total, approximately 15,000 houses benefitted from some kind of improvement.

---

[107] Newport borough council. *Housing committee meeting minutes.* 6 April, 1979.

[108] Newport borough council. *Housing committee meeting minutes.* 6 February, 1976.

[109] Young, John. "Newport wraps up improvement package." *ROOF.* July, 1979, pp 116-117.

[110] Merrett, S. *Owner-occupation in Britain.* London. Routledge, 1979.

By the time the scheme ended in 1982, it employed forty-seven people (compared to six when it started) and provided many elderly and low-income households with modern amenities such as bathrooms and central heating – smart properties that would only have been a pipe dream in the early 1970s.

CHAPTER 5

A CONCRETE MONSTROSITY

The long commute

For many people during their daily commute to work, their biggest frustration occurs on a short 360m section of the M4 motorway that bypasses Newport to the north – the Brynglas tunnels (the only twin-bored tunnels on the UK motorway network – one tunnel for each direction of traffic). This stretch of the M4 is the busiest stretch of motorway in Wales and regularly features on traffic bulletins particularly during the morning and evening rush hours. Numerous plans to build an M4 relief road south of the city have been proposed since the 1990s, but these plans were shelved in 2019 by the First Minister of Wales, Mark Drakeford. For many, this has not gone down well and the comment sections on any media report relating to motorway traffic through Newport invariably leads to criticisms of this decision and of Mark Drakeford in particular.

The route for the northern by-pass of the A48, and what was to become the M4 motorway, as well as the ensuing building of the George Street Bridge (that crosses the river in the middle of the city), was probably the greatest legacy left to Newport by Aubrey and several other post-war councillors. However, for those of you now turning your morning or evening frustration on Aubrey, you need to be aware of what the alternative was in the late 1950s. If it had not been for these councillors, an alternative route of the M4 motorway would probably have resulted in even greater levels of traffic congestion, and talks since the 1990s might have focused on a relief road to the north of the city, rather than to the south.

By-pass or throughway

Before the northern by-pass was built, traffic into Newport and to the west was along the A48, through the centre of Newport, passing over the River Usk at the town bridge (little traffic went across the Transporter Bridge). In 1933, the Ministry of Transport (the Ministry) approved plans for a new road to relieve traffic congestion in Newport, and these plans were revisited during the Second World War as traffic volumes increased.[1,2] This led, in 1945, to the planning of what was to become the Newport by-pass of the A48. At this point, the consulting engineers, Sir Owen Williams and Partners, were invited by the Ministry to undertake preliminary investigations into the construction of a northern by-pass (previously, in 1942, the Ministry had adopted the concept of a trunk road system across the UK in the form of motorways).[3] The northern by-pass was confirmed for Newport following a public enquiry in 1947, and the route was later fixed in 1948.[4,5] The route was fixed despite objections from within the council on the grounds that the by-pass catered only for through traffic – and that the lack of side roads into Newport would cause a barrier to development of the town.[6,7] Plans were then in any case put on hold when the UK was nearly bankrupted during the convertibility crisis of the summer of 1947 and further national economic problems in 1952. In the meantime, Newport council developed proposals for a river crossing between George Street and Wharf Road, as part of its 1953 town development plan.[8]

With car ownership in Newport more than doubling in the 1950s, and the town bridge carrying more than 3000 vehicles per hour by 1958, this had created a major bottleneck for traffic travelling through Newport and across South

---

[1] Government control of transport was reorganised several times at this time, most often coming under the Ministry of Transport. For ease of reference and to avoid confusion, this chapter just refers to "the Ministry".

[2] "New ring road would sever integral parts of town." *South Wales Argus.* 3 June, 1947.

[3] Baldwin, P. Baldwin, R. and Evans, D.I. The motorway achievement-building the network in Wales. Chichester. Phillimore, 2010.

[4] "Newport to have ring road one day." *South Wales Argus.* 13 December, 1947.

[5] Hansard HC. Parliamentary debate on Welsh Affairs. Series 5. Volume 447. 16 February, 1948. Available at: https://hansard.parliament.uk/.

[6] "Minister to hear case for bridge at Newport." *South Wales Argus.* 27 January, 1958.

[7] "Newport by-pass plan 'another Bankside case.'" *South Wales Argus.* 4 June, 1947.

[8] Newport county borough council. Written statement for the development plan for the county borough of Newport. June, 1953.

Wales.[9,10,11] Regular questions were raised in Parliament about the traffic problems in Newport by its MP Peter Freeman, as well as MPs representing constituencies to the west of Newport including George Thomas and James Callaghan in Cardiff.[12,13] Despite this, the various governments of the day refused to give any promises on when, or if, they would sanction a new bridge in Newport, and refused to meet a deputation from the council in 1954 to discuss the matter further.[14]

However, in 1956 there seemed to be a change of heart when the Ministry promised to look into the need for a new bridge and the Minister Harold Watkinson told representatives of the Town Council that the need for a second bridge was agreed in principle but that it was a question of priority.[15] There was initial excitement when, in the following year, a surprise announcement was made that a new bridge had been approved – but this lasted only a few hours before it was admitted that it had been made in error.[16]

In July 1958 a meeting to discuss the 2nd river crossing took place – at the same time as the green light for the Severn Bridge was given (improving the link between South Wales and London).[17,18] Harold Watkinson was keen that the by-pass, or an equivalent scheme, would be agreed and in place as soon as possible. At this meeting he therefore proposed a radical new scheme; a road through the heart of Newport that would provide a second river crossing for local traffic, while at the same time improving the route for through-traffic.

This new proposal intoxicated those present, including Reg Tyack and Arthur Dolman as well as the mayor, Herbert Nock, who described it as a "wonderful piece of work."[19] It later also dazzled nearly all the Conservative

[9] "Second bridge no solution." *South Wales Argus.* 25 November, 1958.

[10] "Another plea for second bridge." *South Wales Argus.* 16 July, 1955.

[11] Hansard HC. Speech by Sir Raymond Gower. South Wales Ports (Road and Rail Communications). Volume 492. 30 July, 1958. Available at: https://hansard.parliament.uk/.

[12] Hansard HC. Usk Bridge, Newport written answers. Volume 544. 27 July, 1955. Available at: https://hansard.parliament.uk/.

[13] Hansard HC. Newport (traffic conditions) written answers. Volume 551. 11 April, 1956. Available at: https://hansard.parliament.uk/.

[14] "This £5½ million scheme will change the face of Newport." *South Wales Argus.* 24 October, 1959.

[15] Ibid.

[16] "Bridge over the Usk Story 'All a Mistake.'" *South Wales Argus.* 20 November, 1957.

[17] Newport county borough council. *Parliamentary and improvement committee meeting minutes.* 7 July, 1958.

[18] "Green light for Severn bridge – Start will be made on project in two years." *South Wales Argus.* 17 July, 1958.

[19] "This £5½ million scheme will change the face of Newport." *South Wales Argus.* 24

and most Labour councillors when the scheme was presented to them, with many seeing the added benefit of quick and easy access to the docks. To almost universal approval, the scheme was approved in principle subject to agreement on the detailed plans and costs.[20]

Traffic on the A48 as it passed over the Town Bridge before the by-pass was built. This bridge not only took all local traffic from one side of Newport to the other, but also traffic travelling further west into South Wales, north to Birmingham and east to Bristol and London.[21]

October, 1959.

[20] "Newport may get a third bridge." *South Wales Argus.* 25 November, 1958.

[21] Source unknown.

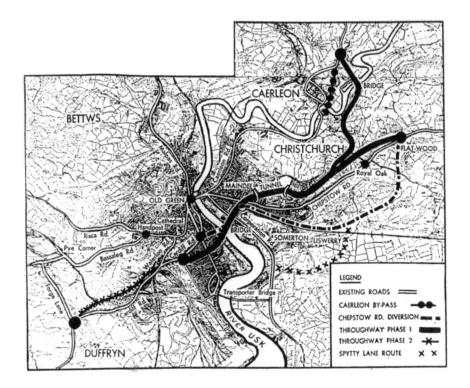

The proposed route of the "throughway" for Newport as depicted by the South Wales Argus, 24th October 1958. The route initially followed the same route of what was to become the M4 motorway before flying over Beechwood Park and under the Maindee area. Emerging from Maindee underground, it would then fly over existing roads before crossing the River Usk approximately where the George Street Bridge was later built. From here it was to link up with Cardiff Road at the eastern edge of Belle Vue Park.

Youth versus experience

The small group of councillors who were not intoxicated by the proposal had three things in common; they were mostly young and had been elected since 1954.[22] This group preferred the idea of a northern by-pass, with five sets of junctions, and a separate second crossing of the River Usk.[23] They

---

[22] Aubrey Hames Freedom of Newport ceremony, 19/02/98.

[23] The original proposal for the by-pass that was agreed in 1947 only offered two sets of junctions. Further discussions with Harold Watkinson had later offered five, which was reduced to two when he proposed the throughway.

considered the throughway to be a "concrete monstrosity" and something that would "scar the town" for future generations.[24] Aubrey was part of this group and called a meeting with the aim of persuading the council to reject the throughway, build the northern by-pass, and continue the fight for a second river crossing in central Newport. And they wanted these achieved at minimal cost to the ratepayers.

Those in favour of the throughway argued that a northern by-pass would ruin the view from the Ridgeway, something that was described as "sacrilege" by Reg Tyack when he was mayor.[25] Those against the throughway felt that the visual impact of the throughway would be far worse, especially as it would rise to a height of 55ft (16.8m) above mean high water in order to accommodate ship traffic.[26] Councillor William Casey claimed that no member of the council would be willing to "live within 500 or 600 yards of the overhead roadway" – an argument that would evidently not convince Reg Tyack as the proposed route of the throughway passed within a few metres of his house.[27] A bigger issue was the impact on tenants whose homes would be demolished. Estimates of the number of properties that would be demolished for the throughway were in the hundreds with as many as 3000 people potentially having to be displaced. Far fewer properties would need to be demolished with the by-pass.[28] The throughway would also have had a greater impact on the number of properties whose view would have changed from open fields or parkland to fast moving lanes of traffic on concrete roads and columns at a time when compensation was only paid if your home was demolished.[29] As debates on the pros and cons of the different schemes raged in various council meetings between the summers of 1958 and 1959, it was the concern about the impact on proprieties and the limited effect on local traffic that began to turn the tide against the throughway.[30] Objections raised against the by-pass in the public enquiry of 1947 – for example that it would be like building "Hadrian's Wall, or cutting Offa's Dyke, right through the middle of the town" now paled into insignificance when compared to the

[24] "By-pass plan gets council vote." *South Wales Argus.* 25 August, 1959.

[25] "By-pass would take away nearly half traffic from town centre, say Ministry." *South Wales Argus.* 18 August, 1959.

[26] Newport county borough council. *Parliamentary and improvement committee meeting minutes.* 15 July, 1958.

[27] "By-pass plan gets council vote." *South Wales Argus.* 25 August, 1959.

[28] Ibid.

[29] Baldwin, P. Baldwin, R. and Evans, D.I. *The motorway achievement-building the network in Wales.* Chichester. Phillimore, 2010.

[30] "Wonder road plan splits council." *Western Mail.* 26 November, 1958.

consequence of the throughway that would segment Newport into four.[31] Aubrey also pointed out that accommodating for ship traffic up the River Usk – traffic that amounted to 2-3 ships per week and that would likely dwindle to none by the 1970s – was illogical.[21] However, the primary concern for most councillors, and the one that was ultimately to decide what scheme was built, was money.

The financial arguments for and against the different schemes were laid out in a series of letters in the South Wales Argus by Aubrey and Arthur Dolman during the December of 1958. Aubrey's main point in favour of the by-pass was simple; it would not cost the council a penny, and local traffic would use it to get from one end of the town to the other rather than drive through the middle.[32] Building the by-pass first, followed by a second river crossing at a later date for local traffic, would attract a 50%, 60/% or even 75% government grant dependent on the extent to which it catered for external traffic. And, he estimated that it would cost the ratepayers in Newport as little as £500,000, or as much as £800,000, dependent on the level of government grant.[33] His argument against the throughway was that the cost to the council would be £500,000, and a second river crossing would be required later for which the Government would not pay more than a 50% grant. This would result in a total cost to the ratepayers for both bridges of approximately £1,500,000.[34] His argument that a later local bridge would be required was based on projected future traffic growth that indicated that the throughway would have become unfeasible by the end of the 1960s. Actual growth in traffic figures over the 1960s suggests he was about right.[35]

Arthur Dolman on the other hand felt that the by-pass was of little if any use to Newport, and that Harold Watkinson had told him that the government would only pay a 50% grant towards a local bridge. Aubrey felt that this was mischief making by the Minister.[36] Dolman argued that a by-pass would take only 80% of through-traffic (although as Aubrey noted, he didn't explain where the remaining 20% would go) and would put the construction of a new

---

[31] "By-pass plan gets council vote." *South Wales Argus.* 25 August, 1959.

[32] "Local traffic on the throughway." *South Wales Argus.* 19 December, 1958.

[33] "Councillor answers alderman." *South Wales Argus.* 8 December, 1958.

[34] Ibid.

[35] Parliamentary Office of Science and Technology (POST). *Peak car use in Britain; briefing document for the Commons transport select committee.* November, 2013.

[36] "Local traffic on the throughway." *South Wales Argus.* 19 December, 1959.

bridge in central Newport back years.[37,38,39] He further argued that improved links between the docks of Newport and the Midlands would be of significant benefit for trade between Newport and Birmingham, would ease transport from Chepstow Road and Caerleon to Cardiff Road, and would solve 90% of Newport's traffic problems.[40,41] Dolman's estimates, however, appeared to be based on nothing more than instinct when he several times disagreed with published estimates that did not suit his arguments.

Regardless of these arguments, the minister Harold Watkinson had another surprise up his sleeve which would ultimately change the minds of nearly all those who had been in favour of the throughway. This was revealed at a further meeting with Reg Tyack, Arthur Dolman and others on 13th July 1959 when Harold Watkinson clarified that his only interest was dealing with through-traffic, not local issues. He told them that if they opposed the Ministry's plan for the throughway, they would build the northern bypass anyway, but if they agreed, the Ministry would go no further than their statutory obligations; this meant that the Ministry would only pay the market value for the properties of residents who were displaced, and that the council would have to pay for any shortfall which was likely to be significant.[42]

Faced with a significant rehousing bill that they were not expecting and could not afford, this put a completely different perspective on the throughway. A meeting on whether or not to approve the throughway was called for the 25th August. Opening the debate, Councillor Frederick Cornford described the decision they were to make as "one of the most important facing us for many years," and despite initially being in favour, he felt that the issues regarding houses and finance now made it unfeasible.[43] With Reg Tyack and Arthur Dolman agreeing with him, there was now little dissension about the most appropriate option, and a free vote saw the proposal on the throughway defeated by 43 votes to 2.[44] This occurred despite the fact that many councillors, such as Arthur Dolman, still felt that the throughway was the better option. And, there was also universal agreement that a second river crossing in central Newport was still essential, and that they should not give

[37] "A better road link with Midlands, says alderman." *South Wales Argus.* 1 Dec, 1958.

[38] "Councillor answers alderman." *South Wales Argus.* 8 December, 1958.

[39] "A better road link with Midlands, says alderman." *South Wales Argus.* 1 Dec, 1958.

[40] Ibid.

[41] "Local traffic on the throughway." *South Wales Argus.* 19 December, 1958.

[42] "Emergency bulletin." *South Wales Argus.* 15 July, 1959.

[43] "By-pass plan gets council vote." *South Wales Argus.* 25 August, 1959.

[44] "The throughway has been buried." *South Wales Argus.* 28 August, 1959.

up the fight to get this approved as soon as possible.[45]

What changed Watkinson's mind?

It was Harold Watkinson who had proposed the throughway, rather than the bypass, for Newport in order to address the dual problem of through and local traffic. But despite being a keen advocate, just one year after his proposal he effectively killed it stone dead and forced the council in Newport to agree to the northern by-pass, and to end the impasse that had existed for the previous 10 years. Many felt that this was a deliberate ploy and that he had "played" the council into accepting the by-pass.[46] Other evidence suggests that a meeting with the Minister of State for Welsh Affairs, Lord Brecon, towards the end of May 1959 may have been the reason why the throughway was confined to the dustbin.

David "Vivian" Lewis was a Brecon County councillor who was plucked from nowhere in December 1957 to be the first Minister of State for Welsh Affairs and became Lord Brecon when he was created a hereditary peer the following month.[47] As a Minister, he was an enthusiastic advocate of economic and industrial development across Wales, and regularly went on fact-finding meetings to see for himself what the problems were, and what could be done about them. One of these fact-finding meetings took place over a two-week period in April/May 1959 when he visited all the ports in South Wales to discuss obstacles to their development, and what could be done to remove them and improve trade.[48] Each of these visits involved a tour of the port and its facilities in the morning, followed by discussions with port representatives in the afternoon.

He visited Newport Docks on 29th April, but it was probably his visit to Port Talbot Docks six days later that convinced him, if he needed convincing, that the problem of through traffic at Newport was a priority that had to be resolved as soon as possible. This was especially the case as construction of the Severn Bridge was due to start within the next two years. At this time, traffic through Port Talbot was along the A48 which snaked through the town and crossed a railway line that meant it was closed for three hours a day. Even though a by-pass for Port Talbot had been approved by Harold Watkinson two years previously in November 1957 (with work due to begin

[45] "By-pass plan gets council vote." *South Wales Argus.* 25 August, 1959.

[46] Ibid.

[47] Lewis, David, Vivian Penrose (1st Baron Brecon). *Dictionary of Welsh Biography.* Available at: https://biography.wales/. Accessed 12/03/22.

[48] "Minister studies docks problems." *Western Mail.* 22 April, 1959.

in early 1958), in May of 1959 when he visited Port Talbot, there was still no indication of when construction would start – and the poor access through Port Talbot was evidently a significant bar to trade across west Wales.[49] This was emphasised by Percy Morris, MP for Swansea West eleven days before Lord Brecon's visit; he stated in Parliament that the best way to ruin the economy in South Wales was "to leave Port Talbot as it is."[50] With Lord Brecon's journey deliberately taken along the road that locals described as the "worst road in Britain," it was clear that the numerous delays to the construction of the Port Talbot by-pass since approval had initially been granted in 1953, had to end. It was also clear that the delays that had plagued Port Talbot while they wasted time discussing alternative schemes could not be repeated at Newport, and this point was raised by officials in Port Talbot who expressed a preference for the by-pass in Newport.[51] Not surprisingly, shortly after visiting Port Talbot, Lord Brecon sanctioned a census of traffic through Port Talbot in preparation for his meeting with Harold Watkinson. He then made several speeches about improving the country's road system and arguing for the urgent need to remove the bottleneck at Newport.[52,53,54,55,56]

Lord Brecon's meeting with Harold Watkinson took place around the end of May 1959. This was not the first time they had discussed the road programme, but this meeting took place shortly after he had witnessed for himself the problems that the inadequate A48 had on trade and development across South Wales – particularly at the bottlenecks of Newport and Port Talbot. With Lord Brecon in a much better position to argue the case for by-passes at both Newport and Port Talbot, six weeks after this meeting, Harold Watkinson effectively forced the by-pass on Newport.

Did Aubrey have an influence on Lord Brecon?

If Lord Brecon was responsible for convincing Harold Watkinson to essentially ditch the throughway at Newport, it could be argued that the small group of councillors who started the fight against the throughway in 1958

---

[49] "Go ahead for Port Talbot's £2½ million by-pass scheme." *Western Mail.* 28 November, 1957.

[50] "Wales 'not a land of despair.'" *Western Mail.* 24 April, 1959.

[51] "Road link-up key to industrial growth." *Neath Guardian.* 18 September, 1959.

[52] "Traffic facts for Minister." *Western Mail.* 26 May, 1959.

[53] "Roads plan helps trade." *Western Mail.* 30 May, 1959.

[54] "Focus on roads." *North Wales Weekly News.* 4 June, 1959.

[55] "No new bridge – no new jobs." *Western Mail.* 4 February, 1958.

[56] "A silver lining to those unemployment clouds." *Western Mail.* 25 February, 1959.

ultimately had little effect on the decision-making process beyond delaying it long enough for Lord Brecon to step in. However, there is the intriguing possibility that Aubrey may have played some part in influencing Lord Brecon beyond his role as a councillor in Newport.

Lord Brecon's visits to the South Wales ports was a major public relations event that received significant press coverage. He would have met the different management staff at all the South Wales ports, including Aubrey who worked for the ports at this time (see Chapter 8), and who oversaw publicity for all South Wales Ports. In this role, he probably arranged Lord Brecon's visits, would have been present at all the meetings and may well have accompanied him on each visit. If so, he would have had plenty of time over a period of four days to talk to him about the traffic problems through Newport, the need for the by-pass, and the potential problems of the throughway, as well of course of their shared love of rugby.[57] But nobody involved in these events is still around, and during the interviews for this book, nobody knew about, nor mentioned the political process that led to the construction of the by-pass at Newport. However, in Aubrey's Freedom of Newport speech, he described this, in collaboration with that small group of councillors, as his biggest achievement in politics. An opinion piece published in the South Wales Argus three days after the throughway was rejected also suggested that Lord Brecon was responsible for Harold Watkinson changing his mind shortly after this tour of the South Wales ports.[58] Considering the significant role that Aubrey played in the development of Newport during his time as a councillor, and the comments he made in his Freedom of Newport speech, it seems unlikely that the only role he played extended to debate in the council chamber.

A by-pass, five motorway junctions, and a second river crossing

Although many councillors, including Arthur Dolman felt that the best scheme for Newport was the throughway, the decision to reject it in favour of the by-pass ultimately came down to money. Many councillors at the time stated that history would judge them on whether they had made the right decision, and there is little doubt that the correct decision was made. Regardless of the current issues at the Brynglas tunnels and whether a southern relief road should be built or not, the same issues would undoubtedly have existed at the Maesglas tunnels, and the throughway would probably have

---

[57] The visits to Swansea and Port Talbot took place the same day, having already visited Cardiff, Barry and Newport on separate days.
[58] "The throughway has been buried." *South Wales Argus*. 28 August, 1959.

made little difference to local traffic issues. The "concrete monstrosity" of the throughway may also have become unfeasible as the future route of the M4, possibly forcing the construction of a later southern relief road anyway.

As for the decision of Harold Watkinson to essentially force Newport to choose the by-pass over the throughway, many councillors at the time felt that he never wanted the throughway in the first place. It was put on the table to address the dual issue of the by-pass, which is what he wanted, and the local bridge, which is what Newport wanted, yet he contrived to make Newport choose the by-pass. However, telling the Newport delegation when he met them in July 1958 that if they turned down the throughway, he might not proceed with the by-pass, does not seem to tally with his desire to have the by-pass built.[59] But if he did change his mind based on any intervention, it almost certainly would have been in the build-up to the meeting with Newport officials in July 1959. This would have been in discussion with someone who he appreciated would understand the problems and issues, and more likely to be someone who was in Government. This description fits Lord Brecon, a man to whom Aubrey probably had unfettered access to in the days before he met Harold Watkinson.

However, things can and do change, particularly in government, and often plans that had once seemed unfeasible can suddenly become feasible very quickly. As far as the George Street Bridge was concerned, the unfeasible became feasible less than two months after the council rejected the throughway on 14th October 1959. This was when Harold Watkinson was promoted to the role of Minister of Defence and replaced as Minister of Transport by Ernest Marples. Ernest Marples was much more open to a new bridge in Newport for local traffic, and before the end of the year agreed to a parliamentary bill to be put forward by Newport Council.[60,61] This was promoted by the council in November 1960, and despite wranglings over the number of lanes (Newport wanted six, yet the Ministry only offered four), the government agreed to the construction of a second Usk crossing.[62]

The grant given by the government for the George Street Bridge was 75% – the maximum figure predicted by Aubrey – and the cost including the Wharf Road approach was £2,105,000. This meant that the total cost of the bridge

---

[59] "Council are not committed to throughway plan." *South Wales Argus.* 20 May, 1959.

[60] Hansard HC. Parliamentary questions to Ernest Marples, Minister of Transport. Volume 629. 8 November, 1960. Available at: https://hansard.parliament.uk/.

[61] "George Street Bridge supplement." *South Wales Argus.* 9 April, 1964.

[62] Ibid.

to Newport was just over £500,000, the same estimate as given by Aubrey.[63]

The bridge that the council had been fighting for since 1945 was completed in July 1964, and the day it was opened was described by the South Wales Argus as Newport's biggest day for a quarter of a century.[64,65] It opened three years earlier than the most optimistic predictions in the early 1950s, three years before the by-pass was completed, and probably several more years before a throughway would have been built.[66] Based on the drive and determination of Aubrey and a few other mainly young councillors, as well as Aubrey's possible influence over Lord Brecon, Newport got its by-pass, its five motorway junctions, and its second river crossing in central Newport, all a lot earlier than they could have predicted. As Aubrey was to say in September 1964, this was all an example of outstanding local government.[67]

---

[63] "Marples gives town £1m grant for bridge." *South Wales Argus.* 8 May, 1962.

[64] "George Street Bridge supplement." *South Wales Argus.* 9 April, 1964.

[65] "Flinging open the gate." *South Wales Argus.* 9 April, 1964.

[66] "Newport's new development plan." *South Wales Argus.* 30 April, 1952.

[67] "The other side." *South Wales Argus.* 30 September, 1964.

CHAPTER 6

ROGUE POLITICS

Reginald Silas Tyack

When Aubrey was elected to the council in May 1954, the leader of the Labour Group was Reginald Silas Tyack, commonly known as Reg Tyack, who had been leader since the early 1940s.[1] With Labour gaining control of the council for the first time in 1945, he could also be considered the first Labour leader of the council, even though a formal leader as we now know it did not exist at this time. Being leader of the Labour group and "ex officio" leader of the council he was to become probably the most powerful and influential local politician that Newport had ever had. He also became slightly dictatorial in the decision-making process and so by the time Aubrey was elected as a councillor, there was a level of dissatisfaction in the party with Tyack's leadership – particularly among the younger members who had seen action in the Second World War.

Consequently, Aubrey's first recorded action as a councillor was a resolution to remove Reg Tyack as leader of the group, as well as chairman of the influential Housing and Parliamentary and Improvement Committees. This was the first ever recorded attempt to remove a Labour leader from office. It was also the start of the process of the removal of certain stale old guard First World War politicians in Newport, who maximised the trappings of office, yet paid minimal attention to the less interesting aspects of the council work

---

[1]Reg Tyack stood down as leader during his mayoral year of 1947/48 but regained the leadership the following year.

for which they had been elected.[2,3]

Although Aubrey failed in this attempt to remove Reg Tyack from office, he did succeed nine years later with a brutal attack on his leadership. Leading the fight to remove Reg Tyack as leader of the group probably ruined his own chances of becoming leader at this time, but it allowed the like-minded Stewart Watson to take over from Reg Tyack, with Aubrey taking over from Stewart Watson when he initially stepped down as a councillor following his mayoral year in 1972.

Alderman Reginald Silas Tyack during his mayoral year of 1947/48 (photo courtesy Civic Centre).

---

[2] This was a common problem with many of the old guard politicians in the 1950s and 1960s as noted by E. Shaw, 1988.

[3] Shaw, E. *Discipline and discord*, 1988.

The original "young turk"

Reg Tyack was born in Bristol in 1893, one of six children of Thomas, a railway guard, and his wife Mary.[4] Like his father and grandfather before him, he worked on the railways initially as a clerk for Great Western Railway (GWR) in Plymouth from 1910 aged 16, before serving with the Royal Engineers in France during the First World War.[5,6] This is where he met his wife Yvonne who he married in Plymouth in 1919.[7] He was later posted to Porthcawl before eventually being moved to Newport in 1920 to work as a booking clerk at Newport railway station.[8,9]

Shortly after arriving at Newport, he started to involve himself in trade union affairs and became the Chairman of the Newport No. 1 branch of the Railway Clerks' Association.[10] After becoming an active member of the Labour Party, he made the first of several attempts to become a town councillor in 1926, before finally succeeding when he was elected for the Liswerry Ward in 1933.

In his early days as a councillor, Reg Tyack proved to be efficient, hard-working, and conscientious – and not afraid of a political fight, particularly with the popular Conservative Alderman Cyrus Thomas Clissitt. Regarded as the hardest working councillor in Newport in the 1930s and early 1940s he was regularly praised for his efforts in various Newport Labour Party minutes and could probably have claimed to have been the first "young turk" of the Labour Party in Newport.[11] It is therefore of little surprise that within six years of becoming a councillor he was elected as deputy leader of the party.[12] He likely then became leader in early 1941 when the long-standing leader Richard Davies stood down.[13]

---

[4] "Widow of GWR Official." *Western Daily Press.* 15 February, 1943.

[5] "Alderman's Rail Ticket Offence." *Wesern Mail.* 15 March, 1952.

[6] "Taunton Police Court." *Taunton Courier, and Western Advertiser.* 11 April, 1866.

[7] "Obituary of Reginald Silas Tyack." *South Wales Argus.* 14 August, 1968.

[8] Ibid.

[9] "Mayor elect's experience of public work." *Weekly Argus.* 9 November, 1946.

[10] Ibid.

[11] He regularly attended more committee meetings than any other councillor, averaging 320 per year at this time, see "Mayor elect's experience of public work" above.

[12] Newport Labour Party. *Labour Party meeting minutes.* 1 December, 1939.

[13] The minutes where Reg Tyack became leader of the Labour Party do not exist. However, he probably became leader in January or February 1941, although certainly before the end of 1942.

A gentleman and a rogue

Working in poorly paid, relatively low status work, Reg Tyack was typical of many Labour Party politicians in urban areas at this time who turned to politics as a means of self-advancement.[14] Having reached the position of ex officio leader of the council, with a position on the aldermanic bench in 1946 and the mayoralty a year later, he had reached the pinnacle of respectability.[15] He was always smartly dressed with a flower in his buttonhole and enjoyed his position of power and the privileges it gave him; unfortunately though, it also provided him the means of abusing those privileges.[16,17]

The clearest example of the abuse of the privileges came in his use of the Mansion House, and the hospitality it afforded. He lived there both when he was mayor, and also when he was leader of the Labour Group – despite it being solely the mayor's residence – and he held regular well-attended and raucous parties there.[18] During this time, council meetings became more sociable; so much so that it became difficult to go home sober.[19] He also took full advantage of the expense system, particularly in his mayoral year when his expenses were over £4,500 (approximately £125,000 at today's prices).[20] This was more than two and a half times the average level, and 95% of it had been for entertaining – over 50% more than the previous highest.[21,22] This caused considerable debate over several weeks in both the local and national press towards the end of his mayoralty, with one letter commenting that he was "living like a lord at the public expense," and one national newspaper referring to Newport as a "hospitality town."[23,24] His excessive use of hospitality did not end in Newport with one example revealing him having spent £34 and 14 shillings treating businessmen in Birmingham to a four-course luncheon with "wines and liqueurs" – a figure that was later

---

[14] Shaw, E,1988.

[15] Newport county borough council. *Council meeting minutes.* 10 December, 1946,

[16] Personal ccommunication with Mrs. Chris Wilson, Reg Tyack's next-door neighbour.

[17] "South Wales viewpoints" (letter from Anthony Pollock), *Western Mail.* 16 January, 1956.

[18] Based on several interviews.

[19] Interview with Ron Jones, former Newport Labour Party councillor. 25 May, 2013.

[20] This included an astronomical £748 6s 4d for entertaining guests in 3 days at the Newport Show held in August (*Daily Mirror.* "They want councillors to pay £18,630 show loss." 24 November, 1947.

[21] "Why Newport may have to stage 1948 show." *South Wales Argus.* 15 October, 1947.

[22] "How the mayor of Newport 'spent his salary.'" *South Wales Argus.* 30 October, 1947.

[23] "The election," (letter). *South Wales Argus.* 28 October, 1947.

[24] "Newport let down," (letter). *South Wales Argus.* 22 October, 1947.

agreed in council to be far too high.[25,26] Reg Tyack defended his expenses and use of privileges as an important part of attracting prospective industrialists to the town – except of course when there was no defence.[27,28]

In 1940 as deputy leader of the Labour Group, he had been fined 10 shillings for drinking in a pub in the early hours when drinking was prohibited.[29] This was made worse by the fact that he was chairman of the Newport ARP committee at this time – a position he no longer seemed to hold after that incident.[30,31] In 1952 as council leader, he was fined £3 for using a first-class ticket issued to him for council business for a travelling companion. This was made more embarrassing when he was caught handing over his companion's ticket at the very station where he worked.[32] The fact that his travelling companion was an unmarried woman with whom he was having an affair further added to his embarrassment.[33,34]

However, his abuse of privilege was not just contained to social and financial affairs. Decisions passed by the Labour Party (locally or nationally) were often conveniently forgotten about or ignored if his opinion differed. When caught in a corner he gave no ground and would resort to crying if necessary to win an argument.[35,36] In the extreme, he would "go missing" to avoid unwelcome meetings, often for considerable periods of time.

In contrast, any member of the Labour Group who threatened his position was dealt with severely. He was primarily responsible for Frederick Morrice (a councillor first elected in the same year as he was elected) having the Labour whip removed prior to the 1945 municipal elections despite disagreements

---

[25] "The £34 bill upsets council." *Birmingham Daily Gazette*. 12 January, 1955.

[26] "Council decide lunch expenses were too high." *South Wales Argus*. 11 January, 1955.

[27] "The £34 bill upsets council." *Birmingham Daily Gazette*. 12 January, 1955.

[28] "How the mayor of Newport 'spent his salary.'" *South Wales Argus*. 30 October, 1947.

[29] "Licensee and guests fined." *Western Mail*. 27 April, 1940.

[30] "Use of premises for ARP purposes." *Western Mail*. 11 October, 1939.

[31] They are several references in the *Western Mail* of Reg Tyack as chairman of the Newport ARP committee prior to this incident, yet none after, although no reference to any successor can be found.

[32] "Regret for 'extremely foolish offence.'" *Hartlepool Northern Daily Mail*. 14 March.

[33] Interview with Harry Williams, former Chairman of Newport Labour Party. 11 December, 2014.

[34] Several interviews mention that Reg Tyack had long standing affairs.

[35] "South Wales viewpoints," (letter from Anthony Pollock). *Western Mail*. 16 January, 1956.

[36] Interview with Sir Harry Jones, Aubrey's successor as Leader of Newport Council, 3 March, 2013.

from many party members and the trade unions.[37,38,39] Frederick Morrice was still nominated by the Central Ward as its candidate but this nomination was later rejected by the party. Frederick Morrice then stood as an independent, with the support of some ward members, who were all sub-sequentially expelled from the party.[40]

However, despite the disquiet felt by many members of the group, there was no clear attempt to remove Tyack as leader. Disillusioned by the way the group was run, several aldermen and councillors started to limit their attendance at Labour Group meetings, yet, when Reg Tyack stood for leader again after his year as mayor, he was comfortably re-elected.[41,42]

Tyack challenged

By the early 1950s, Reg Tyack had a powerful grip on the leadership of the Labour Group and the council. At a time when chairmen of various committees often held more power than group leaders, Reg Tyack was chairman of the most influential committees, as well as president of the Labour Party.[43] It is unlikely that any previous councillor had ever held as much power on the council in Newport as Reg Tyack. Considering his dominant position, it is perhaps not surprising that his leadership had not been directly challenged in the post-war period, even though many members of the party were unhappy with the way he led the Labour Group. But this was to change as soon as Aubrey was elected to the council in 1954.

Prior to the local elections in 1954, Reg Tyack had been mildly rebuked for various comments he had made in council and to the public, and these events seem to have been the catalyst for Aubrey to try and get him removed as leader.[44] This attempt was carried out via a resolution from the Malpas Ward that was read out at the Executive Committee meeting on 18th May 1954,

---

[37] Newport Labour Party. *Executive committee meeting minutes*. 31 July, 1945.

[38] Newport Labour Party. *General committee meeting minutes*. 31 August, 1945.

[39] Newport Labour Party. *Executive committee meeting minutes*. 10 September, 1945.

[40] Newport Labour Party. *General committee meeting minutes*. 9 November, 1945.

[41] Attendance at party group meetings at this time for many aldermen and councillors was less than 25% (see for example; Newport Labour group. *Labour group meeting minutes*. 11 September, 1950, and Newport Labour Party *Executive committee meeting minutes*. 2 October, 1950).

[42] Newport Labour group. *Labour group meeting minutes*. 9 November, 1947.

[43] Jones, G.W. and Norton, A. eds., *Political Leadership in Local Authorities*. Birmingham. Institute of Local Government Studies, University of Birmingham, 1978.

[44] Newport Labour group. *Labour group meeting minutes*. 12 April, 1954.

four days after Aubrey had been elected as a councillor.[45] Without doubt, this resolution was driven by Aubrey and would have been made with the support of many members of the party, including Stewart Watson, who had been elected at the same time. Reg Tyack clearly knew that this resolution was coming – either via Aubrey himself or via a friendly warning – because he did not turn up at this meeting (a regular occurrence if there was an issue he wanted to avoid).

The resolution called for Reg Tyack to be removed as Group leader and chairman of the influential Housing and Parliamentary Committees at the next Annual General Meeting. The stated reason was due to the "criticism of the many party members and in the interest of future party progress."[46] This resolution was carried following a "full and frank discussion." However, the resolution was defeated at the Labour group meeting six days later when Reg Tyack agreed to behave in the future, and asked for a renewal of confidence in his leadership.[47,48]

Although this attempt to remove Reg Tyack as leader failed, it was a remarkable act by Aubrey. Not only was it the first recorded attempt to remove a Labour Group leader in Newport, but it was also his first recorded action as a councillor – Labour's youngest councillor since the war, and one of its youngest ever. Although the vote to remove Reg Tyack as leader failed, six out of twenty-six Labour councillors and aldermen still voted in favour of removing him, which was not an overwhelming vote of confidence. Reg Tyack did though receive some reassuring support from his Union, USDAW (Union of Shop, Distributive and Allied Workers), who later disaffiliated from the Newport Labour Party due to the action taken over him.[49]

Expenses and dinners

Although Aubrey failed in his initial attempt to remove Reg Tyack as Group leader, over the coming years he was to become Newport's most formidable political operator and the clearest threat to Reg Tyack's leadership and his allies, as well as the Conservative Party who saw him as their biggest political threat.[50] A reputation as a "firebrand" and a "political hooligan" in

---

[45] Newport Labour Party. *Executive committee meeting minutes*. 18 May, 1954.

[46] Ibid.

[47] Newport Labour group. *Labour group meeting minutes*. 24 May, 1954.

[48] Newport Labour Party. *Executive committee meeting minutes*. 28 May, 1954.

[49] Newport Labour Party. *Executive committee meeting minutes*. 21 June, 1954.

[50] This was mentioned in the Newport Conservative Party minutes (noted by Jim Criddle). National Library of Wales.

his early political career would not have endeared him to Reg Tyack's allies, and it is likely that most of his fury would have been aimed at them.[51] Indeed, one Conservative elder statesman who did observe the various interactions between Aubrey and the predominately older councillors noted around that time that "Aubrey wasn't all that chummy with his own Labour members."[52]

With Reg Tyack having set a template for how many councillors behaved, it wasn't just Aubrey and the new generation of young politicians who tried to put an end to some of the less salubrious activities of certain, predominantly Labour, council members. Sidney Teece Millar, the Conservative Group leader, was also incensed by these activities – particularly two that he referred to many years later.[53] The first of these was the practice of councillors who lived in the valleys driving to meetings in one car, yet with each claiming their own fuel expenses as if they had driven in by themselves. The second was the practice of deliberately adjourning a morning's discussion for lunch, and then to return in the afternoon for a few minutes so that they could claim two full sessions of expenses.[54] However, as one of the few Conservative members of the council, there was little he could do to end these practices. Aubrey would also have found it difficult to end these privileges as most members enjoyed them, although he made his feelings on council lunches clear by boycotting them and getting his lunch from the local chip shop with his political buddy John Marsh.[55]

However, the political balance of the Labour group was changing. The old guard politicians were retiring to be replaced by members enthused by socialism as children following Labour's post-war general election victories. Reg Tyack's hold on the party was weakening.

A convenient meeting

In July or August 1962, it was agreed that the policy for setting council house rents should be passed from the Housing Committee, of which Reg Tyack was chairman, to the Labour group as a whole. This decision, which removed a level of control over council house rents that Reg Tyack had enjoyed since the end of the war, was strongly resisted by him but he assured the Labour group that he would abide by the decision. However, this policy was

---

[51] "Aubrey steps out of the hot seat." *South Wales Argus.* 29 April, 1987.

[52] Ibid.

[53] Hames, D., telephone conversation with Andrew Millar, Sidney Teece Miller's grandson. 16 March, 2021.

[54] "Aubrey steps out of the hot seat." *South Wales Argus.* 29 April, 1987.

[55] Aubrey and John Marsh were often referred to as the "Fish and Chip" gang.

subsequently ignored as he unsuccessfully tried to push through proposals to substantially increase council house rates behind his colleagues' back – while at the same time going missing for a couple of months so that he could not be questioned about these proposals.

This was not the first time that Reg Tyack had deliberately gone against a Labour group decision, or refused, or "forgotten", to implement an agreed policy. It was at this point that Aubrey decided for the second time that Reg Tyack had to go; and he knew, or suspected, that he had the majority support of the Labour group.

On 16th November 1962, Aubrey informed the general committee that he wanted them to hear a report by him on the affairs of the Labour group at which the persons involved in the report (i.e. Reg Tyack) would be invited to attend.[56] It was therefore agreed to arrange a meeting on a date that was convenient for both Aubrey and Reg Tyack.[57] However, as much as Aubrey wanted the general committee to hear his report, the subject of his report was not interested. Several attempts were made by the Labour group secretary and agent to arrange a date with Reg Tyack, and to ensure that he was present, but a date proved difficult to pin down.[58] Eventually, a "convenient" date was agreed – 21st January 1963 – almost two months later.

But Reg Tyack still had to turn up, and sure enough, when the day arrived, Reg Tyack rang the deputy leader of the Labour Party to tell him that he did not feel well and "would be staying in."[59] A call to his house during the meeting was not answered.[60] A further meeting was called for 28th January, with Newport's MP and the Shadow Home Secretary, Sir Frank Soskice, present.[61] When Tyack again refused to show up, it is not known what excuse he gave – or indeed the excuses he gave in the ensuing 7 weeks – because no Labour Party minutes exist between 26th January and 7th March. But it appears that the meeting finally took place on 4th March.[62]

Although the minutes of this meeting do not exist, the original copy of the report does, and it was a ferocious attack on Reg Tyack, his leadership, and the

---

[56] Newport Labour Party. *General committee meeting minutes*. 16 November, 1962.

[57] Newport Labour Party. *Executive committee meeting minutes*. 27 November, 1962.

[58] Newport Labour Party. *Executive committee meeting minutes*. 21 January, 1963.

[59] Ibid.

[60] It is not clear from the minutes if this was a phone call, or whether someone physically turned up at his house.

[61] Newport Labour Party. *General committee meeting minutes*. 25 January, 1963.

[62] Newport Labour Party. *General committee meeting minutes*. 8 March, 1963.

contempt that he showed to all members of the Labour group.[63] Reg Tyack's response is also not known, but he clearly disagreed with the contents of the report as implied by the minutes of the general committee held on 8th March, which deferred any action on the report until there had been an "an indication of the factual, correctness, or otherwise, of the above-mentioned report."[64] Unfortunately, the various Labour Party minutes do not exist from April to September 1963, and nobody interviewed was aware of the internal politics of the Labour Party over this time. However, it was clear that Reg Tyack no longer had the support from the party that he had enjoyed nine years earlier, and whether he went voluntarily or not, he was to lose his position as leader of the Labour group in probably May or June of 1963.

A new leader

With Reg Tyack gone, Aubrey was his obvious successor. He stood for the position against Reg Lloyd, who, like Aubrey at the time, was not a councillor although he would be elected for the first time the following year. However, the Labour group could not choose between Aubrey and Reg Llyod and there was opposition from members against both candidates. Opposition against Aubrey would have been understandable from those who still supported Reg Tyack. And Reg Lloyd, although competent, was probably considered too young and inexperienced. Although Aubrey was the favoured candidate, it became clear to him that he was too divisive a leader for the Labour Party at this time, and a compromise candidate was proposed – Stewart Watson. So Stewart Watson was elected as leader of the Labour group and would later become Newport's first ever official council leader.[65] He was to remain leader of the Labour group until his mayoral year in 1971 after which he stepped down as a councillor.[66] With the stale, old guard politicians of the 1950s and 1960s now gone, the older, wiser and by now less fiery Aubrey was his obvious replacement. He became leader of the Labour group in 1971, and with Labour holding the balance of power on the council he also

---

[63] Newport Labour Party. Report to the executive committee of the Newport Labour Party and the joint EC and Labour group. 4 March, 1963.

[64] Newport Labour Party. *General committee meeting minutes*. 8 March, 1963.

[65] It is not known when Newport first had an official council leader, or even if the role of group leader just morphed into leader of the council with time. However, the role of council leader would have emerged during Stewart Watson's tenure as Labour group leader when the Labour Party controlled the council. As such, Stewart Watson can be considered Newport's first ever official council leader.

[66] Although leaving the council after his mayoral year, he was later to return in 1976, remaining as a councillor until he retired from politics in 1996.

became leader of the council – a role he was to maintain for all but two of his remaining years as councillor (1977/78 which was his mayoral year, and the year before that when the Conservatives controlled the council). Reg Lloyd, his original opponent in 1963, was elected as his deputy.

As for Reg Tyack, he was to remain an alderman until he died aged 75 in 1968 after a long illness.[67] At his funeral, his coffin was walked down the aisle accompanied by his wife Yvonne, and two more unrelated women.[68]

---

[67] "Obituary of Reginald Silas Tyack." *South Wales Argus.* 14 August, 1968.
[68] Interview with Ron Jones, former Newport Labour Party councillor. 25 May, 2013.

CHAPTER 7

PARLIAMENTARY SELECTION

An MP for Newport

The death of Newport's Labour MP Peter Freeman in 1956 presented Aubrey with the first of what were to be four opportunities to seek the nomination as Labour's prospective parliamentary candidate in Newport – all of which were unsuccessful. Nominated by the Caerau Ward, Aubrey may have felt he had an outside chance of selection, but with the National Labour Party keen to return the ex-Attorney General Sir Frank Soskice to Parliament, there was little doubt who would secure the nomination regardless of who else was nominated.[1] It wasn't until Sir Frank Soskice's subsequent retirement prior to the 1966 general election that Aubrey had his first serious opportunity to secure the nomination for Labour as its prospective parliamentary candidate in Newport. Unlike in 1956, it was generally expected that he would be selected, but he lost out to a trade unionist, Roy Hughes. Although the loss to a trade union candidate should not have been unexpected, the background to Roy Hughes' candidacy masks what is possibly the most serious crisis faced by the Labour Party in Newport in its history; the effects of which were to last into the next century. In 1983, with the creation of two Parliamentary seats in Newport, and Newport's current MP Roy Hughes choosing to stand in Newport East, Aubrey was controversially not nominated by his ward as a prospective candidate for the Newport West constituency. This occurred despite the fact that at the time he was leader of the council, and arguably the best-known and most highly respected local politician in Wales. The

---

[1] Gwent Archives. *Aubrey Hames nomination form.* 6 June, 1956.

reasons for him not being nominated by his ward led directly to him leaving local politics, and almost certainly led to the one failure of Labour to win a parliamentary seat in Newport since the war. At the following general election in 1987, Aubrey was now 64, and his desire to only serve one term meant that he was not considered a serious candidate. The candidacy, and seat ultimately went to Paul Flynn, who went on to represent Newport West for 32 years until his death in 2019.

This chapter highlights the background to Aubrey's failures to secure the nomination as Labour's prospective parliamentary candidate in both 1966 and 1983, with a background for the 1966 nomination which can be traced back to the 1920s.

A "suitable candidate"

In the early 1920s, there was a significant increase in membership of the Newport Labour Party which bucked the national trend. Membership continued to grow throughout the 1920s, and by 1929 (as noted in chapter 3), it was the largest constituency party in Wales, and the fourth largest in the UK.[2] The growth in this support was particularly strong among women, who outnumbered men by 1924 and made up 70% of the party membership by 1933 – a level that they were to maintain for the next 20 years.[3] Membership fees provided an income of more than £400 a year, and the sterling work of the women's sections, who were responsible for most of the fund raising (responsible for 10-20% of the party income at the time) gave a substantial boost to Labour Party funds in Newport.[4] This was a significant boost for a constituency that was considered a safe Conservative seat at the time, and which consequently drew minimal trade union support of less than £50 a year.

Yet despite the money generated by membership fees, the Labour constituency party in Newport struggled to stay in the black. This was not helped by a consistent failure of certain unions to pay their affiliation fees, as well as a failure to collect fees from many individuals via door-to-door collections. Unfortunately, most of these failures could be laid fully at the door of the male members of the party, as indicated, for example, by the party's annual report in 1927, which contained the forlorn hope that the male members

---

[2] Tanner, D., Thane, P. and Tiratsoo, N. eds., *Labour's first century*. Cambridge. Cambridge University Press, 2000.

[3] Hopkin, D., Tanner, D. and Williams, C. eds., *Labour Party in Wales 1900-2000*. Cardiff. University of Wales Press, 2000.

[4] Newport Labour Party. *Annual Report and Balance Sheet, 1927, 1928.*

would "play a more active role in the party."

Therefore with a requirement for more funds, the Labour Party in Newport was open to the adoption of a candidate who could "assist" with their monetary problems. So for the 1929 general election, they adopted James Walker as their prospective parliamentary candidate. With the support of William Bowen, who had been Labour's candidate in all elections since the constituency was established in 1918, James Walker won the seat for Labour for the first time, bringing with him significant financial support from the Iron and Steel Confederation.[5,6] However, when James Walker lost his seat in the 1931 general election and was successfully courted by the Motherwell constituency for the next general election in 1935, the Iron and Steel Confederation withdrew their support to the Newport Labour Party in May 1932.[7,8] This once again placed the party in financial difficulty so an appeal was sent out for financial aid from what was described as a "suitable candidate."[9]

Keen to adopt a parliamentary candidate early, several people were approached, including Ernest Bevin who had co-founded the Transport and General Workers' union (TGWU) in 1922, and was its current General Secretary.[10] They also wrote to all affiliated organisations asking for names.[11] Others applied who were mainly rejected either because they could not supply an appropriate level of re-numeration, or because they were considered too controversial. This included Frank Wise, who was the most prominent member of the Independent Labour Party, and someone who many wanted to see disaffiliated from the Labour Party.[12]

Eventually, after a long and drawn-out process, three candidates were identified for interview. These were Reginald Fletcher, a former Liberal MP who was later to serve as a Minister in Clement Attlee's government after the war; Ivor Owen Thomas, a trade unionist and future Labour MP after the war; and Peter Freeman, who had been elected as MP for Brecon and Radnorshire in 1929 before losing his seat at the 1931 general election.[13] A

---

[5] Newport Labour Party. *Executive committee meeting minutes.* 14 March, 1932.

[6] Newport Labour Party. *Executive committee meeting minutes.* 10 July, 1932.

[7] "Tragic death of Mr. James Walker MP." *Motherwell Times.* 12 January, 1945.

[8] Newport Labour Party. *Executive committee meeting minutes.* 10 July, 1932.

[9] Ibid.

[10] Newport Labour Party. *Executive committee meeting minutes.* 23 November, 1932.

[11] Newport Labour Party. *Executive committee meeting minutes.* 23 October, 1932.

[12] Ibid.

[13] Newport Labour Party. *Executive committee meeting minutes.* 4 January, 1933.

further motion, and not for the first time, was also made to approach James Walker, but this was lost.[14]

Subsequentially only Reginald Fletcher and Peter Freeman were interviewed, and both had to write statements on what "financial assistance" they could provide. Ultimately Reginald Fletcher was to withdraw from the process (probably due to ill health that had dogged him throughout the interview process) so Peter Freeman was adopted as the parliamentary candidate for the 1935 general election.[15]

Peter Freeman

Peter Freeman was an interesting character. He was an accomplished sportsman who could have had a professional career in any number of sports; he won the Welsh Tennis Championships in 1919, and at one point in his tennis career was one half of a double that beat the reigning Wimbledon Doubles champions.[16] He was also an environmentalist and animal rights campaigner at a time when these issues were treated with contempt by many in Parliament. As managing director at J.R. Freeman & Sons, a family business that made cigars, he introduced holiday and sick pay for all employees before it became a legal requirement, as well as social facilities and outings.[17] Unsurprisingly he was a philanthropist, although less surprisingly he was also a non-smoker and teetotaller. More importantly for a prospective parliamentary candidate without the backing of a union, he was independently wealthy.[18]

This wealth enabled him to secure the nomination as the Labour Party candidate for the Brecon and Radnorshire constituency for the 1929 general election after agreeing to bankroll the campaign. He also agreed to pay the salary and expenses of a full-time secretary and agent, Tudor Watkins (later MP for Brecon and Radnorshire 1945-1970).[19] In securing this nomination, he had defeated a former and future cabinet minister, Wedgewood Benn, the father and grandfather of Tony and Hilary Benn respectively, a nomination

---

[14] Newport Labour Party. *Executive committee meeting minutes*. 19 December, 1932.

[15] Newport Labour Party. *Special General Committee meeting minutes*. 13 April, 1933.

[16] Bloxsome, M. *The green Casanova: An affectionate biography of Peter Freeman, maverick MP*. Talybont: Y Lofla, 2004.

[17] Ibid.

[18] Ibid.

[19] The cost of fighting an election at this time was estimated at £650-£900, yet the funds of the Brecon and Radnor Labour Party in January 1927 stood at just £5. In addition, with financial problems in the Labour Party at a National level, there was no financial support available for the appointment of an agent.

clearly secured as he was able to contribute greater funds to the local Labour Party.[20] Unexpectedly winning this seat for the first time for Labour in the 1929 general election, and immediately resigning as managing director at J.R. Freeman & Sons to concentrate on his political career, he was to lose this seat heavily at the next general election in 1931. With no parliamentary seat, and feeling that the constituency party in Brecon and Radnorshire did not match his dedication and commitment, he decided not to seek this nomination again, and chose instead to seek the nomination for Newport in the following general election.

Although the adoption of Peter Freeman improved finances and the consequent election fund of the Newport Labour Party, this was not quite enough to secure the Parliamentary seat in the 1935 general election in which the Conservative Reginald Clarry won with a majority of just over 1,500. Despite this loss, Peter Freeman agreed to nurse the party through to the next election, and to contribute £100 to party funds each year – a sizeable sum considering that an MP's salary at this time was only £400 per year. This enabled the party to feel confident enough to appoint Reginald Ley as a full-time agent (who co-incidentally had done the same job for Peter Freeman in Brecon and Radnorshire).[21]

However, despite Peter Freeman's contributions, the finances of the party remained tight. No delegate was sent to the National Labour Party conference from 1935 to 1940, and the party received sympathetic treatment from the Co-operative Bank regarding its overdraft.[22,23,24,25] But Peter Freeman's continuing support kept the party going to the next general election, agreeing to fully clear their debts by 1941.[26]

The complacent years 1945-1956

The next election for an MP in Newport came on 17th May 1945 following the death of Reginald Clarry after a short illness on 17th January.[27] Co-incidentally this was just 12 days after his predecessor James Walker had

---

[20] Brecon and Radnor Labour Party. *Executive committee meeting minutes*. May, 1927.

[21] Newport Labour Party. *Executive committee meeting minutes*. 5 June, 1935.

[22] Newport Labour Party. *Executive committee meeting minutes*. 2 December, 1935.

[23] Newport Labour Party. *General committee meeting minutes*. 17 July, 1936.

[24] Newport Labour Party. *General committee meeting minutes*. 3 May, 1940.

[25] The Newport Labour Party executive committee meeting minutes of 30 December 1936 indicate that the Co-operative Bank had sanctioned an overdraft of £150.

[26] Newport Labour Party. *Annual meeting minutes*. 25 January, 1941.

[27] He was Sir Reginald Clarry at the time of his death.

been killed in a road traffic accident in Brighton. As the last by-election of the 1935-1945 Parliament, the seat was not contested by the Labour and Liberal parties under a war-time electoral pact which meant that by-elections would only be contested by the party which previously held the seat. This pact though did not apply to other parties or individuals, and the Conservative candidate Ronald Bell was required to stand against and defeat an Independent Labour Party candidate. With the date of the next general election announced just six days later, he was heavily defeated by Peter Freeman within two months of winning his seat. This was only three days longer than the tenure of the shortest-serving Member of Parliament whose time in office was not ended by death.[28] With Peter Freeman finally elected as an MP for Newport, he increased his funding to the party, pledging £400 per annum to the constituency in addition to the £100 he had already pledged to the election fund.[29]

Over the next eleven years, Peter Freeman proved to be one of the hardest working and most popular Members of Parliament, and one of the most well-respected MPs both within and outside the party.[30,31] By the end of his time as Newport's MP, membership of the Newport Labour Party had increased to levels near its peak in the mid-thirties.[32] However, during these eleven years, the party still had to meet the costs of a full-time agent, and the problems of collecting membership fees continued. This was a particular problem with regard to fees paid by the unions; for example, nineteen unions did not pay any of their affiliation fees, and not a single affiliated union paid all their due annual fees over the period 1954-1960.[33] Increasing demands were made on Peter Freeman to make up any shortfall, and this caused contention within the party.[34] However, the financial contributions that Peter Freeman made to the party ensured its financial stability, and this would have been expected to continue for as long as he remained their MP.

---

[28] This record belongs to Henry Francis Compton who won a by-election for the New Forest constituency on 6 December 1905, which he lost at the 1906 general election which was held from 12 January to 8 February.

[29] Newport Labour Party, *Finance committee meeting minutes*. 27 August, 1945.

[30] Bloxsome, M., 2004.

[31] Interview with Clive Shakesheff (interview carried out by Jim Criddle). *Former member of the Newport Labour Party*, circa December 2014.

[32] South Wales Regional Council of Labour. 10 May, 1943.

[33] Newport Labour Party Study Group. *The Finances of the Newport Labour Party*. 10 December, 1961.

[34] Interview with Clive Shakesheff (interview carried out by Jim Criddle), former member of the Newport Labour Party. circa December 2014.

However, by the time of the 1955 General Election, his tenure as MP for Newport was near an unexpected end, and many familiar issues that he had resolved were re-emerging. The continual demands on his finances were also beginning to concern him, something that he raised prior to the 1955 General Election.[35] Despite winning this election, he was noticeably grumpy while campaigning, and by the end of the year it was clear that he was not well. Suffering from cancer, he died on 19th May 1956, having been in great pain towards the end of his life after refusing morphine as it had been tested on animals.[36]

A new agent

With the loss of Peter Freeman, there was a desire to secure another candidate for the up-coming by-election who could meet the financial demands of the constituency. However, his death had occurred a year after a general election, and in common with many by-elections that occur shortly after general elections, this presented the national party with a perfect opportunity to return a high-profile politician to Parliament.

That high-profile politician was Sir Frank Soskice, the Attorney General in the last Parliament, who had not fought a seat in the 1955 General Election after his Sheffield Neepsend constituency had been abolished and he had failed to secure the nomination for the Manchester Gorton constituency. With pressure exerted from the national party, he secured the nomination and won the by-election comfortably. However, the agreement to adopt Sir Frank Soskice did not come with any of the financial guarantees that Peter Freeman had made, and even though he contributed money regularly, the sums were a long way short of the level given by Peter Freeman. He was also known to be careful with his money, as indicated by Dora Gaitskell, wife of Hugh who declared that he was "too fond of money."[37]

However, despite the loss of financial security provided by Peter Freeman, the party continued to employ a full-time agent, Edwin Plaistow, on the grounds that it was a marginal seat, as well as a clerk, Lorna Kennedy, who had been in place since 1945.[38,39] Membership of the party was also starting to fall, and by the early 1960s, there were approximately 500 members, a sixth of the number at its peak. The collection of membership and union affiliation

---

[35] Newport Labour Party. *Finance committee meeting minutes.* 17 January, 1955.

[36] Bloxsome, M., 2004.

[37] Benn, T. *The Benn diaries: 1940-1990.* London. Random House, 2013.

[38] Jones, E. Letter to Newport Labour Party executive committee, 26 April, 1965.

[39] Newport Labour Party. *General committee meeting minutes.* 18 May, 1945.

fees also continued to be a problem. In 1960, Reg Ley referred to a report on the party finances as "the most gloomy report he had ever read."[40] By 1962, Edwin Plaistow's salary had reduced by a quarter from what had been "agreed in principle" two years earlier, and candidates in local elections were asked to approach their respective unions to cover their expenses[41,42] With the Co-operative Bank refusing to lend the party any more money, despite guarantees from 16 members of the party, morale amongst party members started to fall, and unsurprisingly by mid-1963 Edwin Plaistow resigned, and certain members of the party implored the party not to replace him.[43,44]

These pleas were ignored, and against the wishes of those same members, a decision was made to appoint another full-time agent.[45] However, with the finances of the party made clear to any potential applicants, as well as the poor salary on offer, only one person applied.[46] This was David Thorndell who had been the full-time agent for Brecon and Radnor, Peter Freeman's former constituency. Although not considered a particularly strong candidate, the decision was made to appoint him, rather than to re-advertise the post.[47]

Even though David Thorndell was aware that the party was in financial difficulties when he became the agent, it probably wasn't until he started his employment that he realised just how serious their difficulties were. This was not helped by the decision of Labour Central Office to classify Newport as a safe Labour seat after 1964 which removed some funding from the party. With little or no money available, within a year of being appointed he took some drastic, and unwise measures to reduce the flow of money out of the party. He stopped paying certain bills, as well as party affiliation fees. More crucially, he stopped paying National Insurance and Pension contributions for himself and the party clerk.[48] Falsifying the accounts to hide any discrepancies, nobody in the party was aware of the financial time-bomb that was building up, something that would inevitably explode at some point

---

[40] Newport Labour Party. *General committee meeting minutes.* 4 November, 1960.

[41] Newport Labour Party. *General committee meeting minutes.* 27 July, 1962.

[42] Newport Labour Party. *Executive committee meeting minutes.* 23 May, 1960

[43] Newport Labour Party. *Executive committee meeting minutes.* 11 October, 1961.

[44] Newport Labour Party. *General committee meeting minutes.* 26 July, 1963.

[45] Newport Labour Party. Special executive committee meeting minutes. 1 August, 1963.

[46] Newport Labour Party. *Executive committee meeting minutes.* 14 August, 1963.

[47] David Thorndell was regarded internally as "unwise" in several public statements he made as indicated in: Newport Labour Party. *Executive committee meeting minutes.* 14 August, 1963.

[48] Newport Labour Party. Emergency meeting of party officers meeting minutes. 26 August, 1967.

in the future. He did not take all his due salary increases, and in some cases did not draw all or part of his monthly salary; the accounts still indicated a worsening situation, but due to their falsification were even worse than they appeared. Many members of the party blamed David Thorndell for the financial problems, while others, notably Sir Frank Soskice, felt that he was being unfairly treated, and also demanded that monies owed to him should be paid.

Running up to the next general election in 1966, Thorndell remained in his post, and when Sir Frank Soskice decided not to stand due to ill health, it opened up the possibility of a new candidate who could hopefully bring in significant funds to the Labour Party.[49]

A satisfactory financial settlement

Sir Frank Soskice not standing gave Aubrey the perfect opportunity to return to politics after resigning as a councillor in 1961, and his first serious opportunity to represent Newport as its MP. Announcing his candidacy at the general committee meeting on 21st January 1966 he knew that it was likely he would face stiff competition from a trade union candidate, but as a safe Labour seat, he probably expected a large number of nominations.[50]

Behind the scenes though, David Thorndell was taking significant measures to secure a financially attractive candidate. Foremost amongst these was a candidate from the largest trade union, the TGWU, who had agreed to implement a "satisfactory financial settlement" if their candidate was successful.[51] Approaches were probably also made to all unions, clarifying what would be expected from them, should their candidate be successful. The polices that David Thorndell put in place to secure a "suitable candidate" proved to work spectacularly well, and by the closing date at midnight on 5th February, 110 nominations had been received, almost five times the average number.[52] This was the highest number of nominations ever received in a Welsh Labour constituency as well as possibly the UK as a whole.[53] The nominations came in from every union except the National Union of Mineworkers. For the first time in months David Thorndell probably slept soundly in his bed that night. This was not the case for Aubrey; early the

---

[49] "Soskice not to stand again." *South Wales Argus.* 17 December, 1965.

[50] Newport Labour Party. *Executive committee meeting minutes.* 25 October, 1965.

[51] Newport Labour Party. *Executive committee meeting minutes.* 31 January, 1966.

[52] Rush, M. *The selection of parliamentary candidates.* London. Nelson, 1969.

[53] The highest known number of applicants for a Labour nomination prior to the 1966 general election was 70 for the safe Labour seat of Erith and Crayford, see Rush, M., 1969.

next morning, his youngest child entered the world and I was determined to do my best to ruin his selection chances – especially as I was supposed to arrive two days after the selection conference. These nominations were reduced to a more manageable 19 for the shortlisting meeting held on 10th February 1966 at which a further-reduced shortlist, of five candidates, was compiled.[54] The five were: Calvin Kerr, a barrister; David Marquand, a journalist and university lecturer; Richard Leonard, an editor; Roy Hughes, a member of the TGWU; and Aubrey, the only candidate whose choice was unanimous.[55,56,57] This shortlist did not include the council leader Stewart Watson who was disappointed by the decision but accepted that a difficult year for the Labour council would have counted against him.[58] It did however contain five people, which was probably four more than certain members of the Labour Party and the TGWU wanted.

Selection conference

The selection conference on 18th February was attended by at least 110 people compared to a usual attendance of about twenty.[59,60] Most of the attendees were trade union delegates who were there as representatives of different organisations, including John Wright who was one of four representatives from the British Transport Docks Board. At the time, he did not know Aubrey, though just over twenty years later he was to celebrate with Aubrey the birth of their first grandchild, Tomas.

There to listen to the speeches and choose who he believed was the most suitable candidate, John Wright decided to vote for Aubrey although he was equally impressed with David Marquand.[61] This appeared to be the view shared by most others at the selection conference, with some placing David Marquand above Aubrey; Roy Hughes was considered the weakest of the

---

[54] Newport Labour Party. Special executive committee meeting minutes held to shortlist for the parliamentary candidate. 10 February, 1966.

[55] David Marquand was the son of Hilary Marquand, a famous economist, and former Labour Cabinet Minister. It is also believed that David Marquand had been nominated by Transport House, then the Labour Party headquarters in London, see Hughes, R., 2003.

[56] Newport Labour Party. *Special general committee meeting minutes.* 11 February, 1966.

[57] Newport Labour Party. Special executive committee meeting minutes held to shortlist for the parliamentary candidate. 10 February, 1966.

[58] "Looking for Sir Frank's successor." *South Wales Argus.* 18 February, 1966.

[59] Based on recorded voting figures.

[60] Interview with Clive Shakesheff, 2014.

[61] Interview with John Wright, former trade unionist. 7 July, 2012.

candidates particularly as regarding his knowledge of Newport.[62,63]

After the speeches, the delegates retired to discuss the candidates and consider their votes. It was at this point that John Wright realised why he had been asked to attend; together with all the other trade union delegates, they were told to vote for Roy Hughes as he was the sponsored trade union candidate. Disillusioned by the process, particularly at the concept of a shop-floor worker being told what to do, he refused to vote and abstained.[64] Having never attended a political meeting before in his life, he never attended one again – something that he probably shared with a large number of the trade union delegates. However, with the backing of the trade unions, who supplied most of the delegates at the conference, Roy Hughes won on the second ballot with Aubrey finishing as runner-up after Calvin Kerr and Richard Leonard had been eliminated in the first round.[65] This clearly delighted David Thorndell who rather tellingly said "I am very happy with the result. I'm delighted with the management committee's choice."[66] Many delegates were less happy, particularly the more left-wing members of the party who thought (quite rightly) that the seat had been "bought" by the TGWU.[67]

The David Thorndell affair

With Roy Hughes selected as the Labour candidate for Newport, and easily winning the seat at the general election six weeks later, it was now time to negotiate with the TGWU regarding their contribution to the Labour Party. In theory, this should have been straightforward, as even though unions were prohibited from specifying what level of sponsorship they would provide until their candidate was selected, there were set rules on what unions could contribute to a Labour constituency for a sponsored candidate.[68,69] However, collusion between constituency Labour parties (CLPs) and unions did occur to "buy" a seat and it was not unusual for "additional" contributions to be

---

[62] This was based on several interviews with people who were either at the conference and voted, or who were aware of the events at the time.

[63] Interview with John Wright, former trade unionist, 7 July, 2012.

[64] Ibid.

[65] Hughes, R. *Seek Fairer Skies*. Spennymoor. The Memoir Club, 2003.

[66] "To fight Newport." *South Wales Argus*. 19 February, 1966.

[67] Interview with Clive Shakesheff, 2014.

[68] Shaw, E., 1988.

[69] This was under something called the Hastings Agreement of 1933, which had been introduced to control the maximum amount which unions could contribute towards sponsored MPs.

hidden in the accounts.[70,71]

The announcement of the result of the 1966 general election result for Newport outside the Civic Centre by the Mayor Alfred Lovell. Roy Hughes is on the left, with his defeated opponent, Peter Temple-Morris on the right. In later life Peter Temple-Morris was to defect to the Labour Party, sitting with Roy Hughes in the House of Commons and the Lords.

Negotiations with the TGWU regarding their contributions were to prove long-winded and fairly fruitless over the next few months. The minutes from various Labour group meetings during this period indicate that whatever the TGWU may have suggested or hinted at initially, this was not what they intended to contribute once Roy Hughes had been selected.[72] At one stage, this included a proposal to "reduce" their affiliation fees by half – something that did not go down well with the party membership.[73] Exhaustive discussions with Roy Hughes himself also took place to try and mediate with the TGWU

---

[70] Ranney, A. *Pathways to Parliament. Candidate selection in Britain.* London. MacMillan, 1965.

[71] Harrison, M. *Trade unions and the Labour Party since 1945.* London. Ruskin House, 1960.

[72] See for example: Newport Labour Party. *Executive committee meeting minutes.* 27 June, 1966.

[73] Newport Labour Party. *Executive committee meeting minutes.* 27 June, 1966.

and see what contributions he could make, but this met with little success.[74] Moreover, falling membership numbers, a lack of support from the National Labour Party and local trade union branches, and his decision to live in Chepstow (as opposed to Newport) did not reflect favourably on him.[75] The limited financial support from the TGWU meant that the financial difficulties of the Labour Party did not ease as expected, and continuing attempts by David Thorndell to hide the problem had inevitable consequences.

By the summer of 1967, the finances of the Newport Labour Party were the worst they had ever been, and they dominated general and executive party meetings. Pleas for extra funds from members had mainly proved fruitless, and various loans had been sought.[76] Wards were told they had to take more responsibility for funding their elections and yet again comments were made regarding the lack of effort from certain members and wards.[77] The pressures on David Thorndell were also growing, with a motion of confidence placed in him that he passed – but with several abstentions.[78] Later, there was a recommendation that the party should dispense with the services of an agent.[79] There were also concerns about the pressures placed on members of the party who acted as guarantors at the bank, as well as the loans they had made that had to be repaid.[80,81] This included Aubrey whose donations were described as "very generous."[82]

The discovery of the true nature of the finances of the Labour Party appear to have occurred in late August 1967 when it emerged that a company called Roneo Ltd were owed £595 (equal to approximately £10,000 today) – a sum that had been due since 1961.[83] This and other issues were raised with David Thorndell on 23rd August and outlined to the astonishment of the party officers at an emergency meeting on 26th August.[84] This meeting highlighted,

---

[74] See for example: Newport Labour Party. *Executive committee meeting minutes*. 25 July, 1966.

[75] Less than 1000 by November 1966: Newport Labour Party. *General committee meeting minutes*. 25 November, 1966. Interview with Clive Shakesheff, 2014.

[76] Newport Labour Party. *Executive committee meeting minutes*. 26 September, 1966.

[77] Ibid.

[78] Ibid.

[79] Newport Labour Party. *Special committee meeting minutes*. 6 October, 1966.

[80] Ibid.

[81] Newport Labour Party. *General committee meeting minutes*. 6 January, 1967.

[82] Interview with Clive Shakesheff, 2014.

[83] Newport Labour Party. Emergency meeting of party officers meeting minutes. 26 August, 1967.

[84] Ibid.

among other things, that National Insurance and pensions contributions of the agent and clerk had not been paid for several years, despite being marked as paid on each year's balance sheet. Cheques had bounced, and depts owed to several organisations, including the bank, amounted to over £1,200 (later this figure was estimated to be over £2,000).[85,86] Whether embezzlement of funds had taken place or not was not clear, however, David Thorndell's defence that the party was not paying him his due salary certainly mitigated any such claim.[87]

Offering his resignation, David Thorndell was subsequentially suspended on full pay until a further investigation had taken place. He had to hand over his keys, and the money in the safe was counted in his presence.[88] At a further meeting on 19th September David Thorndell admitted fraudulent entries in the books and falsifying the balance sheet, as well as having received warnings from Labour's head office regarding non-payment of affiliation fees. There was a unanimous vote to dismiss him and to call in the police and inform Labour's head office that they would be taking criminal proceedings against him.[89] However, there was no evidence that David Thorndell had profited from his actions, committed any offence or been dishonest or negligent. At a subsequent meeting, a solicitor named Bryn John pointed out that they would have no control over any police investigation.[90] Despite several members feeling that the police should be involved, it was also clear that the party could be irretrievably damaged by any police investigation.[91] It was the party's responsibility to pay their employees' National Insurance contributions and the agent's salary, and David Thorndell had voluntarily reverted back to his original salary when appointed, amounting to a reduction of more than 25%. Party members had not been aware of this.[92]

David Thorndell appealed against his dismissal, and the party accepted that they were partly responsible for their lack of supervision and management of Thorndell's work. It was therefore decided to defer taking further action until the appeal that Thorndell had lodged had been heard.[93] The constituency

---

[85] Ibid.

[86] Newport Labour Party. *Special executive committee meeting minutes.* 19 September, 1967.

[87] Interview with Clive Shakesheff, 2014.

[88] Newport Labour Party. *Emergency meeting.* 26 August, 1967.

[89] Newport Labour Party. Special executive committee meeting minutes. 19 September, 1967.

[90] Newport Labour Party. *Special party officers meeting minutes.* 24 September, 1967.

[91] Ibid.

[92] Ibid.

[93] Newport Labour Party. *Executive committee meeting minutes.* 25 September, 1967.

appeal against David Thorndell's dismissal was heard in a five-hour meeting on 3rd November 1967. The CLP concluded that not having their attention drawn to non-payment of bills amounted to deceit and incompetence, and information that the party should have known about had been concealed. In his defence, Thorndell quite rightly pointed out that this included his salary decreases.[94] Labour Party headquarters agreed with the CLP's decision to dismiss David Thorndell, although they also found that the CLP bore some responsibility for failing to supervise his work.[95] David Thorndell's dismissal therefore stood. It was also agreed that no criminal action should be taken against him and that he be permanently debarred from the party.

He ran off with all the money

When I started this book in 2010, the priority was to interview as many of Aubrey's contemporaries as possible and as soon as possible. At that time, I did not know what the stories or events to cover would be, never mind any specific details. Quite quickly the stories of interest started to emerge, and consequently I started to work out the questions to ask, as well as who else to interview. Unsurprisingly one story mentioned by many of Aubrey's contemporaries was what I have outlined above as the "David Thorndell affair" of which two subtly different versions emerged. These versions depended on whether the person being interviewed knew the story first hand or second hand. For those who had not been present or around when these events unfolded, David Thorndell had run off with all the money and was responsible for the severe financial problems of the Labour Party in Newport that lasted into the 20th century. For those who were there at the time, they saw David Thorndell more as a victim rather than perpetrator; a pleasant man who was maybe naïve, but not dishonest.

Undoubtedly, David Thorndell panicked when he first realised the financial situation that he faced as party agent. He could have responded in one of two ways: by being upfront and honest and possibly losing his job, or as he did, initially hiding and managing the situation while hoping that he would finally be able to turn it around. Some may see this as deceitful and dishonest. Yet, the fact that he voluntarily forewent salary increases when he was already poorly paid, and the fact that he did not pay his own National Insurance and pension contributions, indicates that (in his own mind at least) he was doing things for the right reasons. This of course then spiralled out of control when the consequences of doing what he thought would help, actually made things

---

[94] Newport Labour Party. *Appeal inquiry meeting minutes*. 3 November, 1967.

[95] Newport Labour Party. *General committee meeting minutes*. 5 January, 1968.

worse.

David Thorndell was also not helped by the actions of the unions and their representatives. This was demonstrated, for example, by the Boilermakers Union, who had paid no affiliation fees since 1964 despite multiple reminders (yet paid enough to attend the selection conference).[96] Other unions also made demands on the constituency party that could be considered unreasonable had they been paying their affiliation fees, but downright insulting when they hadn't paid any for years. He was also let down by the inactivity of many party members, particularly in their failure to collect membership fees and take an active part in fundraising. In fact, the only group who pulled their weight were the women's section, who consistently over-reached themselves when it came to fundraising. It is also of interest that in his defence, David Thorndell only mentioned Aubrey's name as someone who was sick of coming to meetings and hearing of the financial crisis – a clear swipe at the failure of certain members of the party to pull their weight.[97]

Remarkedly, apart from the sacking of David Thorndell and his threat to stand as an independent Labour MP, these events were mainly kept out of the papers. However, it was now clear that the party could not afford an agent and had to find some means of rescuing itself from its perilous financial position. Before David Thorndell had been sacked, donations totalling £500 had been received from various wards and sections yet other depts were to emerge, including non-payment of PAYE dating back to 1964.[98,99] Party members continued to step in including a "Mr X" who was noted to have made a large donation to the party in September 1969, as well as another member who mortgaged his house to cover the shortfall in National Insurance contributions when the clerk left in the 1970s.[100] Only about three people were aware of this shortfall at the time and how it was covered, and it was over 20 years later when the member in question told his wife what he had done when the truth finally came to light.[101]

The process of bringing the Labour Party back into the black was undertaken by John Newnham as unpaid party agent, and by Aubrey as honorary

---

[96] Thorndell, D. Letter to Dan McGarvey, President of the Amalgamated Society of Boilermakers. 2 June, 1967.

[97] Newport Labour Party. *Appeal inquiry meeting minutes*. 3 November, 1967.

[98] Newport Labour Party. *General committee meeting minutes*. 15 September, 1967.

[99] Newport Labour Party. *General committee meeting minutes*. 16 February, 1968.

[100] Newport Labour Party. *Executive committee meeting minutes*. 8 September, 1969.

[101] From various interviews, including the party member in question.

secretary.[102,103] Finances gradually improved, and in 1972 the finances were briefly in the black.[104] However, finances were not considered robust enough to send a delegate to the national party conference until 1976 and they were to remain a concern for the rest of the century.[105]

As regards the (lack of) contributions from the TGWU, this was a bone of contention with the Newport CLP for many years to come – and certainly up to 1977 for when minutes of the Newport Labour Party are available. At least every couple of months, meetings were held either with TGWU officials, or with Roy Hughes, to discuss their contribution, and it is clear from the various Newport CLP minutes that members of Newport CLP were becoming increasingly exasperated with the TGWU, as well as with Roy Hughes. Roy Hughes' best interests were clearly with the TGWU not the Newport CLP. This was best illustrated on 12th September 1969 when he referred to a donation of £500 to Newport CLP as "another generous donation" by his union.[106] Funds were also sought from Roy Hughes, and although he did make some contributions, it is believed it was not much, and probably nowhere near the level of other members of the Newport CLP, nor those of his predecessors.

By the early 1970s the TGWU appeared to be paying the Newport CLP the maximum allowable under something called the Hastings Agreement – which only applied as Newport did not now have a full-time agent.[107,108] By 1976, the rates had remained unchanged for the previous eight years – which was an effective 60% reduction once the high levels of inflation had been accounted for. This caused Gerald Powell, secretary of the Labour party, to refer to trade union sponsorship as a sham after Roy Hughes commented on how generous the TGWU had been to the Newport CLP over the years.[109]

Was Newport unique?

The problems of finance and candidate selection within the Newport CLP was little different to many Constituency Labour Parties over most of their history. Almost without exception, CLPs struggled to stay in the black, and

---

[102] Newport Labour Party. *Annual meeting minutes*. 29 March, 1968.

[103] Newport Labour Party. *Annual meeting minutes*. 28 March, 1967.

[104] Newport Labour Party. *Executive committee meeting minutes*. 7 February, 1972

[105] Newport Labour Party. *62nd annual general meeting minutes*. 19 March, 1976.

[106] Newport Labour Party. *General committee meeting minutes*. 12 September, 1969.

[107] Newport Labour Party. *Executive committee meeting minutes*. 10 December, 1973

[108] Newport Labour Party. *Executive committee meeting minutes*. 8 November, 1976.

[109] Newport Labour Party. *General management committee meeting minutes*. 9 July, 1976.

many were always on the lookout for either a trade union or independently wealthy candidate. Many trade unions colluded with CLPs to "buy" seats with lavish contributions, and many CLPs were always demanding more money off them.[110] The lack of finance from the trade unions and the constant demands from CLPs irritated both sides.[111] There were also repeated squabbles between CLPs and their MPs who renegaded on promises of payments once they were elected; MPs knew that once they had been elected, they had a job for life provided the voters kept them in.

As for full-time agents, this was an intended outcome of the new party constitution adopted by Labour in 1918, and by 1963 there were 208 full-time agents in CLPs despite the fact that few constituencies appeared to be able to afford them.[112,113] They were poorly paid, inadequately trained, and suffered from chronic insecurity "scraping round to find the current month's salary." Not surprisingly they were of an uneven calibre.[114]

All CLPs also had the same problem with the collection of subscriptions from members on a regular, usually weekly, basis. If members were not called on, they did not pay.[115]

Newport therefore appeared to be no different from any other constituency in the country apart from having a larger membership (many of whom did not pay their membership fees) and a large and very effective women's section. Whether other agents or party officials behaved in the same way as David Thorndell is unknown, but it would not be surprising. Indeed, in November 1974, the treasurer of the Conservative Party in Newport, the rather elaborately named Vicomte Alwyn John Eugene Manso-Reesare di Villa, had to repay almost £2,000 for what was described as "unauthorised spending."[116] It is not known what this unauthorised spending was, and whether it was fraudulent or not, but he left Newport a year or two later moving to a village called Pinxton on the border between Derbyshire and Nottinghamshire. Here, he became both a district and parish councillor and clearly had a rather selective memory in his new home. This is indicated by his biography which was

---

[110] Ranney, A., 1965.

[111] Harrison, M., 1960.

[112] Thorpe, A. *Parties at war: Political organisation in Second World War Britain.* Oxford. Oxford University Press, 2009.

[113] Leonard, R.L. and Mortimore, R. *Elections in Britain.* London. van Nostrand, 1968.

[114] Shaw, E., 1988.

[115] Thorpe, A., 2009.

[116] Newport Conservative Party. *Special Executive Council meeting minutes.* 18 December, 1974.

published after he died and where the rather telling comment was made that "it is inconceivable that he didn't join the Conservative Association in the years before coming to Pinxton."[117] Also at the same meeting in November 1974, the Young Conservatives in Newport were disbanded as a result of spending £200 at a barbecue, a pretty impressive sum now let alone in 1974. However, the Conservative Party in Newport is clearly better at keeping its secrets than the Labour Party. Neither of these stories made the papers, and they weren't mentioned to me in any of interviews carried out for this book, even though several people interviewed were at this meeting.

Roy Hughes MP

The candidates who stand for Labour seats in a general election can be broadly divided into three groups. Firstly, there are the politically ambitious, whose sole aim is to become an MP and possibly more, with no attachment to the constituency they represent (which probably applies to most MPs, regardless of their political affiliation). Secondly, there are the trade unionists who are there to represent their union – again with no attachment to the constituency they represent. And finally, the local men or women who are there to represent the constituency where they live and where they were probably born. In the first group, you also have the candidates who will seek nominations in multiple constituencies, and often get shortlisted or nominated multiple times before securing a seat. Across both the Labour and Conservative Parties this includes every Prime Minister from Margaret Thatcher in 1979 until 2022 when Liz Truss became Prime Minister. This group also includes David Marquand and Richard Leonard, who went on to get nominated and to win seats in Ashfield in 1966 and Romford in 1970 respectively. The second group, the trade unionists solely exist for candidates in safe Labour seats. So, for example, of the 138 trade union candidates who stood in the 1966 general election, only six weren't elected.[118] Of the third group, the local men and woman, their battle to get into Parliament is now a difficult task yet was an almost impossible one in 1966. Of the 23 seats held by Labour going into the 1966 general election where the sitting MP did not stand for re-election, only one, Stoke-on-Trent North, was contested by a local, John Forrester, who wasn't sponsored by a trade union and hadn't stood as a candidate in a previous general election.

Against this background, Aubrey essentially had no chance of securing the Labour nomination, regardless of his abilities and his presentation to the

---

[117] Zmith, Z. *Eugene Di Villa – a friend to Underwood*, 2014.
[118] Rush, M., 1969.

selection committee (notwithstanding my attempts at sabotage). Just making the short-list was a remarkable achievement. Across the 21 general and by-elections in the Newport constituency from 1918 when it was formed until it was split into Newport West and East in 1983, Aubrey was the only local person ever short-listed by Labour.[119] Not surprisingly, across the Labour Party, few constituencies were, and are, represented by someone who has a genuine attachment to the area, and any talented socialist politician who just wants to represent their constituency has little chance of getting into Parliament unless they are a representative of a trade union. Local candidates also often have local enemies, and it is not unusual for a local candidate to fail to get a nomination even when they are the best candidate. This is particularly the case when those local enemies hold undue influence over the short-listing process. This appears to have happened when David Marquand went on to secure the nomination for Ashfield, where he believes he was selected over a better local candidate due to local politics.[120]

Conversely, a zealous trade unionist with little interest in politics and its intricacies, can almost guarantee a seat in Parliament regardless of his or her abilities – ultimately acting as a potentially poor representative of both the Labour Party and their constituents.

As for Roy Hughes, although originally from Pontllanfraith, and therefore relatively local to Newport, his main interest in parliament seemed to be as a representative of the unions rather than the people who voted for him. Without exception, everyone interviewed from both sides of the political spectrum found it a travesty that he was nominated over Aubrey, with many expressing the view that having arrived in Newport in 1966 as a councillor on Coventry City Council, he should have been sent straight back there. Better candidates than him failed to get shortlisted and he was clearly the worst of the shortlisted candidates.[121] Despite this, and not for the first time in a Labour constituency, trade unionists voted for him who felt the same.[122] As for Aubrey's feelings about Roy Hughes, I do not know. I never heard him say a bad word about him, and in Roy Hughes' autobiography he noted that

---

[119] This is based on an analysis of various sources including Labour Party minutes, newspaper reports, and other historical records.

[120] Interview with Professor David Marquand, former Labour MP for Ashfield 1966-1977. 18 April, 2014.

[121] There is no known list of the 110 people nominated for selection of the Labour Party candidate. The only person known to be nominated who was not on the shortlist was Stewart Watson, who was considered a better candidate than Roy Hughes by everybody interviewed for this book.

[122] Rush, M., 1969.

Aubrey was "always most friendly and helpful to me."

However, Roy Hughes' decision to suggest to someone in the upper echelons of the Labour Party in 1997 that he would stand down as an MP if he obtained a life peerage would have appalled Aubrey if he had known about it at the time.[123] This decision, which enabled the Labour Party to secure a safe seat for Alan Howarth (the previous Conservative MP for Stratford-on-Avon who defected to the Labour Party in 1995) was inappropriate, although frustratingly not uncommon.[124]

East and West

After failing to be nominated in 1966, Aubrey probably felt that his chance of representing Newport in Parliament had gone. Roy Hughes was not likely to stand down as its MP and Hughes came nowhere near failing to retain his seat when another opportunity for Aubrey may have emerged at the following general election.[125] However, the creation of two seats in Newport in 1983, Newport East and Newport West, presented an unexpected opportunity for Aubrey to stand for Labour in Newport.

With Roy Hughes offered the choice of seats and choosing Newport East, Aubrey was therefore one of sixteen candidates who put themselves forward for selection for the Newport West seat.[126] One of the sixteen was a sitting MP, Reg Race, whose constituency had disappeared in the same boundaries revision that had created two seats in Newport. Another candidate was a former MP, Bryan Davies. Despite these two candidates, and although Aubrey was strongly favoured by many in the party, a local man was expected to secure the candidacy – Adrian Jones. The influence of the trade unions was also not as great in 1983 as it had been in 1966, so a good candidate from the short-list could have reasonably expected to secure the candidacy, whether sponsored by a trade union or not.

However, in the Labour Party, you cannot apply to become a Labour

---

[123] BBC 4. *Today programme.* 22 March, 2001.

[124] Alan Howarth was the first MP to defect directly from the Conservative Party to the Labour Party.

[125] A selection conference only took place if there was no sitting MP, or in the rare case of an MP being deselected, which did not happen with Roy Hughes. In Richard King's book *Brittle with Relics* published in 2022 (pages 120-121), it says that there was a selection conference in Newport in the early 1970s, but this is incorrect. It is believed that this referred to the Monmouth constituency in one of the two General Elections that took place in 1974.

[126] "Race for Labour nomination." *South Wales Argus.* 4 May, 1983.

Party candidate. You can put your name forward to be considered, but you must be nominated by a branch or an affiliated organisation. For Aubrey, the assumption was that this would come from his own Stow Hill Ward, which through its various guises he had always represented, and the only ward where it is believed he looked for a nomination. His chances were also probably increased with the Stow Hill members meeting with the ward where he lived, Allt-Yr-Yn, although they split when they chose their respective candidates.[127] Although his nomination appeared to be a forgone conclusion, inexplicitly he was not nominated, and Reg Race secured the nomination instead. Although Reg Race came with the sponsorship of the National Union of Public Employees (NUPE), and many Labour Party members wanted him as their parliamentary candidate, this decision astounded the majority of the members of the party.[128,129] Sir Harry Jones (Aubrey's successor as leader of the council) described the decision as "unbelievable."[130] Paul Flynn described it as "outrageous" and "shocking" going further to say that Aubrey was "by far the strongest candidate" and that the injustice and ingratitude of the Stow Hill ward was "shocking."[131]

The lack of a nomination for Aubrey initially mystified and surprised him, but later turned to anger when he found out that the reason he didn't get the nomination was not because he wasn't the best candidate, but because his ward did not want to lose him from local politics. Returning from his ward that evening was the only time in my life when I saw my father outwardly angry. This includes the time when I kicked a football through a window, and when my brother set fire to the coal shed. Feeling let down by the party, and by his ward for their selfishness, he immediately announced that he was standing down from politics. This initially caused panic and confusion in the party as the local elections were the next day – but he won his seat and stayed only until the next election when he kept his promise and did not seek re-election. He left despite members such as John Marsh urging him to stay. Ultimately the failure to nominate Aubrey backfired spectacularly on the Labour Party in Newport; it resulted in them losing one of the most respected and admired local politicians they had ever had, and almost certainly also losing a Newport parliamentary seat for the only time since Peter Freeman

---

[127] Interview with Shirley Newnham, member of Labour Party and Stow Hill Ward. 23 February, 2013.

[128] Now part of UNISON.

[129] Interview with Paul Flynn, Newport West MP 1987-2019. 22 September, 2012.

[130] Interview with Sir Harry Jones, leader of Newport City Council 1986-2003. 3 March, 2013.

[131] Interview with Paul Flynn, 2012.

took the Newport constituency seat in 1945. Although it is not possible to measure what Aubrey's personal vote would have been, his vote share in local elections in the Stow Hill Ward was typically the order of 15% more than the other Labour candidates in the same ward. This suggests the increased share from this ward alone with Aubrey standing would likely have wiped out the 581 winning margin for Mark Robinson, the Conservative candidate. General opinion at the time also suggested that the personal qualities of a candidate could make a difference of up to 3,000 votes, even though personalities count less in general elections.[132] In addition, Mark Robinson fought a considerably better campaign than Brian Davies, the Labour candidate chosen to fight the seat, who spent little time in the constituency before the election. However, the greatest indication that Aubrey would have won this seat in 1983 came from Trevor Warren, the leader of the Conservative group on Newport Borough Council at this time. Interviewed in 2014, he believed that Aubrey would have won easily, and moreover that he, together with many members of the Conservative Party, would probably have voted for him and given him their full support as their MP.[133]

The consequences of Labour not winning the seat in 1983 did give Aubrey another opportunity in 1987, when the CLP were determined to choose a local candidate after believing that this was what lost them the election in 1983. Unfortunately however, Aubrey was now 64 years old and his desire to only serve one term probably counted against him. He was now up against an impressive younger candidate, his former deputy Paul Flynn, and he did not get nominated. Paul Flynn went on to win this seat, becoming Newport's longest serving MP until he died in post in 2019.

Aubrey Hames MP

After being snubbed by the Stow Hill Ward in 1983, Aubrey paid no interest in the management of his ward although he worked tirelessly, as always, among his constituents and within other wards. Many of the people interviewed for this book noted how angry and bitter he was with his ward, and others shared this frustration. Ron Jones, who served as a Labour councillor in the Pill Ward for over 30 years described it as "the biggest afront to him in politics" and agreed with almost everyone else interviewed who said he would certainly have been nominated by several, if not all the other wards, if he had asked for their nomination.

---

[132] Ranney, A., 1965.

[133] Interview with Trevor Warren, former Conservative leader of Newport Borough Council. 31 October, 2014.

However, if Aubrey had been nominated, and ultimately elected in 1983, or more likely in 1966, it is interesting to speculate on how he would have fared as an MP. Putting this question to various members of the Labour Party in Newport, there was a similar response from all of them; Bob Bright said that Aubrey would have been "a superb MP", Sir Harry Jones said he would have been "a wonderful MP", Dame Rosemary Butler said, "a brilliant MP", and Paul Flynn, "a great MP."[134,135,136,137] Others said he would have been "a breath of fresh air in Parliament."[138] Nobody doubted that he would have been ministerial material.

These were not unexpected responses from people in Newport, but these were also views shared by others outside of Newport. Paul Murphy, who was Labour MP for Torfaen from 1987 to 2015 and served as both Welsh and Northern Ireland Secretaries under Tony Blair, thought he would have become a Minister quite soon within the 1974-1979 Labour government and would have been a good one. Had he been Prime Minister at the time, he would have chosen Aubrey as a Minster.[139] This was a view shared by Don Touhig, Labour MP for Islwyn from 1995 to 2010 and former Government Minister who now sits in the House of Lords with Paul Murphy.[140] The view of Neil Kinnock, Don Touhig's predecessor as MP for Islwyn, and leader of the Labour Party from 1983 to 1992, would have been the most insightful, but I was unable to secure an interview with him. A Cabinet or Shadow Cabinet position could well have followed a ministerial role, but those posts are at the whim of the party leader and have little to do with experience or ability. However, Aubrey's prospects would have been significantly enhanced by a succession of leaders of the Labour Party from James Callaghan, through Michael Foot to Neil Kinnock who knew him well, and who all represented Welsh constituencies adjacent to Newport.

Although it would have been very difficult to find an argument against him

---

[134] Interview with Bob Bright, former Labour leader of Newport City Council. 17 August, 2013.

[135] Interview with Sir Harry Jones, leader of Newport City Council 1986-2003. 3 March, 2013.

[136] Interview with Dame Rosemary Butler, former Presiding Officer of the Welsh Assembly and former Newport Borough Councillor. 29 September, 2012.

[137] Interview with Paul Flynn, 2012.

[138] Interview with Harry Williams, former Newport Borough councillor. 11 February, 2014.

[139] Interview with Lord Paul Murphy, member of the House of Lords, and former Secretary of State for Wales and Northern Ireland and former MP for Torfaen. 12 May, 2021.

[140] Interview with Lord Don Touhig, member of the House of Lords, and former MP for Islwyn and Gwent County Councillor. 12 May, 2021.

securing a senior role in government or opposition based on abilities alone, we will never know. However, there is little doubt that he would have made a "wonderful" and "brilliant" constituency MP as predicted by Bob Bright, Sir Harry Jones, Dame Rosemary Butler, and Paul Flynn respectively, as well as many others.

CHAPTER 8

MISFEASANCE IN PUBLIC OFFICE

Cardiff Docks

Following Aubrey's return to Newport in May 1950, he joined the British Transport Docks Board (BTDB) in June 1950 as a clerk in the accounts department at Newport. As the ports in South Wales had grown massively due to the coal mining industry (the most significant export from this area) this was a sound career move, especially as he soon started to move up the career ladder.

However, with the expansion of the oil industry, demand for coal started to reduce dramatically, leading to a deliberate rundown of the South Wales coalfields and a consequent reduction in exports from the ports. By 1970, the number of collieries was to reduce to less than a third from when Aubrey first joined the BTDB, and the ports in South Wales started to suffer an economic slowdown as a result.[1] This prompted the Rochdale Committee, (which had been appointed by the government in March 1961 to investigate port investment in Great Britain) to conclude that there were too many ports in South Wales. They recommended the closure of Barry Docks and part of the docks at Port Talbot, with a gradual transition of the Barry trade to Cardiff and Newport, and the Port Talbot trade to Swansea. However, by the time the Committee's report was published, Barry Docks' fortunes had revived, and it had become financially viable. As a result, the remaining ports in South Wales, which were all heavily in the red with massive operating

---

[1] Williams J. *Digest of Welsh Historical Statistics*. Volume 1., 1985.

157

losses became even more vulnerable.

It was against this background of massive operating losses, and the continuing reduction of the South Wales ports' primary export, that Aubrey obtained his first managerial post in 1963 as Assistant Docks Manager at Newport. He was later to be appointed as Assistant Docks Manager at Port Talbot in 1964, before finally becoming Assistant Docks Manager at Cardiff in February 1965, where he was to remain for the rest of his working career.

With Cardiff Docks losing in the region of £100,000 annually at this time, and many of the port's facilities inadequate or obsolete, promotion of the port was difficult, and it was the general opinion in the shipping fraternity in Cardiff that it would soon close.[2] But within a year of Aubrey's appointment, Cardiff's fortunes, together with the remaining South Wales ports had changed dramatically. Over the remaining period of Aubrey's active management at Cardiff Docks, net profits typically averaged £100,000 per year, primarily driven by port charging procedures and commercial practices introduced by Aubrey that were without precedent in the UK.[3] With two-thirds of the BTDB's net profits generated by the South Wales ports at this time, Aubrey's contribution to the change of fortunes at Cardiff did not go unnoticed, and consequently he was offered dock manager positions at two other ports, one of which was believed to be at Southampton in the early 1970s. He turned these down due to the failing health of his father, as well as a desire to guide Cardiff Docks through what was a critical period at the time. He was also in line for a new post of docks manager at Barrow until the BTDB decided to upgrade the docks superintendent's role rather than appoint a docks manager when it became clear the port might close. Aubrey therefore remained as Assistant Docks Manager at Cardiff until 10th February 1979, when as a direct result of events two years previously, and significant media attention, he ended up in court on spurious charges of corruption and conspiracy and was dismissed from service. This chapter highlights the background to the events and personalities that led to Aubrey's dismissal, as well as the subsequent consequences for Aubrey that lasted for nearly a decade afterwards and resulted in a British record payout (at the time) to Aubrey for unfair dismissal. This chapter also discusses the unexpected implications of recently uncovered evidence and consequential events that call into question the motives and integrity of the investigating officers on this case, and their advocacy and protection of arguably the most corrupt

---

[2] Interview with Aubrey Hames (interview by David Williams of HTV Wales) for *Wales this Week* documentary title "Corruption." 14 February, 1983.

[3] "Aubrey steps out of the hot seat." *South Wales Argus.* 29 April, 1987.

police officer of the second half of the 20ᵗʰ century.

Much of the information in this chapter is based on police statements and private notes written by Aubrey over this time. In some cases, it is not clear what the source of the material is, and where this is the case, these statements are not referenced. Where possible, alternative references have been sought, however, no contradiction of any of the notes made by Aubrey have been found. This suggests that the outline of the events he gave at the time are a true reflection of what happened. This chapter also draws extensively on several interviews with, and publications by, Graham Satchwell. Although he was not involved in Aubrey's case, and was unaware of it when I first talked to him, he worked with the investigating officers involved in the investigation in the 1980s. He was later to become the most senior investigating officer of the BT Police. The source of some of the information by Graham Satchwell is unknown to me as it was only provided to him on condition of anonymity. However, where possible I have sought other evidence to back up claims made.

Seeds of industrial tension at the docks

In 1972, Australian lead importers Austral Metals decided to move their business from Ellesmere Port down to Cardiff. They employed their traditional agents from Liverpool, H.A. Watson, to act on their behalf.[4] As part of their duties, H.A. Watson chose British Road Services (BRS) as the exclusive haulier of these lead cargoes, which they did without going through a competitive tendering process.[5,6] Over the next two years, this traffic proved to be very lucrative for BRS, and they often sub-contracted their work to private haulage companies, at substantially lower haulage rates. At the same time, they proposed increasing their haulage rates to Austral Metals by 20% from January 1975.[7]

Concerned by the proposed increased haulage rates for the lead traffic, Hubert Walsh of Austral Metals met with Aubrey on 11ᵗʰ November 1974 to discuss his company's transport arrangements. Aubrey was asked if the BTDB could obtain competitive fixed haulage rates to certain destinations – initially for the period January to June 1975 – in preparation for a further visit by Hubert Walsh on 19ᵗʰ November.

---

[4] Later taken over by W H Stott & Co.

[5] Walsh, H. Letter to Isidore Rosen (solicitor). 7 November, 1983.

[6] Hames, A. Letter to the Attorney General Michael Havers (draft, marked "not sent"). May, 1983.

[7] Evans, H. Letter addressed "to whom it may concern". 21 November, 1978.

Aubrey therefore requested quotations from BRS, as well as at least two other companies. This included, at Hubert Walsh's request, a relatively new company to Cardiff Docks called Quay Pak. This was a clearing house that specialised in matching the transport needs of an importer with hauliers who had no goods for return journeys.[8] These quotations, presented to Hubert Walsh on 19th November, indicated significant savings for Austral Metals, so they decided to dispense with H.A. Watson's services, and asked the BTDB to arrange the haulage of their cargo.[9]

This new involvement of the BTDB in the tendering process concerned British Road Services who had a dominant position in Cardiff, particularly in the transport of lead. This traffic was one of the most lucrative at Cardiff Docks and they saw this as one of their traditional cargos, even though when this traffic first came to Cardiff it was carried by a company called Gommes.[10,11,12] Horace Yates (who was the local manager of the BRS depot at Cardiff Docks) therefore arranged a meeting with Aubrey in his office on 22nd November to complain at what he saw as the BTDB's interference in the lead traffic movement. At this meeting, Aubrey highlighted that the role of the BTDB was to secure the best coordinated service for all its customers, or traders, at the most competitive rates – but Horace Yates did not accept this explanation. Later, Douglas Thomas, the general manager of BRS Cardiff, met with Aubrey and Ray Wareham, the Docks Manager, to further discuss the issue – but he too expressed dissatisfaction with the outcome of that meeting. These events infuriated BRS and raised tensions between BRS and the BTDB with Aubrey as the main target of the anger coming from BRS. This sentiment was later confirmed when the marketing executive for BRS (Western) in South Wales, Michael Tilley, also went to see Aubrey sometime in 1975. When Tilley reported the outcome of this meeting back to Ron Irons (the BRS divisional manager at Bristol) he allegedly said that he was going "to break Hames."[13]

Despite BRS's attempted interventions, haulage rates for the lead traffic from Austral Metals were submitted to the BTDB, and Austral Metals accepted the lowest tenders which, for the rest of 1974, were from BRS, and from

---

[8] Several Interviews with Derek Mason, former operations manager of Quay Pak. April-May, 2022.

[9] Watson, H.A. Letter to Amalgamated Metal Corporation Limited. 3 December, 1974.

[10] Curtin, D. *Police witness statement.* 4 January, 1978.

[11] Yates, H. *Police witness statement.* 2 November, 1977.

[12] Rich, A. *Police witness statement.* 5 October, 1977.

[13] This statement was allegedly made by Michael Tilley in the presence of Glyn Short when Michael Tilley was later employed by Eurolease in Cardiff.

the beginning of 1975 were from Quay Pak (resulting in an immediate 15% saving).[14] This resulted in a saving for Austral Metals of approximately £27,000 per annum.

This loss of this haulage was a severe blow to BRS who, after significant changes to the company structure in 1972, were suffering poor trading conditions and were losing money.[15,16] They had also recently invested in a new fleet of vehicles to serve the port, which were now idle.[17] At the same time, and due to an initiative by Aubrey, Cardiff Docks was also offering demurrage to certain vessels to help attract steel imports from Immingham, through which ¼ million tons were imported annually.[18] Demurrage meant that if there were any delays or interruptions in a ship's discharge, and/ or if the speed of discharge was below average, the BTDB would pay the ship demurrage, typically about £2,000 to £3,000 per day.[19] This was an attractive incentive to importers, particularly as they had to pay a penalty of £2,000 for each day that their vessel was in port beyond their allotted time. Although this ploy had proved to be highly effective in attracting new trade to Cardiff Docks since the mid-1960s, it put extra pressures on the BTDB to discharge vessels on time. This often led to additional traffic on the quayside and consequential difficulties with haulage companies – and resulted in an increase in the number of labour disputes during discharge. Transport co-ordination at the quayside was therefore key, particularly bearing in mind that hauliers only contracted to move cargo on their own terms. They would also not accept liability for ship demurrage even if this arose from their own supply failures.

Aubrey therefore proposed that the BTDB should set up a transport consortium at Cardiff, which would outline a suitable method of organising transport arrangements.[20] This would improve the service offered to the port traders at Cardiff by arranging the inland transport of imported goods.[21] It would also

---

[14] Walsh, H. Letter to Isidore Rosen (solicitor). 7 November, 1983.

[15] Unpublished notes of Mike Houle, BRS historian.

[16] Lewis, G. *Corporate strategy in action. The strategy process in British Road Services.* London. Routledge, 1988.

[17] This is based on a confidential email to the author which is believed to be credible and reliable.

[18] Port charges at Immingham were cheaper than Cardiff, and this was seen as the only way in which Cardiff could attract some of this trade.

[19] Cardiff was the first port authority in the UK or the continent to attempt this form of inducement.

[20] BTDB. Meeting minutes for the proposed establishment of the transport consortium. 2 December, 1974.

[21] Walsh, H. Letter to Isidore Rosen (solicitor). 16 November, 1983.

protect the BTDB's interests. The BTDB had little control of movement of goods from the port (some of which had gone disastrously wrong over the previous 2-3 years) and it was hoped that an organised consortium would bring some measure of control to significant levels of minor corruption in the transport world at this time – including payments, or backhanders, to local agents to secure haulage. It would also remove the concerns of several importers who in recent years had expressed concern at the haulage rates they were being charged.[22]

Provisional agreement for a transport consortium – to be responsible for all future haulage – was agreed on 2nd December 1974 between BRS, Glyn John Transport, Freightliners, and Quay Pak.[23] The inclusion of Quay Pak, who had started to attract new trade to the port, gave some measure of control to the BTDB because they offered periodic access to private transport rates and helped to prevent the traditional hauliers from fixing rates by collusion.[24,25] The transport consortium also proposed that haulage arrangements were to be organised under a single transport coordinator, paid by the BTDB, who ideally was to be independent of the organisation employed to unload the vessel. Future haulage could also not be sub-contracted (apart from Quay Pak, who could sub-contract only once), and if the contracted haulier failed to provide the necessary vehicles from their own resources, the haulage would be offered to one of the other consortium members. Implicit in any contract that the BTDB negotiated with the consortium members was the acceptance of the demurrage charges if it could be shown that they had failed in their job. This was a significant change from the previous situation, where hauliers had no interest in charges to the BTDB due to any failure on their part.

The proposed transport consortium was received favourably by all members except BRS, who felt it was not to their advantage and particularly disliked the clause on the acceptance of demurrage charges.[26] Horace Yates of BRS also expressed his dissatisfaction with Quay Pak being part of the consortium, and the inconsistent rules that applied to them. This was particularly because they had no road transport of their own at this time, so would not be able to

---

[22] Hames, A. *Police interview*. 9 August, 1977.

[23] BTDB. *Meeting minutes for the proposed establishment of the transport consortium*. 2 December, 1974.

[24] Hames, A. *Police interview*. 9 August, 1977.

[25] Unaware of this at time, Lihu Ichilov later felt he had been "taken for a ride" by Aubrey as he believed most of the rates he quoted were used as a guide by the BTDB on rates (interview with Lihu Ichilov, interview by David Williams of HTV Wales, *Wales this Week* documentary "Corruption." 21 February, 1983).

[26] Thomas, D. *Police witness statement*. 8 November, 1977.

assist in the supply of road transport.[27] However, despite BRS's concerns, the transport consortium as proposed was established.

Over the following year, the transport consortium proved to be difficult to manage, and there were many disagreements and complaints, with Aubrey in the chair often acting as a mediator between different hauliers. Even though it brought improved profits to the BTDB and offered substantial savings to the traders, it was disbanded with immediate effect by the Docks Manager Ray Wareham at a meeting on 5th December 1975.[28] This followed a particularly heated meeting regarding haulage allocations, and the resignation from the transport consortium of Glyn John Transport as a direct result of a dispute with Freightliners.[29] Aubrey, clearly dissatisfied with this decision, later expressed this view to Ray Wareham, who replied by saying that if Aubrey was unhappy with his management at Cardiff, he would ask the South Wales Ports Director Tommy Roberts to transfer him to another port.[30]

The decision of Ray Wareham to disband the transport consortium was because, in his own words, he had "become fed-up with the arguments and complaints by members." Many of these complaints had been instigated by Ron Irons, Douglas Thomas and David Manners, all of BRS, who were aggrieved at the loss of the lead cargo to Quay Pak.[31] This unrest had spread amongst BRS staff, leading to rumours of conspiracies between Quay Pak and the BTDB to remove traditional traffic from BRS, resulting in redundancies of BRS drivers. Aubrey, as chairman of the transport consortium, and Lihu Ichilov as managing director of Quay Pak, were central to these conspiracies. Rumours of conspiracy were fuelled by the friendship that Aubrey and Lihu Ichilov had – a friendship that dated back to Lihu Ichilov's time as the Port Manager of the Citrus Marketing Board of Israel (CMBI) for Wales and the Southwest of England (i.e. the Jaffa Organisation).

These rumours increased when, in December 1975, Douglas Thomas visited Stan Jones, Terminal Manager of Freightliners Cardiff, and told him that, among other things, Ron Irons had proof that a family holiday by the Hames family to Israel in August of that year had been paid for by Lihu Ichilov.[32,]This

---

[27] Yates, H. *Police witness statement.* 2 November, 1977.

[28] Wareham, R. *Police witness statement.* 10 January, 1978.

[29] Kemble-Dunn, I. *Police witness statement.* 2 December, 1977.

[30] Wareham, R. *Police witness statement.* 10 January, 1978.

[31] Ibid.

[32] Aubrey had made a vow to return to Israel following his service there in the Second World War. As a committed Catholic, and with a long-standing invitation by Lihu Ichilov's mother to stay with her in Israel at a time when cheap foreign travel was opening up, this presented Aubrey with an ideal opportunity to return to Israel, this time with his family.

was shortly after Quay Pak's offices had been burgled, and the only document taken related to a down payment for a trip to Israel by Lihu Ichilov.[33] Douglas Thomas added that Ron Irons said that he was going to "do something about it."[34][35] Stan Jones, concerned by these allegations, went to see Aubrey, who in turn reported these accusations to the South Wales Port Director Tommy Roberts. However, no further action was taken as unfounded allegations were commonly made in the transport world at this time, and Aubrey was told to ignore the matter.[22] BRS also approached Stan Jones three times to suggest that BRS and Freightliners jointly try and squeeze Quay Pak out of business, although Stan Jones refused to cooperate.[36][37]

With industrial unrest increasing on the dockside in 1976, the rumours alleging a conspiracy between Quay Pak and the BTDB intensified. The unrest was partly a result of a change in the system of remunerating Dock workers on piecework – and these workers were members of the Transport and General Workers Union (TGWU) – the same union as the BRS drivers.[38] This was most evident when cargo handling operations had to be halted due to insufficient numbers of vehicles to take cargo from ships. This resulted in Graham Phillips, the District Secretary of the TGWU, writing to Ray Wareham to complain about the BTDB's involvement in road transport and threatening to take appropriate industrial action if there were consequential redundancies among his members. In addition, Ron Irons, met John Williams, the new South Wales Port Director, in January 1977 with a suggestion that they co-ordinate their commercial activities at Cardiff Docks to exclude companies like Quay Pak – even if consequently haulage rates would increase by about "£1 per ton" (this was just after the MV *Doryforos* incident, which is discussed below). This request was refused. The situation developed further in February 1977, when the total dock labour force withdrew their labour for four days because two haulage companies (D&N Transport and Holmans) were unable to maintain an adequate supply of vehicles to discharge a butter and cheese cargo. At a joint management/TGWU meeting held on 14th February to enquire about the cause of this strike, the dockworkers' representatives re-iterated their complaints about the BTDB's interference in

---

[33] Hames, A. Letter to Mark Robinson, Newport West MP (draft). 1 February, 1984.

[34] Spear, M. Letter to Isidore Rosen (solicitor). 20 November, 1983.

[35] Interview with Aubrey Hames (interview by David Williams of HTV Wales for *Wales this Week* documentary "Corruption." 14 February, 1983).

[36] Spear, M. Letter to Isidore Rosen (solicitor). 20 November, 1983.

[37] Ichilov, L. *Police interview*. 16 November, 1977.

[38] Type of employment in which a worker is paid a fixed price for a piece of work, regardless of the time taken to complete that piece of work.

the haulage of cargo by BRS. They also claimed that the cause of the strike was the BTDB's denial of work to BRS that resulted in lorry shortages at the dockside. This accusation against BTDB occurred despite that fact that it was the repudiation of a haulage contract by BRS – the day before the vessel was due to commence discharge – that meant it was too late to order in alternative transport.[39] As a result of the increasing problems with dairy produce vessels in particular, Ray Wareham threatened that if contracted hauliers failed to supply vehicles, they would be struck from the BTDB list.

Attempts at what may have been industrial sabotage failed, and things did start to settle down. They did, though, resurface in June 1977 as a result of the case of the MV *Doryforos*, and after Aubrey had taken a year's leave of absence to become Mayor of Newport in May 1977.

MV Doryforos

Aubrey first became aware that a cargo of steel coils and angles transported by a vessel called the MV *Doryforos* was due to arrive in the UK in October 1976, with its cargo destined for the Midlands. As an inducement to discharge at Cardiff, Aubrey offered the ship charterer, Retla Steamship Company (Retla), a rate to offload the cargo alongside the vessel, with delivery to its final destination. Aubrey also offered Retla a "demurrage-free" arrangement of US $6,000 (about £3,500) per day.

With Retla accepting this rate, Phillip Condliffe, 2nd Assistant Docks Manager at Cardiff, took responsibility for compiling haulage rates for the transport of this cargo to its inland destinations – which were approved by Aubrey before they were offered to the traders. The MV *Doryforos* was then put on the arrivals list for "sometime" in October 1976, discharging about 4,600 tons, which included approximately 2,900 tons of steel coils and 1,750 tons of steel angles which were to be immediately transported to the Midlands by rail. However, the arrival date of the MV *Doryforos* was delayed, and its arrival date was later estimated as 13th/14th December 1976.[40]

With the new expected arrival date of around the 13th/14th December, it was at some point in November 1976 when Quay Pak was awarded the haulage contract after a tender process involving several hauliers.[41] Phillip Condliffe

---

[39] A memorandum (probably from Ray Wareham) dated 24/01/76 before this strike had noted "I believe BRS have let us down on several occasions during 1976 in not supplying an adequate number of vehicles to keep vessels going."

[40] BTDB. Letter to Mr Thomas of Cory Bros Shipping. 24 November, 1976

[41] Retla Steamship company had specifically invited Quay Pak to quote for this cargo.

then negotiated with Quay Pak to discharge the cargo from the MV *Doryforos* and to sort it for delivery to the respective customers. This was to be done in a warehouse offsite as it was not practical and safe to sort the cargo during discharge, and the dock's warehouses had limited space. Since customers could not accept their consignments of cargo as quickly as the vessel could offload them, a phased operation was calculated by Phillip Condliffe to take 3 weeks. This included a probable arrival of the MV *Doryforos* on 13th/14th December 1976, and potential problems with deliveries to the customers over the Christmas period. The charges for sorting and delivering the steel angles was given to Retla as £2.85 or £2.92 a ton with an additional stipulation that a charge of £1 per week per ton would be raised if the cargo was delivered in full within three weeks.[42]

MV Doryforos at sea

Unfortunately, the MV *Doryforos* continued to be delayed, and it did not finally dock at Cardiff until 20th/21st December. The ship's papers giving details of the cargo were also not delivered until either the day before or the actual day the ship docked. This meant that there was no firm information on which to plan the sorting, discharge and disposal of its cargo until the last minute. Before arriving, it also became clear that additional cargo was now to be discharged at Cardiff Docks – a total of 7,140 tons instead of

---

[42] Condliffe, P. Letter to Retla Steamship company. 24 November, 1976 (it is not clear why two rates were given).

the original 4,676 tons. The additional cargo of 2,463 tons of steel angles had been sold to another importer whilst in transit, and this importer had immediately instructed local shipping agents Lambert Bros & Co. to receive and arrange inland delivery at Cardiff – and they engaged BRS to undertake the haulage of this cargo.[43]

Based on the additional cargo to be discharged, Aubrey called Retla and withdrew the demurrage-free arrangement as he now had no control over the BRS consignment. With the extra cargo, and the date of arrival, he also informed them that there was a possibility that some of the cargo might not be unloaded until the Christmas holiday period (which later proved to be correct), leading to problems of potential work closures of up to 10 days. In addition, if any of the receivers' works closed for Christmas, some cargo may have been stored on the quayside and forwarded after the holiday period at a cost over and above the special "all-in" rate. Moreover, the receivers informed Aubrey that all cargo had to be warehoused, and not stored in the open.[44] Subsequently, Phillip Condliffe asked Quay Pak to re-quote for warehousing and delivery of the original 4,676 tons of steel coils and angles, and these revised quotes were accepted by him.

Aubrey, although not happy with the increase in charges, agreed to accept them on the understanding that all cargo would be cleared within 4 weeks, and that he could not accept more than £4 per ton from Quay Pak for the total cargo handled.[45] Aubrey and Phillip Condliffe then met with Lihu Ichilov where he was warned of possible dockside problems if his company's staff did any work that was perceived to be the job of the dockers (e.g., unloading the cargo). Lihu Ichilov was confident that provided he was given uninterrupted discharge from the MV *Doryforos*, he would complete the job within 4 weeks; it was known that this may be difficult to achieve if bad weather were to occur, but Lihu Ichilov agreed to take this risk.

Meanwhile, in danger of losing their demurrage-free terms, Retla decided to cancel Lambert Bros & Co.'s instructions yet still unload all 7,140 tons of cargo at Cardiff. They informed the BTDB that the MV *Doryforos* would only dock at Cardiff if the demurrage-free terms were maintained on all 7,140 tons of cargo. In danger of losing this trade, the BTDB reluctantly agreed. The BTDB were also informed that the receivers of the cargo, rather than Retla, would be responsible for the handling of the cargo on the quayside and

---

[43] Condliffe, P. *Police witness statement*. 19 December, 1976.

[44] Besser, A.D. Letter to Aubrey. 15 November, 1976.

[45] This rate was similar to the BTDB's rate for banking steel billets/angles on the quayside.

the inland haulage charges.[46]

Aubrey now had to determine how to deal with the additional 2,463 tons of steel angles. Although Retla had cancelled the instructions from Lambert Bros & Co., BRS had still been engaged to move this cargo. Now that BRS and Quay Pak would attempt to take their mixed (but separately marked) cargo out of the ship's holds at the same time (something that was not apparent until the vessel's papers were received), this would almost certainly cause difficulties and increase the risk of demurrage being paid. One solution – to sack BRS and have them hand their work to Quay Pak – would have exacerbated an already difficult relationship between these two organisations. There was also the risk that labour trouble might occur on the quayside if it was alleged that BRS drivers' jobs were jeopardised – especially considering that BRS drivers and the Cardiff dockers belonged to the same union.

Aubrey therefore called Horace Yates of BRS and Lihu Ichilov of Quay Pak to the General Cargo Office and explained the situation to them. Having earlier agreed this with Ray Wareham, it was proposed that BRS would unload their cargo of 2,463 tons, and they would be managed in this by Quay Pak who would be employed as the transport coordinator – as this was a role in which Quay Pak were considerably more experienced in.[47] Quay Pak was responsible for making sure that the ship was unloaded on time so that the BTDB would not incur demurrage costs. Although both companies accepted these terms, BRS did not provide a continuous supply of vehicles which resulted in some cargo being misplaced for several weeks.[48] And they also did not undertake the promised warehousing of the steel. Subsequently, a substantial claim, believed to be of the order of £40,000, was lodged by the receivers which was passed to BRS for settlement.

Meanwhile, the delay in the docking of the MV *Doryforos* had resulted in additional unforeseen up-front costs to Quay Pak, who had been unable to re-negotiate the warehouse hire for the cargo from the MV *Doryforos*. Quay Pak would now be responsible for interest charges if the warehousing rents were not paid on time. Lihu Ichilov therefore approached Aubrey to ask if the BTDB would pay 50% of their warehousing charges in advance once the

---

[46] The cargo had been purchased on what is known as CIF (Carriage, Insurance, Freight) terms, where the seller pays for the carriage and insurance to the named destination point, with all risks passing over to the buyer (or receiver) when the cargo is handed over to the first carrier.

[47] Several Interviews with Derek Mason, 2022.

[48] Cardiff Docks Managers Office. Confidential memorandum, unsigned but probably written by Ray Wareham. 2 January, 1976.

vessel was in dock. During this meeting it was pointed out, much to Aubrey's embarrassment, that the BTDB currently owed Quay Pak £28,745.40 for non-payment of haulage charges, most of which were several months overdue.[49] In the circumstances, an advance was authorised for £5,461.67, which was to be deducted from the final account after the vessel had completed discharge and all the steel had been delivered.

Unfortunately, the original rates quoted to Retla when it was anticipated that it would dock on 13th or 14th December had not been withdrawn by Phillip Condliffe (rates that would not have been quoted if the arrival date of the MV *Doryforos* had been known to be on the 21st December).[50] Therefore, with the increased charges from Quay Pak, he was asked to look for savings. Quay Pak agreed to several reductions in charges which included an agreement not to increase rates after 1st January 1977 when new rates were due to kick in.

With the delay in the arrival of the MV *Doryforos* and therefore also in the necessary warehousing of the vessel's cargo, Phillip Condliffe contacted the receivers to get confirmation that they would accept the revised charges. However, the receivers of the steel coils, Metal Enterprizes, proved difficult to contact, and when Aubrey later contacted them, after the MV *Doryforos* had been unloaded, they refused to pay the warehousing charges. Retla's representative also tried to get Metal Enterprizes to accept these revised charges, but without success.

This now presented Aubrey with another problem. If the steel coils were warehoused by Quay Pak, and Metal Enterprizes refused to pay these costs, the coils might end up being warehoused by Quay Pak beyond the 4 weeks stipulated as the maximum storage period. This would mean the BTDB would incur unacceptable costs. Aubrey therefore stopped the coils going to Quay Pak (who had already started unloading) and ordered for space to be made in the BTDB's warehouses and stored as best as they could. This was despite a lack of space and floor-loading tolerances being exceeded. These coils could then be stored for weeks at no charge to the BTDB, although it would mean that they had to be moved regularly before they were finally cleared. It also meant that a lien could be enforced if required.[51]

Aubrey contacted Quay Pak and told them of the changed position. Desperate

---

[49] Quay Pak eventually issued a writ on 17/03/78 against the Docks Board seeking payment of fees due, including the MV *Doryforos* invoices. An out of court settlement of £1,500 was eventually agreed in May 1981 after Quay Pak had gone into voluntary liquidation, and this was paid to the receivers.

[50] Condliffe, P. *Police interview*. 11 October, 1977.

[51] A right to keep property belonging to another person until a debt is paid.

to avoid demurrage, he asked them to continue their original supply of vehicles to service the ship, despite the lesser quantity of steel to be carried away. He also promised Lihu Ichilov an immediate review of the position after the vessel had completed discharge and assured him that additional warehousing or local transport costs to Quay Pak based on the lesser tonnage of steel would be covered. This assurance was on the clear understanding that the BTDB would not meet any costs incurred by Quay Pak after the fourth week. Lihu Ichilov expressed serious concern at this turn of events, maintaining that potential payment based on the substantially lesser tonnage going into his warehouse would result in a serious financial loss. However, even though Quay Pak could have terminated their contract at this point as the terms of contract had varied substantially, he agreed to the amended conditions.

In the end, the MV *Doryforos* was unloaded successfully and on time, and no demurrage was incurred despite several delays. However, agreement could still not be reached with Metal Enterprizes on the warehousing charges. In view of the value of the coils, and to not unnecessarily clash with the receivers, Aubrey eventually agreed to the release of all the coils except three, later reduced to one following representations from Retla's representative, Colin Harrison.[52] This more than covered the Board's warehousing expenditure.

A negotiated settlement for this expenditure was finally agreed about 3 months later, but not before Aubrey had visited Metal Enterprizes on 3rd March 1977, accompanied by Colin Harrison, who withdrew a charge of several hundred pounds for shipwright's services which Retla had earlier claimed from Metal Enterprizes.[53] This facilitated settlement, and a cheque for £5,278.57 was obtained from Metal Enterprizes, with the remaining coils released by the BTDB. This cheque which later went missing and appears to have been re-issued several months later, formed a central part of the court case against Aubrey and his dismissal as discussed later.

Quay Pak submitted an invoice for warehousing based on the original contract, i.e., a declared weight of about 2,731 tons of angles and coils at £4 per ton. This was discussed with Ray Wareham, and it was agreed that this invoice should be paid, particularly bearing in mind that all the cargo had not actually been cleared from Quay Pak's warehousing until the 5th or 6th week, rather than the maximum agreed 4th week. Accordingly, payment of £5,961.96 (£5,520 + £441.63 VAT) was authorised, being £10,982.06 minus the £5,461.67 previously paid. Later, Quay Pak produced a summary of the

---

[52] Hames, A. *Police witness statement*. 9 August, 1977.
[53] Ibid.

local transport costs payable to Freightliner and Hills Transport. This was based on additional costs which were caused by interruptions at the quayside, and to which Quay Pak was entitled to as part of its contract with the BTDB. Quay Pak only requested payment based on actual expenditure, and this was given to Phillip Condliffe to discuss with Ray Wareham.

However, with no action taken on this for a couple of months, Lihu Ichilov approached Aubrey. With Ray Wareham abroad, Aubrey authorised an interim payment of £1,000 which was accepted by Lihu Ichilov, and which Aubrey was to discuss with Ray Wareham on his return.[54] Outlining the problems that had occurred with the MV *Doryforos*, he recommended that Quay Pak be reimbursed the actual excess haulage expenditure, which Ray Wareham agreed.

Shortly after the MV *Doryforos* had completed her discharge, Brian Anthoney of BRS wrote to Ray Wareham on 20th January 1977 to express his disappointment regarding the loss of work to Quay Pak. His complaints solely related to trade lost to Quay Pak, in particular the continuing loss of the Austral Metals lead traffic, as well as not being appointed as transport coordinator for the MV *Doryforos*. Crucially, this letter also contained information that suggested that BRS had access to confidential rates information for other haulage firms, with a suggestion of industrial tension via the TGWU due to lost work for their members. This prompted Ray Wareham to write to Brian Anthoney of BRS on 24th January, to ask how they had access to the rates information. Over the following two days, two unsigned memorandums were issued from the Docks Manager's office in relation to BRS's apparent knowledge of these rates and their apparent attempts to squeeze its competitors out of the haulage business from Austral Metals. These memorandums stated that previous experience suggested that BRS would have no hesitation in bumping their rates up again once the threat of competition had been removed. It was also noted that BRS had let the BTDB down on several occasions during 1976 when they had not supplied an adequate number of vehicles, including as noted above, for the MV *Doryforos*. They also struggled to co-ordinate transport within their own division let alone acting as a coordinator for other or subcontracted hauliers.

Nothing more occurred as a result of these events, and then four months later in May 1977, Aubrey was elected Mayor of Newport, starting 12 months leave of absence from the BTDB.

---

[54] Hames, A. Letter to BTDB Accountant. 19 April, 1977.

Police investigation

Sometime around June or July 1977, a complaint was made to the then Prime Minister James Callaghan, who was the constituency MP covering Cardiff Docks, of alleged corrupt practices at Cardiff Docks involving the management and local hauliers.[55] This complaint was made by Ken Bulpin, who was the regional security manager for BRS, and who was probably used as a pawn by BRS as he lived in James Callaghan's constituency.[56,57] Bulpin was acting on instructions from one or more senior members of BRS – one of which would almost certainly have been Ron Irons. Crucially, as discussed later, this complaint was almost certainly sent to James Callaghan at 10 Downing Street, and not to his local constituency office.[58] Central to these allegations was an alleged corrupt relationship between Aubrey and Lihu Ichilov, and apparent proof that a Hames family holiday to Israel in August 1975 had been paid for by Lihu Ichilov. Other allegations were also made – mainly relating to the handling of the MV *Doryforos* and the lead traffic from Cardiff. The complaint was passed onto the British Transport Police (BT Police) in South Wales.

The serious nature of the allegations, and the involvement of a senior public official who was also a prominent politician, made this a potentially high-profile case, and a five-man team was dispatched by the BT Police from London to Cardiff. The investigation was led by Chief Superintendent Maurice Woodman, the most senior investigating officer of the BT Police Criminal Investigation Department (CID), and Detective Inspector Edward John Innes (known as John Innes).[59]

The initial investigation appeared to concentrate on the involvement of Quay Pak in the haulage business at Cardiff, as Maurice Woodman and John Innes could not appreciate how a relatively small company such as Quay Pak was getting this business.[60] As a result, the first recorded interview was with Hubert Walsh of Austral Metals in July 1977 (the "lead traffic").[61] In this interview, Hubert Walsh explained how he had gone to see Aubrey at

---

[55] Williams, J. Letter to Aubrey. 10 August, 1980.

[56] This is based on a confidential correspondence with a former member of the British Transport Police, 25/11/16.

[57] Hames, A. Letter to Ruth Sharpe, James Callaghan's Personal Secretary. 26 August, 1980.

[58] Callaghan, J. Letter to Aubrey. 9 September, 1980.

[59] Interview with Graham Satchwell, former Det. Superintendent British Transport Police. 25 November, 2016.

[60] Interview with Maurice Woodman, former Det. Superintendent British Transport Police. 13 June, 2012.

[61] Hames, A. Letter to Isidore Rosen (solicitor). 8 November, 1983.

Cardiff in November 1974 to obtain his advice on the escalating transport costs that his company were facing. Explaining how Aubrey had obtained much more competitive haulage rates for his company, saving them in the region of £30,000 per annum, clearly surprised the investigative team. Presumably, having only heard BRS's side of the story, they commented that this had "put an entirely different picture on the case," and that it was Hubert Walsh's view that it would be surprising if this inquiry was pursued.[21] However, the statement later prepared by the BT Police for Hubert Walsh only included Austral Development's relationship with Quay Pak, which was stated as "100% in all respects."[62] No other details from this interview were given, such as why the consortium was established or the resultant (substantial) savings in haulage.[63] The omission was later noted by Hubert Walsh as "surprising," although he still signed his statement.[64] Stan Jones of Freightliners was also interviewed at this time; in his interview, he mentioned BRS's attempts to squeeze Quay Pak out of business, but this was also not included in his prepared statement – and as a result he did not sign it.[65,66]

Later in July, or early August, the investigation moved on to the BTDB, so the BT Police went to see the Managing Director of the BTDB, Keith Stuart. As a result, on 4th August 1977, a meeting was held between Maurice Woodman, John Innes, Alan Tomsett (the BTDB finance director), and Edward Jordan (the BTDB's internal audit manager).[67] Neither John Williams (the South Wales Port Director), or Ray Wareham, (the Cardiff Docks Manager) were present – nor were they aware at this time of the allegations or the ongoing police investigation. At this meeting, a request was made to Edward Jordan to carry out a special audit of the BTDB's accounts at Cardiff Docks with particular attention being paid to transactions between the BTDB and Quay Pak relating to cargo carried by the MV *Doryforos* as well as a contract for the transportation of lead (the Austral Metals contract).[68] This request was made despite the fact that an audit of the MV *Doryforos* had already been carried out by a member of Edward Jordan's staff a month previously, on 7th July, and had concluded that there was no discrepancy in the charges

---

[62] Walsh, H. (undated) *Police witness statement.*

[63] Walsh, H. Letter to Isidore Rosen (solicitor). 16 November, 1983.

[64] Walsh, H. Letter to Isidore Rosen (solicitor). 7 November, 1983.

[65] Spear, M. Letter to Isidore Rosen (solicitor). 20 November, 1983.

[66] Although interviewed twice, no statement was given to, or received from, Stan Jones (Jones, S. Letter to Aubrey. 10 November, 1983).

[67] BTDB. *Memorandum.* 27 October, 1977.

[68] Ibid.

made by, or to, Quay Pak.[69,70] A draft of the new audit was later presented at a meeting between Keith Stuart, John Williams, and Ray Wareham, on 24th October 1977, and the final report was to be prepared by 27th October subject to minor amendments.

Five days after the meeting on the 4th August, Keith Stuart rang Aubrey and requested that he attend an interview in London. Prior to this call, Aubrey had been contacted several times by Vernon Snow, the BTDB manager at Newport who was due to retire at the end of 1977. Vernon Snow told Aubrey that he had been suggested as his possible replacement. He said that despite the senior management at BTDB questioning whether Aubrey's political activity might interfere with the appointment, he should expect an imminent call from Keith Stuart in connection with the post. So when Aubrey set off for London the day after Keith Stuart's call, he anticipated discussion on the potential new post of docks manager at Newport. However, when he arrived, he was informed by Keith Stuart of the allegations that had been made concerning haulage and other work at Cardiff Docks, and that the BT Police had been asked to conduct a domestic inquiry into the allegations. With the BT Police waiting in the adjoining room, Aubrey agreed to assist them, and after they had talked to him, Aubrey was told not to contact any colleagues at Cardiff Docks when he returned to Newport.

At what was described as a preliminary interview, Aubrey was interviewed by Maurice Woodman and John Innes over a period of two hours.[71,72] Detective Sergeant Roger Mayers was also present and took notes during the meeting so that enquiries could be made as quickly as possible.[73,74] Aubrey was not cautioned, and was told that they would contact him again later, although they never did.[75,76]

One of the crucial questions put to Aubrey during this interview related to the family trip to Israel in August 1975 that had allegedly been paid for by Lihu Ichilov. Aubrey explained that this allegation had been made by BRS in November 1975, and that he had reported this to his superiors. Although

---

[69] Aubrey later identified that this audit had not been undertaken by a member of Edward Jordan's staff, but by a Brian Harding, the acting Assistant Docks Manager at Cardiff during Aubrey's absence.

[70] Jordan, E. Evidence at Cardiff Stipendiary Magistrates. 28 February, 1979.

[71] Mayers, R. *Witness statement.* 15 February, 1978.

[72] Innes, E. *Witness statement.* 31 January, 1978.

[73] Mayers, R. *Witness statement.* 15 February, 1978.

[74] Innes, E. *Witness statement.* 31 January, 1978.

[75] Hames, A. *Police witness statement.* 9 August, 1977.

[76] Interview with Maurice Woodman, 2012.

Aubrey told the investigating officers that he had paid by cheque for this trip and should be able to produce it if required, they did not follow this up and the cheque was never requisitioned or seen by the BT Police.[77,78,79]

Left: Keith Stuart, Managing Director of BTDB and later Chairman of Associated British Ports (ABP) after the BTDB was privatised (1977-2011). Right: Chief Superintendent Maurice Woodman (photo courtesy of Graham Satchwell)

Aubrey was also asked about alleged discrimination against BRS in the transport of the lead traffic, as well as on the handling of the MV *Doryforos* and transport arrangements at Cardiff Docks – including the transport consortium and the alleged lack of corporate substance of Quay Pak (an allegation frequently made by BRS staff at Cardiff). This interview was recorded, but Aubrey was not aware of this until he was later issued with a court summons and the trial depositions.[80,81]

The nature of the questions that Aubrey was asked during his interview indicated to him that these accusations had probably been instigated by BRS.

---

[77] Hames, A. *Police interview*. 9 August, 1977.

[78] Interview with Maurice Woodman, 2012.

[79] HTV Wales. *Wales this week,* documentary. 24 March, 1983.

[80] Mayers, R. *Witness statement*. 15 February, 1978.

[81] Innes, E. *Witness statement*. 31 January, 1978.

Further evidence came in the first people to be interviewed after Aubrey; Ron Irons (BRS Divisional Manager Bristol) and David Manners, (BRS Bristol) who were interviewed on 17th August, Michael Tilley (BRS Potters Bar) who was interviewed on 19th August, and Horace Yates (BRS Cardiff) who was interviewed on 24th October.[82] When interviewing Lihu Ichilov at a later date, Superintendent Maurice Woodman also stated that the investigation had been initiated by the then Prime Minister, James Callaghan.[83,84] James Callaghan later strenuously denied this, stating that the suggestion that he, as Prime Minister, was responsible for initiating police enquires was "rubbish."[85]

The following morning, Aubrey rang Keith Stuart to express his concern at the questions he was asked and requested a personal interview to clarify certain matters. At this time, he believed that a range of allegations had been made involving not only him, but also several BTDB officials. The same day, a reporter and a photographer from the Daily Mail turned up at Aubrey's house to ask him questions about his police interview, which he refused to answer.[86] However, they did tell him that a case of corruption was being investigated, which was the first time that this had been mentioned to him. Aubrey immediately rang John Williams to express his concern that what he believed was a domestic inquiry had been leaked to the press. John Williams although sympathetic was not able to help. The next day, the *Daily Mail* headlined a report written by Peter Burden, their chief crime reporter, that Aubrey Hames, the Mayor of Newport was involved in police enquires into allegations of corruption at Cardiff Docks, and that millions of pounds of contracts had been awarded possibly because of friendships, or in return for favours. The need to establish the truth as quickly as possible reflected the sensitivity felt at the time regarding any hints of corruption in relation to senior public officials, particularly because of the fallout from the John Poulson affair.[87] The Poulson affair had rocked British politics just a few years earlier, and later became a major driving force in the initiation of the Register of Members' Interests in the House of Commons. The fact that this

---

[82] Ibid.

[83] Williams, J. Letter to Aubrey. 10 August, 1980.

[84] Rosen, I. Letter to Aubrey. 22 May, 1980.

[85] Callaghan, J. Letter to Roy Hughes MP. 20 May, 1980.

[86] Aubrey and his family were away on this day, not returning until about 6:30 in the evening. According to neighbours, the Daily Mail reporters had turned up at about 10:00am and waited all day for Aubrey's return.

[87] John Poulson was a British architect and businessman who caused a major political scandal when his use of bribery to obtain building contracts resulted in him being charged and convicted of fraud for seven years in 1974. This case also forced the Conservative Home Secretary, Reginald Maudling to resign, and almost resulted in the jailing of three MPs.

article was written by someone who was well known for his scoops via police contacts, and who was friendly with Maurice Woodman, suggests Maurice Woodman was responsible for the leak.[88,89]

Headline in the Daily Mail, 11th August 1977 following Aubrey's police interview.

Despite Aubrey's offer to provide the cheque that proved he had paid for the family holiday to Israel, the police investigation proceeded on the basis that Lihu Ichilov had paid, or supplemented the trip, and that Aubrey had benefitted from accommodation owned by Lihu Ichilov's mother.[90] This was based on the travel agent's invoice which had the reference "Hames care of Ichilov" – probably because Lihu Ichilov had organised the tickets for Aubrey.[91] At the time, a deal known as a "home accommodation holiday" was available to anybody visiting Israel provided you could give an address in Israel where you were staying. The deal paid for the flight and provided a voucher for payment to the host, which Aubrey gave to Lihu Ichilov's mother.[92] The investigating officers only asked the travel agent for the price

---

[88] "Obituary of Peter Burden." *Press Gazette*. 19 October, 2017. Available at: http://www. pressgazette.co.uk/they-trust-me-and-i-trust-them-how-police-contacts-took-daily-mails-peter-burden-who-has-died-aged-77-to-the-top/. Date accessed: 15/03/17.

[89] Interview with Graham Satchwell, former Det. Superintendent British Transport Police. 25 November, 2016.

[90] Havers, M. Letter to Roy Hughes MP. 29 April, 1983.

[91] Interview with Maurice Woodman, former Det. Superintendent British Transport Police. 13 June, 2012.

[92] Aubrey had got to know Lihu Ichilov's mother during her visits to the UK between 1967 and 1975. During these visits, she had been entertained by various BTDB officials, including

of scheduled flights and package holidays to Israel. They did not ask the agent if there were any others offers through which one could travel there.[93]

As a result of this investigation, on 3rd October 1978, Aubrey, together with Lihu Ichilov, were served with summonses from the Director of Public Prosecutions alleging corruption, returnable at Cardiff Magistrates Court at the end of November. A week or two later, Derek Mason who had been Lihu Ichilov's Operations Manager was also served with a summons – a particular surprise as he had never been interviewed and had no idea that he was being investigated.[94]

Two charges were laid before Aubrey, which are given below. Lihu Ichilov was jointly charged on both charges, and Derek Mason was charged on the second of these. As a public official, the first, and most serious of these charges for Aubrey, would have resulted in a jail sentence if he had been found guilty.

1. That at Cardiff on a day between the 2nd July 1975 and the 30th August 1975, as an agent of the BTDB and as an inducement or reward for showing to Izhak Lihu Ichilov and Quay Pak Limited favour in relation to your principle affairs you correctly accepted for yourself from Izak Lihu Ichilov a consideration namely the obtaining for yourself and your family of air passages to and from and accommodation in Israel – contrary to the Prevention of Corruption Act, 1906 Section 1.

2. That at Cardiff on a day between the 7th December 1976 and the 10th February 1977, you conspired together with Izak Lihu Ichilov and Derek Mason to defraud the BTDB by falsely claiming £5,898.60 as two weeks rent in advance of a warehouse and falsely claiming that £10,982.60 was due to Quay Pak Limited in respect of the warehousing of steel coils and steel angles landed from the motor vessel MV *Doryforos* – contrary to common law.

John Williams and Aubrey. In return, she had offered an invitation to reciprocate the hospitality she had received and had subsequently offered accommodation to Aubrey and his family during their time in Israel. She had also entertained at least one other BTDB official during their time in Israel.

[93] Hames, A. (undated) Letter to Paul Flynn MP.

[94] Several Interviews with Derek Mason, former operations manager of Quay Pak. April-May, 2022.

Independent to these police charges, Aubrey then found himself the subject of formal disciplinary charges by the BTDB. This was based on the second audit into the MV *Doryforos* that had been completed a year earlier, even though this audit found no discrepancies in either the haulage arrangements at Cardiff or the dealings over the MV *Doryforos*. In accordance with the formal disciplinary procedures of the BTDB, on 19th October, the South Wales Port Director Ronald Bury, who had been appointed during Aubrey's year of absence for mayoral duty, issued Aubrey with a document known as a DIS Form I, under the staff disciplinary code. This required him to answer certain charges arising from the audit manager's report of 27th October 1977.[95] Advised by his solicitors, Aubrey informed the BTDB on 24th October, that he would not be able to co-operate in these disciplinary proceedings as the matters referred to were sub judice, and he might therefore be held in contempt of court if he took part. The BTDB replied on 10th November stating that they agreed and accordingly withdrew its request, accepting that they could not follow their normal disciplinary procedure.[96] However, they finished their letter by dismissing Aubrey, giving him 3 months' notice under the terms of his contract.[97] Aubrey was dismissed on 10th February 1979 after 29 years of service to the BTDB, presumably on the authority of the BTDB Managing Director Keith Stuart, without being given any opportunity to respond to the charges laid before him.

Time for court

The court case against Aubrey, Lihu Ichilov, and Derek Mason was heard at Cardiff Stipendiary Magistrates over a five-day period between 26th February 1979 and 2nd March 1979.[98] Aubrey, now unemployed, was granted legal aid to fight the charges against him.

Over the first two days, the case for the prosecution was laid out by Keith McHale. The main witness for the prosecution was the BTDB accountant

---

[95] Aubrey had already been suspended on full pay on completion of his mayoral year because of the ongoing BT Police investigation (Stuart, K. Letter to Aubrey. 19 April, 1978.)

[96] Knight, E. Letter to Leo Abse & Cohen solicitors. 10 November, 1978.

[97] David Burn, Transport Salaried Staffs Association divisional secretary wrote to Ron Bury on 12/12/78 requesting that the decision to give notice to Aubrey be reconsidered until he had the opportunity to instigate formal disciplinary proceedings. This request was denied.

[98] Lihu Ichilov at this time was recovering from a back operation, and against doctors' advice had returned from Israel to answer these charges. He ultimately spent the entire proceedings lying on his back.

Edward Jordan, who was cross examined over the conspiracy charges against all three defendants. The crucial evidence of Edward Jordan came at the end of the 2nd day. Having outlined the case for Quay Pak having been overpaid by about £4,600 for the warehousing of steel coils and angles from the MV *Doryforos*, he admitted that he did not know the whole terms of the contract between the BTDB and Quay Pak. He therefore could not say whether the sums claimed by Quay Pak were properly or improperly made.[99] Unable to produce any evidence for payments paid to or from the BTDB, at the start of the third day, Edward Jordan did not return to the stand, and the prosecuting counsel did not continue with their evidence. By this time, the conspiracy charge against Derek Mason had already been dismissed. The magistrate, Sir Lincoln Hallinan, added that he was beginning to worry about whether there was a conspiracy charge at all and advised the prosecution to consider a substitute charge.[100,101]

On the third day of the trial, the prosecution therefore dropped the conspiracy charge, and said that new charges of deception were to be substituted instead.[102] This was based on the settlement for the steel coils from Metal Enterprises that had been obtained by Aubrey for Quay Pak. Over the next two days, the case therefore concentrated on the charge of corruption, for which the alleged free passage to Israel and accommodation was central. However, this line of enquiry collapsed at the end of the fourth day on the evidence of the travel agent who confirmed that the Hames family trip to Israel in 1975 was available to any member of the public on the same terms and conditions that had been obtained by Aubrey.[103] With Aubre's counsel having already produced the cheque that proved Aubrey had paid for the holiday, there was no case to answer and the corruption charges against Aubrey and Lihu Ichilov were dismissed.

The substitute deception charges were heard on the fifth day of the trial. However, these were soon also dismissed, with Sir Lincoln Hallinan saying that the real issue in this case was the "interpretation of a commercial arrangement."[104] Aubrey and Lihu Ichilov left the court with the decision that there was no case to answer on the charges laid before them. Despite the paucity of the evidence presented, the British Transport Police considered

---

[99] "Corruption charges ruled out." *Western Mail.* 2 March, 1979.

[100] Sir Lincoln Hallinan was a Conservative former Mayor of Cardiff.

[101] "Magistrate's worry in conspiracy court case." *Western Mail.* 28 February, 1979.

[102] "Docks hearing is told of new summonses." *South Wales Echo.* 1 March, 1979.

[103] Hames, A. Letter to Sir Cecil Clothier QC, Parliamentary Commissioner. 31 August, 1982.

[104] "Hames and importer are cleared." *Western Mail.* 3 March, 1979.

appealing but did not ultimately pursue it – not least because any appeal would have been expensive.[105] Graham Satchwell, who worked with Maurice Woodman in the BT Police for a number of years, could not remember him ever appealing a case. He suggested that having spent a lot of time and money pursuing this case, the real reason for considering an appeal was because it hurt him professionally.[106] Maurice Woodman may also have presumed that Aubrey, Lihu Ichilov, as well as Derek Mason, were guilty, regardless of the absence of evidence – a common occurrence with many policemen.[107]

Although the case had been dismissed, this was certainly not the end of the matter for Aubrey. He now started a lengthy campaign, that was eventually to last nearly nine years, to restore his reputation and bring to book those people who he believed were responsible for the charges against him – both from the BTDB and the BTP.

On 11th April 1979, just a month after the conclusion of the court case, Aubrey took his complaint of unfair dismissal to an Industrial Tribunal where he asked that he be re-instated to his previous position as Assistant Docks Manager at Cardiff. On 9th May 1979 an answer was filed by the BTDB, and the case went to Tribunal in Cardiff on 23rd July 1979.

The key witness called by the BTDB in the Industrial Tribunal was the South Wales Port Director Ron Bury. Explaining Aubrey's dismissal, Ron Bury said that it was important that the BTDB had to clear up outstanding questions from Aubrey regarding the audit report into the MV *Doryforos*. As Aubrey was unable to answer these questions, he said "there were grounds for issuing this letter of dismissal so that we [the BTDB] could proceed to fill the vacant post."[108] In response, Aubrey's counsel replied that it was not correct to dismiss Aubrey "without giving him the reasons." Further, the tribunal chairman said that after the charges had been dropped, "there was no reason why Mr Hames should not have been asked the questions in the document [i.e., the DIS Form I]."[109]

After two days of evidence, the Industrial Tribunal concluded that Aubrey had been unfairly dismissed, stating: "There can be no doubt in our opinion, that in this case there was a serious breach of the principles of natural justice which require that no one shall be condemned before he has had

---

[105] Interview with Maurice Woodman, 2012.

[106] Interview with Graham Satchwell, 2016.

[107] Caldero, M.A., Dailey, J.D. and Withrow, B.L. *Police ethics: The corruption of noble cause*. London. Routledge, 2018.

[108] "Sacked Docks man slams his employers." *South Wales Argus*. 25 July, 1979.

[109] "£11,655 award for sacked docks man." *Western Mail*. 25 July, 1979.

an opportunity of stating his case." Laying down the criteria upon which a dismissal must be judged, the Industrial Tribunal continued, "the employer must firstly show the principal reason (or reasons if more than one) for the dismissal," which they said that the BTDB had failed to do. Finally, giving their opinions on the real reason for Aubrey's dismissal, the Industrial Tribunal stated that this was because of his leave of absence which at this time had extended to 17 months. Therefore, the tribunal ordered the BTDB to re-instate Aubrey which, after an adjournment to contact the BTDB Managing Director Keith Stuart, they refused.[110]

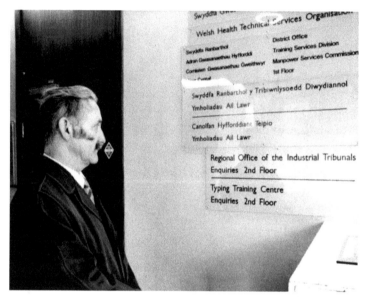

Aubrey turning up for the tribunal (courtesy, HTV Wales.

Compensation to Aubrey was therefore fixed on the basis that he in no way contributed to his dismissal, and he was awarded £11,635 in compensation. At the time this was the highest amount ever awarded by an Industrial Tribunal, and the maximum award that they could make.[111] From his final award, Aubrey had to pay back all benefits that he had accrued over the period of his unemployment, as well as legal costs of about £2,500.[112] Aubrey's annual salary at this time was about £18,000, and he had 9 years left until normal retirement age. With loss of pension (as well as probable

---

[110] Hames, A. Letter to the Consumers Association. 13 January, 1981.

[111] HTV Wales, *Wales this week* documentary, 24 March, 1983. As a comparison, the record as of the end of 2011 was £4.5 million (*Daily Mail*, 17/12/11).

[112] Hames, A. Letter to the Consumers Association. 13 January, 1981.

promotion either at Cardiff or Newport Docks and other rights), his total loss would have exceeded £200,000 (in excess of £1,000,000 today accounting for inflation). And, as a prominent Welsh politician, Mayor of Newport at the time of the accusations, and leader of Newport Borough Council as the case was ongoing, and with significant press coverage both locally and nationally, the defamation of his character was undoubtedly an even greater loss.

The case against Aubrey

The loss of the Austral Metals lead traffic – to Quay Pak – at the end of 1974 was a severe blow to BRS. After suffering significant losses in the early 1970s following a decline in Britain's traditional manufacturing industries, the company (which was part of the nationalised National Freight Corporation) was regionalised into eight companies in 1972 under the Conservative government. Despite this, they continued to make losses, with the BRS Western and South Wales branches in particular performing badly.[113] This would have put a significant strain on the BRS depot at Cardiff to become profitable, and the capture of the Austral Metals lead traffic around this time would have been a significant boost to the company. It would also have been a major boost for the BRS depot at Cardiff, who in common with the other South Wales branches, did not like being managed from Bristol.[114]

The effective appointment of the BTDB as agents for Austral Metals for the lead traffic at the end of 1974 would have been worrying. As a nationalized company, BRS had become used to automatically receiving haulage contracts from the BTDB, and there was also an expectation amongst some BRS staff that haulage contracts would naturally come their way.[115] The effective use of the BTDB as agents could also have been considered as "interference" by some members of BRS, even though this was at the request of Austral Metals, and followed large increases in haulage rates from BRS for 1975. However, Quay Pak had been included on the tender list at Austral Metals request and had been awarded the contract at the start of 1975 as they had the lowest tender. Austral Metals were delighted with the savings they achieved following the tender process, and the service they received from Quay Pak

---

[113] Lewis, G. *Corporate strategy in action. The strategy process in British Road Services.* London. Routledge, 1988.

[114] Ibid.

[115] Aubrey had a heated meeting with Ron Irons in his office over haulage contracts when Ron Irons stated that as both BRS and the BTDB were both nationalised industries all haulage contracts should automatically come their way (see Hames, A. *Police interview.* 9 August, 1977).

was later described as "100% in all respects."[116] Under these circumstances, it is difficult to see how BRS could claim the tender process was unfair. In addition, their claim of collusion or similar between the BTDB (or more specifically Aubrey) and Lihu Ichilov would have been difficult to justify, as any interference in the tendering process would have been highlighted by several witnesses interviewed by the BT Police. This did not happen. In addition, no evidence was uncovered or presented at the court case to indicate that the loss and subsequent award of the Austral Metals lead traffic had not been just, and as already noted, the key witness in this case, Hubert Walsh, later expressed surprise that the inquiry had been pursued, let alone the court case.

The loss of the lead traffic to BRS can therefore only be considered as the natural consequence of a tendering process – and moreover, a process that might be considered to have been necessitated by BRS's own greed and complacency. Having said this, the significant and erratic inflation at the time – inflation that peaked at around 25% by 1975 – would have been the main driver for the large increase in BRS's charges.

The establishment of the transport consortium (that followed soon after the loss of the lead traffic) was another potentially serious blow to BRS, although the BTDB benefitted from an increased control of rates and the reduced risk of paying demurrage. The transport consortium also maintained the key interest of the BTDB in keeping importers and receivers of cargos happy. Glyn John Transport was seen as a long-term threat to BRS, and the inclusion of Quay Pak who had no road transport of their own at the time, was considered questionable by the investigating officers.[117,118] Yet, this was common practice for clearing houses and it is surprising that the investigating officers did not seem to be aware of this.[119] Combined with the recent loss of the lead traffic to Quay Pak, this may also have increased suspicions amongst BRS staff of a potential corrupt relationship between Aubrey and Lihu Ichilov, even though Freightliners and Glyn Jones Transport, the other two members of the consortium, raised no objections to Quay Pak's inclusion or to the establishment of the transport consortium.[120] These suspicions would

---

[116] Walsh, H. (undated) Police witness statement.

[117] Manners, D. *Police witness statement.* 8 November, 1977.

[118] Interview with Maurice Woodman. Former Det. Superintendent British Transport Police. 13 June, 2012.

[119] Several Interviews with Derek Mason, 2022.

[120] Stan Jones of Freightliners later sent a letter of support to Aubrey stating that he was pleased to see the outcome of the court case (Jones, S. Letter to Aubrey. 10 November, 1983).

also have intensified as Lihu Ichilov was well liked among members of the BTDB, and having known Aubrey for a number of years, had a good relationship with him.

However, there was no doubt that Quay Pak was a well-run and successful company that had been established at the instigation of the then Docks Manager John Williams in 1974 and had started to attract new trade to the port. Lihu Ichilov had been very successful in his previous position as the port representative of the CMBI, which was one of the biggest customers at Cardiff Docks.[121] Under his tenure, Jaffa imports into Cardiff increased from around 8,000 tons a year in 1967 to a peak of 83,000 tons by 1971.[122] This fact later persuaded Outspan to move their trade to Cardiff. In 1972, Ichilov had successfully taken over the role of transport coordinator for unloading by Tasfruits Proprietry Limited (TPL) – a company who later threatened to remove their trade from Cardiff Docks because of two disastrous unloadings by BRS.[123,124] However, the emergence of Quay Pak had not gone down well with everyone at Cardiff Docks, and there was a certain amount of jealousy linked to their success – particularly as their general efficiency limited the opportunity for overtime payments for clerical staff. Consequently, payments due to Quay Pak were often deliberately withheld for periods up to 5-6 months which was serious enough for a member of the General Cargo Office to be issued with a verbal warning by Aubrey as a result.[125,126,127] Lihu Ichilov also noted that after this, that this person became more aggressive and even suggested to potential clients that they should not use Quay Pak.[128] Now holding a prominent position in the community where he now lives, it is no surprise that this former member of the General Cargo Office did not want to talk to me about this book.

With the new trade that Quay Pak was bringing to Cardiff, combined with their potential and expertise as a transport coordinator, it is not surprising that they were a welcome addition to the transport consortium. As previously stated, only BRS raised any objections to their inclusion, and indeed, Quay Pak had maintained a very good relationship with Freightliners throughout their time at Cardiff Docks. The periodic access that they provided to the

---

[121] Wareham, R. *Police witness statement*. 10 January, 1978.

[122] This was the equivalent of about 6-10 oranges for every person in the UK.

[123] BTDB. Unsigned internal BTDB memorandum. 18 May, 1973.

[124] Ichilov, L. *Police interview*. 16 November, 1977.

[125] At times these amounted to £50,000-£60,000.

[126] HTV Wales. *Wales this week*. 24 March, 1983.

[127] Wareham, R. Letter to Lihu Ichilov. 31 December, 1975.

[128] Ichilov, L. *Police interview*. 16 November, 1977.

BTDB on private transport rates would have been invaluable, and Lihu Ichilov's belief at the time that he had been used by Aubrey to give him access to these rates was not evidence of an unhealthy relationship.[129]

The basis of the prosecution case and the corruption charge against Aubrey, was laid out in a letter from Michael Havers the Attorney General to Roy Hughes MP, in 1983. The case was brought on the basis that over a considerable period of time, "Mr Hames had abused his position as the Assistant Docks Manager at Cardiff to extend favourable treatment to Quay Pak in relation to the allocation of contracts and other ancillary matters."[130] However, the only evidence that they could uncover was the alleged free holiday in Israel and the potential charge of "utilizing accommodation owned by a relative."[131] Michael Havers now accepted that Aubrey had paid for this holiday, and had benefitted from travel tariffs that were available to anybody entering Israel at this time. As the Department of Public Prosecution's (DPP) decision to prosecute was fundamentally based on the fact that Lihu Ichilov had paid for this holiday, there were therefore no grounds for a corruption charge against Aubrey. Also, as this charge was considered the key charge, and the basis for the case, it would almost certainly not have reached court if the DPP had been in receipt of all the facts when the decision to prosecute was made.[132]

For the second charge of Aubrey's preferential treatment of Quay Pak which arose from the handling of the MV *Doryforos* – the defence revolved around the fact that the change in the contract was caused by the late arrival of the vessel. Despite the change in the contract, the BTDB were still contractually obliged to pay Quay Pak the agreed sums. The charge of the false rent being paid to Quay Pak was based on the BTDB auditor Edward Jordan's calculations. Jordan based his calculations on the basis of reduced tonnage in Quay Pak's warehouse as the cargo was cleared – and did not take account of the fact that a reducing tonnage was of no financial benefit to Quay Pak who had to pay the same warehousing costs regardless of how much cargo was stored. The argument against Aubrey also ignored the terms of the BTDB contract with Quay Pak. Indeed, Edward Jordan was unaware of the terms of the contract with Quay Pak, and he could not produce any documentary evidence at the court case to back up his claims that the BTDB had been over-charged. Ironically, had Aubrey sacked BRS and given their cargo of

---

[129] Interview with Lihu Ichilov HTV Wales, *Wales this Week*, 21 February, 1983.

[130] Havers, M. Letter to Roy Hughes MP. 29 April, 1983.

[131] Ibid.

[132] Ibid.

steel to Quay Pak, there may well have been no conspiracy charge. Quay Pak would have had a greater tonnage than they had contracted for, and the BTDB would possibly still have only paid Quay Pak £10,982.60 for four weeks warehousing. This for a greater tonnage than originally calculated would also have given the BTDB a greater profit. No transport co-ordination fees would have been paid, nor would there have been a damage claim for storing the steel in the open. There also would have been no aggrieved receiver. However, the consequent risk of someone fermenting labour trouble on the quayside was significant, and this would have added to the grievance of BRS, potentially adding more weight to the corruption charge.

Crucially, the claim that Quay Pak had overcharged was based on the settlement from Metal Enterprises for the steel coils – a settlement that Aubrey was alleged to have obtained for Quay Pak by deception or other dishonest means. However, the cheque dated 24th August 1977, had in fact been received and cleared in the BTDB accounts by 31st August. The reason for the discrepancy of Aubrey receiving this cheque in March 1977, yet a presumed re-issued cheque being cashed in August 1977 are not known. However, this would have had nothing to do with Aubrey or Lihu Ichilov – particularly bearing in mind that Aubrey had been on leave from the BTDB for 3 months by this time.

The Attorney General Michael Havers later accepted that the prosecution of conspiracy was incorrect but dismissed it as of minor relevance compared to the corruption charge.[133] Even though he stated that the prosecution would not have proceeded purely based on the conspiracy charge, his response later caused Isidore Rosen, Aubrey's solicitor in the aftermath of the case, to comment that he had "left it open as to whether or not the investigation was negligent."[134]

An independent review of the case by Simon Goldblatt QC and Christopher Llewellyn-Jones in March 1985 concluded that the investigation was "incompetently authorised" and "incompetently conducted."[135] They felt that the evidence given by Phillip Condliffe and Edward Jordan was false in respect of the MV *Doryforos* contract – especially in relation to Aubrey having received sums from Metal Enterprizes for Lihu Ichilov by deception or other dishonest means, when the BTDB had in fact already been paid. This they felt was incompetence on behalf of the BTDB. The fact that Aubrey had

---

[133] Ibid.

[134] Rosen, I. Letter to Aubrey. 11 May, 1983.

[135] Christopher Llewellyn-Jones was later a Judge, but at the time a recorder (essentially a part-time judge).

told the investigating officers, at an early stage of the investigation, that he had personally paid for the trip to Israel – would have been a simple fact to verify. The reviewers agreed that it should have been incumbent upon those concerned to find out who had paid for the holiday before a charge was laid. For the second charge (initially of conspiracy, subsequently reduced to deception), they stated that there was a welter of evidence dealing with the consortium arrangements, and that the invoices that Quay Pak raised in respect of the MV *Doryforos* cargo was money for which they were contractually entitled, and which was clearly stated as such in the invoices. They stated, "a charge which relied for its proof upon establishing beyond reasonable doubt that the terms of contract were other than what Quay Pak and Mr Ichilov asserted, was misconceived."

On the face of it, the evidence certainly suggests that the investigation was "incompetently conducted" – at the very least because no serious effort was made to establish if Aubrey had paid for the holiday to Israel – the key charge on which the whole prosecution case rested. Indeed, when I asked Maurice Woodman why he had not attempted to get hold of this cheque, he replied that he "did not think that it was important."[136] Yet Maurice Woodman was an extremely experienced investigating officer at this time with a knowledge of police procedure that was probably unmatched – so "incompetent" is not an adjective that accurately fits.[137] If not incompetent, this suggests that the investigation was carried out purely in pursuit of a conviction, regardless of the truth. However it is also perhaps unfortunate that at this point Aubrey's solicitor, Leo Abse, apparently refused permission for a second interview with Aubrey.[138]

Considering the evidence, or lack of evidence, against Aubrey and Lihu Ichilov, there was a belief that this case could have been politically motivated. Maurice Woodman stated that Aubrey would not have been charged if he had not been a politician – something that Aubrey had also suspected.[139] At the time of the police investigation, there had been several corruption trials involving prominent councillors both in South Wales and nationally. In 1977, Ernest Westwood, chairman of the Mid Glamorgan Planning Committee, was jailed for four-and-a-half years in the first major corruption trial at Cardiff and other corruption trials also resulted in jail sentences for local authority

---

[136] Interview with Maurice Woodman, 2012.
[137] Interview with Graham Satchwell, 2016.
[138] Interview with Maurice Woodman, 2012.
[139] Ibid.

leaders in South Wales.[140] The John Poulson affair, one of the biggest political scandals of the 1970s, had resulted in the former council leader of Newcastle City Council, T. Dan Smith, being jailed for corruption in 1974. This was probably the main factor leading to a certain level of McCarthyism against officials in local government. The similarities between T. Dan Smith and Aubrey, and their cases, would also have been difficult to ignore in this climate. T. Dan Smith was very prominent in the Labour Party in the North-East of England and known locally as "Mr Newcastle."[141] Aubrey at this time was the dominant personality in local government in Welsh politics and was known locally as "Mr Newport."[142,143] As Mayor of Newport and leader of Newport Borough Council – as well as having the reputation of being straight and incorruptible – the opportunity to secure a conviction against him, regardless of the truth, may have been difficult for opponents to resist.

The apparent tailoring of Hubert Walsh's statement to exclude his evidence on the lead traffic, as well as the apparent omission within Stan Jones' statement of BRS's attempts to squeeze Quay Pak out of business, certainly suggests that the police investigation's sole focus was to get a prosecution. Exhibits that would have hindered the prosecution case were also omitted as evidence, even though in some cases this evidence would have come from the same location as evidence that was submitted. This therefore raises the question as to whether Maurice Woodman and John Innes were guilty of something called "Misfeasance in Public Office" – which would have resulted in them facing criminal charges. In addition, it is known that despite John Williams of the BTDB being interviewed in early 1978, no statement from him was presented at the Magistrates Court.[144] This was probably because he made it clear in his interview that he felt that the allegations would be found to be untrue. At the time, there was no statutory requirement for the prosecution to disclose material that either undermined the prosecution case or assisted the defence. This lack of disclosure was not illegal as it is now, although it would still have been considered inappropriate.[145,146] Either way, the morality and reasoning of these decisions were then, as now, considered

---

[140] "Honeymoon fiddler jailed." *Daily Mirror.* 25 February, 1977.

[141] Foote-Wood, Chris. *T. Dan Smith, Voice of the North: Downfall of a Visionary*, 2010.

[142] Interview with Paul Flynn, 2012.

[143] Ironically Newport in Welsh is Casnewydd, meaning "New castle."

[144] Williams, J. Letter to Aubrey. 10 August, 1980.

[145] Hames, D. Email correspondence with John Jones, Head of Investigations Criminal Cases Review Commission. 9 May, 2018.

[146] Hames, D. Email correspondence with Graham Satchwell, former Chief Superintendent of the BT Police. 20 April, 2018.

highly questionable, as were the original leaks to the press.

Faced with what he felt was an incompetent investigation, and an ill-conceived prosecution, Aubrey understandably had little sympathy for the investigative team, in particular for Maurice Woodman and John Innes. He notoriously expected high standards of people in positions of authority. An accusation of corruption – something that he had successfully fought against with such vigour in local politics in his early career in Newport – would also have been deeply hurtful.

Over the next nine years, Aubrey maintained a sustained fightback against the police investigation and the BTDB, and explored every avenue to pursue court action – most noticeably against Maurice Woodman and John Innes, but also to fight for reinstatement to the BTDB. Central to Aubrey's complaints were that the police investigation was criminally incompetent, and that the British Transport Police may have been implicated with the BTDB in the criminal charges and his subsequent dismissal – possibly acting in collusion with the Managing Director of the BTDB, Keith Stuart.[147]

A complaint by Aubrey that one or more persons had unlawfully conspired to secure his wrongful dismissal from the BTDB was independently investigated by the South Wales Constabulary. This was investigated on the basis that factual information was falsified and given to the BT Police with the consequence that the Director of Public Prosecutions was misled into authorising a prosecution.[148] However, this complaint failed as, in Aubrey's own words, "I would say that I have no direct evidence to show that any particular individuals have criminally conspired against me to get me falsely charged with the offences for which I appeared before the court."[149]

Further complaints to Robert Reid, Chairman of British Rail, via Mark Robinson, the Conservative MP for Newport West, also drew a blank.[150] Robert Reid refused to entertain Aubrey's complaint against the BT Police despite the complaint being deemed his responsibility by the Attorney General, Michael Havers.[151] He stated that under the Police Complaints Procedure, the requirements to record a complaint under Section 49 of the Police Act (Public complaint), "does not extend to complaints about the general administration, efficiency or procedures of the force," which he

---

[147] Hames, A. Letter to Roy Hughes MP. 19 March, 1982.

[148] Reid, R. Letter to Mark Robinson MP. 1 March, 1984.

[149] BTP. Letter to Aubrey. 29 November, 1982.

[150] Several correspondences took place between Mark Robinson MP and Robert Reid over the first three months of 1984.

[151] Havers, M. Letter to Roy Hughes MP. 21 April, 1983.

felt was the basis of Aubrey's complaint. [152] Although Aubrey later clarified that his complaint was about the investigation, actions, and motives, of Maurice Woodman and John Innes, Robert Reid did not address this point, commenting, "it is maintained, and always has been, that the investigation of the allegations against Mr Hames and two others, was properly carried out,"[153,154] These statements astounded Graham Satchwell who said that this was not a matter for Robert Reid to adjudicate on, and he should have forwarded this to the Chief Constable of the BTP.[155] A further complaint about the police investigation – to the Parliamentary Commissioner Sir Cecil Clothier – was also unsuccessful as he had no powers to investigate the actions or decisions of the police force or the BTDB.

Despite Aubrey's failure to get what he felt was a proper investigation into the police charges and possible criminal incompetence, he did not give up. Three times Aubrey sought counsel's opinion on legal remedies in his case, and on at least two occasions drafted writs against the BTDB, and Maurice Woodman and John Innes. However, he was finally persuaded by counsel that any civil action against them would be vigorously defended and would be hopeless.

With all avenues in a British court exhausted, Aubrey's final action, in 1987, was to take his case to the European Court of Human Rights via his European MP Llewellyn Smith.[156] In his application to the European Court on 13th June 1987, he stated that his aim was "to clear my name and have the libellous scandalous allegations publicly expunged" and, "to have his complaint of misconduct of the BT Police recorded, thoroughly investigated, and properly dealt with, so that the Police Complaints Board may finally adjudicate, as provided for under the appropriate Police Acts." On 7th December 1987 his case of serious professional incompetence against Maurice Woodman and John Innes was discussed by the court. However, it was deemed inadmissible as it fell outside the time limit for considering these cases. This was within six months of the time when all legal avenues in his home country had been exhausted, which was considered to be his final complaint against the BT Police in July 1982.

---

[152] Reid, R. Letter to Mark Robinson MP. 9 January, 1984. This was a repeat of a letter previously sent to Aubrey, which was before Aubrey's letter of 01/02/84.

[153] Hames, A. Letter to Mark Robinson MP. 1 February, 1984.

[154] Reid, R. Letter to Mark Robinson MP. 31 October, 1983.

[155] Interview with Graham Satchwell, 2016.

[156] Smith, L. Letter to the Legal Officer of the European Commission. 14 October, 1986.

Grounds for dismissal

When Aubrey went on one year's leave of absence from the BTDB on 23rd May 1977, there was no reason to suggest that his performance as Assistant Docks Manager at Cardiff had (at worst) not been competent. Promotion in his early years in management at the South Wales ports had been rapid, and he had been offered two docks manager positions during his time at Cardiff. At the time that the investigation came to the attention of the BTDB, he was possibly the favoured candidate for the position of Docks Manager at Newport, which was due to become vacant in a few months' time. In addition, there had never previously been a single adverse comment on his performance as Assistant Docks Manager, and during his time in office, Cardiff Docks had been transformed from a heavy loss maker into a viable and profitable undertaking.

The police investigation into alleged corrupt practices at Cardiff Docks had been instigated via a complaint to the Prime Minister's Office, and whether based on factual evidence or personal grievance, the police would have been duty-bound to investigate it. This therefore prompted the special audit of the BTDB's accounts at Cardiff, which covered transactions between Quay Pak and the BTDB, as well as the cargo carried by the MV *Doryforos* and the Austral Metals lead traffic. As a result of this audit (completed on 27th October 1977), the recommendation from Keith Stuart, the managing director, was only a tightening up of management procedures at Cardiff Docks. There was no reason, at the time, to assume that any further action would be likely or necessary.

However, a year later, on 19th October 1978, the BTDB proceeded to issue formal disciplinary charges against Aubrey based on this audit. This, they stated, had nothing to do with the criminal proceedings even though the timing of these charges – in lieu of the pending court case – meant that Aubrey would not be able to answer them, and this was a fact that they would have been well aware of. With Aubrey away from his position of Assistant Docks Manager at Cardiff for 17 months, and in view of the upcoming court case, it was not clear if or when he was likely to return, and it was imperative that his position was filled. Delaying the disciplinary charges until after the BT Police had completed a criminal investigation and issued summonses, therefore made the case sub-judice and enabled the BTDB to dismiss Aubrey and fill his post. Based on the conclusion of the audit in October 1977, and the timing of the disciplinary charges a year later, it would be difficult to draw any other conclusion than that these two events were linked. John Williams, by now Port Director at Southampton, was certain this was the case.[157] This was also rather naively admitted by the South Wales Port Director, Ron Bury, in the Industrial Tribunal and was the conclusion of the Industrial Tribunal. In addition, Brian Harding who was the acting Assistant Docks Manager at Cardiff during Aubrey's absence was allegedly heard to say – as early as September 1977 – that "Aubrey Hames wouldn't be coming back to Cardiff." Other evidence though suggests that this statement might have been wishful thinking based on personal ambition or other reasons.[158]

Under these circumstances, it is not surprising that Aubrey's case and subsequent treatment created considerable anger and interest amongst several prominent individuals. Questions were raised in Parliament by several political figures including (the now ex-Prime Minister) James Callaghan, and Albert Booth who had been Secretary of State for Employment in James Callaghan's Cabinet.

Over a four year-period between 1979-1982, Albert Booth (Shadow Secretary of State for Transport) and Roy Hughes in particular, made sustained efforts to secure Aubrey's re-instatement – including repeated correspondence with officials from the BTDB. Finally, at a meeting with the Chairman of the BTDB, Sir Humphrey Browne, on 10th February 1982, they raised their objections to Aubrey's treatment, which he dismissed. Sir Humphrey Browne stated that the reasons for Aubrey's dismissal were unrelated to the criminal charges, and that he judged the Industrial Tribunal to be wrong. Norman Fowler, the then Secretary of State for Transport, much to Albert Booth's dissatisfaction, also refused to intervene as he had previously done in a letter to James Callaghan on 6th November 1979.[159,160,161] Albert Booth, clearly exasperated by his lack of success on the matter, expressed his dissatisfaction that he could do no more and apologised to Aubrey for the fact.[162]

Sir Humphrey Browne's comments regarding Aubrey's case were severely criticised by the former South Wales Ports Director, Tommy Roberts.

---

[157] A letter from John Williams to Aubrey dated 23/09/80 stated "have again checked from three different sources and I am certain that no action on any activity at Cardiff was commenced until after the BT Police began their investigation."

[158] The reference to this statement has been withheld to protect the source.

[159] Booth, A. Letter to Aubrey. 2 July, 1981.

[160] Fowler, N. Letter to Albert Booth MP, Shadow Secretary of State for Transport. 8 June, 1981.

[161] The reply by Norman Fowler to James Callaghan had been forwarded to Tommy Roberts by Ruth Sharpe, James Callaghan's Private Secretary. Tommy Roberts was very scathing of the comments in this letter.

[162] Booth, A. Letter to Aubrey. 22 February, 1982.

Roberts was forwarded a letter about the case from Norman Fowler to James Callaghan in which Norman Fowler had quoted Sir Humphrey Browne. Tommy Roberts referred to one of Sir Humphrey Browne's comments as "one of the most contradictory statements I've ever read" and another as "comical."[163] It was clear from Tommy Roberts' reply that he had little respect for Sir Humphrey Browne. This probably stemmed from his time as chairman of the National Coal Board when Browne, in 1966, kept an engagement to be invested as the first chancellor of Surrey University rather than drop everything to visit the scene of the Aberfan disaster.[164]

On 22nd September 1980, having not had the opportunity to officially reply to the charges laid against him by the BTDB, Aubrey replied in detail to these charges in a letter to Ron Bury. This happened with the encouragement of Ron Bury's predecessor as South Wales Port Director – John Williams.[165,166] In his reply (dated 30th September 1980), Ron Bury refused to enter into any further correspondence on the matter.

However, with all political efforts failing for Aubrey's re-instatement, the media now stepped in. On 24th March 1983, a *Wales this Week* documentary was aired on HTV Wales about Aubrey and Lihu Ichilov's case after a 5-month investigation. This was the biggest case ever covered (at the time) by HTV Wales and uncovered certain (now unknown) facts that could not be disclosed due to fears of potential libel.[167,168] Not surprisingly, the BTDB refused to co-operate with the documentary and both Keith Stuart and Ron Bury refused to be interviewed. Senior staff at the BTDB were also warned that they would be subject to disciplinary action if they talked to the documentary team.[169] On the same day as the documentary aired, Roy Hughes, together with the Cardiff North East MP Ian Grist, called on the government to hold a public inquiry into this case.

Not surprisingly, Aubrey was never re-instated as Assistant Docks Manager at Cardiff, and the BTDB never responded in any positive way to the many letters and meetings with the media and the many Parliamentary members

---

[163] Roberts, T. Letter/note from Tommy Roberts. 17 December, 1979. It is believed this letter/note was sent to Ruth Sharpe, James Callaghan's constituency secretary.

[164] King, R. *Brittle with relics: a history of Wales 1962-1997.* London. Faber, 2022.

[165] Williams, J. Letter to Aubrey. 10 August, 1980.

[166] Williams, J. Letter to Aubrey. 23 September, 1980.

[167] Interview with Bruce Kennedy, HTV Wales researcher for *Wales this Week.* 27 June, 2012.

[168] Ibid.

[169] HTV Wales. *Wales this week.* 24 March, 1983.

who asked questions on Aubrey's behalf. In 2012, I asked Keith Stuart, who was now Sir Keith Stuart, for an interview. He refused, stating that he had no recollection of specific details of the events. A further request to interview him about accusations made about him by Aubrey at the time was also refused for the same reason and the additional request to interview him about general management procedures at the BTDB at the time was ignored. Despite the 30-35 years between the events of 1977-1983 and 2012, it is nevertheless surprising that Keith Stuart struggles to remember any specific details. 1977 was the first year of Keith Stuart's position as managing director of the BTDB (at the rather young age of 37) and this case, involving a very senior member of the BTDB, made national headlines and was possibly the biggest scandal ever faced by the BTDB. Over the next 6 years, questions were asked in Parliament by an ex-Prime Minister, and a one-hour television documentary was made which would have made for uncomfortable viewing for his organisation. He may indeed not remember specific details with the passage of time, however, having refused to be interviewed by the Wales this Week documentary team in 1983, it would also be reasonable to assume that he would refuse in 2012 – particularly as it was Aubrey's son who was asking for the interview. The passing of a further 30 years could also provide a convenient excuse for someone who was later to be described as "an expert at being economical with the truth."[170]

Conclusions and aftermath

The evidence drawn from the court case as well as from the Industrial Tribunal suggests that Aubrey, as well as Lihu Ichilov and Derek Mason, were falsely and unfairly accused. The investigation, as Simon Goldblatt QC and Christopher Llewellyn-Jones concluded in March 1985, appeared to be incompetently conducted. However, I now believe that there were reasons for this that were not understood at the time, and that have only recently come to light. The prosecutor's case was described at the time by Philip Thomas (now Professor Thomas) of the Cardiff Law School, as worthless. And Thomas further commented that the treatment of Derek Mason in particular was unique.[171]

The accusations made by BRS were almost certainly as a result of a perceived injustice – and were probably driven more by the gradual erosion of their once dominant position in the transport world within the National

---

[170] Feickert, D. *Britain's civil war over coal: An Insider's view*. Cambridge. Cambridge Scholars Publishing, 2021.

[171] HTV Wales. *Wales this week.* 24 March, 1983.

Freight Corporation rather than any substantive reason. BRS accused Aubrey of fixing haulage rates for the benefit of Quay Pak, yet four different BRS employees admitted that they had access to confidential rates quoted by other hauliers.[172] This leak of information almost certainly occurred via a certain member of the General Cargo Office at Cardiff Docks, with whom Horace Yates of BRS was friendly and who, like Yates, had a dislike for Lihu Ichilov. Based on this confidential information they set, or "fixed" their rates accordingly. In addition, Horace Yates and other employees of BRS would often ask to re-quote for haulage if they did not get the work – a policy encouraged by the Managing Director of BRS at the time.[173,174] Ron Irons' claim that he had proof that the Hames' holiday to Israel had been paid for by Lihu Ichilov never emerged, nor did any evidence of whether there was any link between this and the break-in at Quay Pak's offices. As a result, the special audit carried out by the BTDB in October 1977 had clearly indicated that there were no discrepancies or irregularities in any transactions between Quay Pak and the BTDB – and therefore between Aubrey and Lihu Ichilov. This should have been the end of the matter for the BTDB as well as the BT Police.

Aubrey's absence from the BTDB for his mayoral year however undoubtedly caused some friction at management level within the BTDB. In mid-1976, with one week's notice, leave for BTDB management staff for public service had been reduced from 40 days to 20 days – a decision that caused Aubrey to withdrawn from Gwent County Council. In his early years in management, it had also been made clear to Aubrey that his service as a councillor would not enhance his career prospects, and as a result he withdrew from public service for a while.

Aubrey's absence from his position as Assistant Docks Manager at Cardiff for his mayoral year was therefore probably not looked on favourably by many at the BTDB headquarters – as well as possibly by one or two members at Cardiff Docks. His prolonged absence as a result of the court case could therefore have been seen as the final straw. The decision to dismiss him – almost certainly on Keith Stuart's instruction – and possibly based on discussions with Ray Wareham – was clearly based on business rather than performance reasons. This was the conclusion drawn by the Industrial Tribunal. Aubrey's comment after the court case was perhaps more telling in

---

[172] This was contained in the police witness statements of Brian Anthoney, David Manners, Michael Tilley and Ron Irons.

[173] Hames, A. *Police interview*. 9 August, 1977.

[174] Lewis, G., 1988.

terms of future industrial relations at the time: "The implications of this case are serious for local management at the South Wales ports. No manager can now be fully assured that his commercial judgment will not be the subject of malicious innuendo or slander, to be seized upon by the Docks Board in London as justification for a BT Police investigation."[175]

The behaviour of certain members of the BTDB before, during, and after the investigation can only be described as poor at best, and criminal at worst. Aubrey's role as Assistant Docks Manager was to protect the BTDB traders against large haulage costs which were greater than the established or published rates for the Cardiff area. He understood the necessity for increases in haulage costs to be kept to a minimum to safeguard against possible switches from Cardiff to cheaper ports. And the establishment of the transport consortium was seen as a positive move by the traders.[176] Evidence from internal BTDB memorandums at this time indicate that he had the full support of the Cardiff Docks Manager, Ray Wareham, in this respect. However, in his police statement, Ray Wareham distanced himself from the transport consortium and the dealings with the MV *Doryforos*.[177] This is despite it being clear (for example) that he was fully aware of the warehousing arrangements for the MV *Doryforos* and indeed approved the advance payment of £5,898.60 to Quay Pak.[178] His claim in his police statement that he would not have authorised this advance payment had he known the actual warehousing costs to Quay Pak also appears contradictory. The request for advance payment was caused by the BTDB's current and overdue debt to Quay Pak of over £28,000 (about 20% of Quay Pak's annual income from the BTDB) and less than a year earlier he had written a letter of apology to Lihu Ichilov about continued late payment of invoices.[179] Ray Wareham's witness statement also noticeably omits mention of his frequent absences from work due to illness, and the fact that the Port Director never felt it necessary to appoint a temporary replacement during these times. In fact, evidence presented in Ray Wareham's witness statement presents, at best, a neutral viewpoint of Aubrey's dealings with the transport consortium and the MV *Doryforos*, yet coincidently strong leadership, or ignorance, on his part when convenient. On the other hand, in Ray Wareham's defence, it cannot be discounted that his statement may have been tailored to suit the BT

---

[175] "£11,655 award for sacked docks man." *Western Mail*. 25 July, 1979.

[176] Walsh, H. Letter to Isidore Rosen (solicitor). 16 November, 1983.

[177] Wareham, R. *Police witness statement*. 10 January, 1978.

[178] Wareham, R. Confidential memorandum to N.F. Copeland, BTDB accountant Cardiff. 20 December, 1976.

[179] Wareham, R. Letter to Lihu Ichilov. 17 December, 1975.

Police case – as appeared to be the case for the statements made by Hubert Walsh and Stan Jones. In addition, it appears strange that no police statements appear to exist for either John Williams or Tommy Roberts – who at the time and subsequent to this investigation expressed strong support for Aubrey. This is particularly true in the case of John Williams who was interviewed at least once by the BT Police and (from Aubrey's police interview) it was clear that they were as interested in John Williams' relationship with Lihu Ichilov as they were in Aubrey's.[180]

When Aubrey first heard about the allegations against him in around 1975, Tommy Roberts told him to ignore them as these were common in the transport world at the time. It would therefore be reasonable to assume that the BTDB would have supported Aubrey unless there was any evidence that the allegations were true. Despite this, the BTDB's response, when Aubrey's absence from the BTDB became difficult for them, was to sack him. Perhaps the worst behaviour of all was demonstrated by the Chairman of the BTDB Sir Humphrey Browne. Browne's attitude and response to Aubrey's case exasperated Albert Booth, a man described by Tam Dalyell (a former Father of the House) as "the most principled politician of my time in the House of Commons."[181] Sir Humphrey Browne's attitude towards Aubrey's case also clearly angered Tommy Roberts.

The Police investigation – driven by the incorrect belief that it had been initiated by the Prime Minister James Callaghan himself – gave little regard to any evidence that would indicate that Aubrey and Lihu Ichilov were innocent. The suggestion that the investigation had been initiated by James Callaghan, rather than some anonymous civil servant, also caused some discomfort to James Callaghan, who knew Aubrey well and later apologised to him.[182] These factors, combined with the initial leaking of the story to the Daily Mail does not indicate a fair and just investigation.

Following his dismissal from the BTDB, Aubrey made considerable efforts to secure another post and applied for managerial positions all over the UK. However, possibly because of a combination of his age and his recent history with the BTDB (which he did not hide from any job application) he never secured another position. His sole income from 1979 until drawing his BTDB pension in 1988 was therefore a basic council allowance as a member

---

[180] Williams, J. Letter to Aubrey. 10 August, 1980.

[181] "Albert Booth," Obituary. *The Independent.* 11 February, 2010. Available at: https://www.independent.co.uk/news/obituaries/albert-booth-principled-labour-mp-who-served-as-secretary-of-state-under-james-callaghan-1895853.html.

[182] Callaghan, J. Letter to Aubrey. 9 September, 1980.

of Newport Borough Council as well as interest and capital from his savings and shares.

The accusations and court case also left its scars. Despite the significant support that he and his family had been given both before and after the court case, there would always be the belief among some people that there couldn't be any smoke without fire. He admitted that occasional, and probably innocent, comments along the lines of "I see you got away with it," were hurtful. Similar comments were also made against Derek Mason, although always behind his back.[183] Sometimes, these were made by people unaware that a member of their family was in earshot, as happened to me and Derek Mason's son.

In addition, at the time of the case, there were occasions when Aubrey was excluded from certain functions.[184] His political career suffered, with the accusations contributing, at least in part, to his failure to get the Labour nomination for the Newport West Parliamentary seat in 1983, as well as the South Wales East seat for the European Parliament in 1984. Other events and people also suffered indirectly as a result. For example, several years after the court case, port officials at ABP Newport (BTDB were renamed Associated British Ports (ABP) after privatisation in 1981) suddenly withdrew (just as the contract was about to be signed) sponsorship of the Newport International Piano competition when Aubrey's name as leader of the council was mentioned.

As for Lihu Ichilov, Quay Pak gradually became isolated from port trade at Cardiff (apart from the lead traffic that they were getting directly from Austral Metals). Their last job for the BTDB was on 13th December 1977, after which Bernard Pearson, the new BTDB Manager at Cardiff, wrote to Quay Pak informing them that they were no longer an accredited haulage firm. Lihu Ichilov took little part in Quay Pak business during 1978 with back trouble and the court case taking up most of his time, and during this time the company was kept going by Mike Spear the Quay Pak manager. With the loss of trade from the BTDB, and in an attempt to keep Quay Pak going, Lihu Ichilov stopped drawing wages in January 1980 and survived instead on family assistance. However, Quay Pak could not survive, and this once thriving dockside business finally went into voluntary liquidation in August 1980, with some bills from the BTDB still not paid after several years. At its height, Quay Pak had a turnover of about £350,000 a year and employed 25 people.

---

[183] Several Interviews with Derek Mason, 2022.
[184] HTV Wales. *Wales this week.* 24 March, 1983

HOUSE OF COMMONS
LONDON SW1A OAA

From:

The Rt. Hon. James Callaghan, M.P.   30th May, 1980.

Dear Roy

      Thank you for your letter of 21st May about
Aubrey Hames. It seems to me that he did have a
raw deal, but I did not initiate this matter. It
only came to me because Mr. Roberts, who was the
former Chief Docks Manager of the South Wales Ports,
asked me to look into it and I did so, but from now
on I think it would be far better if you were to take
over the issue and see if there is anything further
that can be done.

      I would be grateful if you would contact
Aubrey Hames, who wrote to me again on 17th May,
and indicate to him that you are ready to do so.

      As regards the suggestion that I was responsible,
as Prime Minister, for initiating police enquiries,
that is, of course, rubbish. Prime Ministers do not
instigate enquiries of that sort.

Yours sincerely
Jim Callaghan

Roy Hughes, Esq., M.P.

*Letter to Roy Hughes from the then ex-Prime Minister James Callaghan,
refuting the suggestion that he was personally responsible for initiating
enquires into Aubrey's case while he was Prime Minister.*

200

HOUSE OF COMMONS
LONDON SW1A OAA

From:

The Rt. Hon. James Callaghan, M.P.   9 September 1980

PERSONAL

Dear Mr. Hames

    Mrs. Sharpe showed me your letter of 26 August and I thought I would reply to you direct.

    I am very sorry to hear that we are supposed to be responsible for the beginning of the police enquiries. Mrs. Sharpe has looked through our constituency records and cannot trace any correspondence of this sort. As you may know, she keeps a complete record of all letters from Cardiff South East.

    Of course, if the letter had arrived from another part of Cardiff or from Newport, then it would not have been dealt with by her by by the general correspondence section at No. 10. As you know, when I was there we received over 1,000 letters every month from the public, and such a letter would have been dealt with by one of the correspondence clerks in that section. I have made some enquiries but no record can be found of the receipt of such a letter.

    I am very sorry that neither Mrs. Sharpe nor I can help.

Yours sincerely

Jim Callaghan

A. Hames, Esq.
56 Western Avenue
Newport, Gwent

Letter to Aubrey from ex-Prime Minister James Callaghan apologising for No. 10 Downing Street apparently being responsible for initiating enquires into Aubrey's case.

Finding it difficult to work in this country, Lihu Ichilov and his family finally emigrated to America to start a new life. Before he left, Ichilov tried to bring a case of malicious prosecution and defamation against the BTDB but this was dropped because he was advised that the BTDB would fight any case made against it – and he probably would have had all costs awarded against him if he lost. As for Derek Mason, he had moved on from Quay Pak by the time the case came to court and he deliberately worked away from the area as much as possible when the case hit the papers. This was to avoid the presumption of guilt from some people, including from his own father.[185] Interestingly, despite his clear recognition of all the characters involved in the court case when I interviewed him, the one name he didn't recognise was the man who led the investigation, Maurice Woodman. No member of the BT Police ever talked to him; when he appeared in court, he was never asked a question, and nobody ever told him why he had been charged; it goes without saying, that nobody ever said sorry.[186]

Finally, there was one amusing event to come out of the charges against Aubrey, and this came towards the end of his term as Mayor of Newport in May 1978. When Aubrey was due to award the Freedom of Newport to the 104th Light Defence Regiment, Royal Artillery (Volunteers), several BTDB employees at Cardiff were due to be invited. As Aubrey had been advised by Keith Stuart not to contact anybody at Cardiff Docks while the internal investigation was ongoing, Aubrey's wife Mary sent the invites via Ray Wareham. However, in her letter she pointed out that if anybody from the BTDB turned up, then the host (Aubrey) would not be able to attend the ceremony. Ron Bury, replying on Ray Wareham's behalf, was clearly not impressed with the letter. He returned the invites asking for them to be sent directly to the people involved under the circumstances.[187] Aubrey possibly had little idea of this correspondence between Ron Bury and his wife. Mary certainly enjoyed mischief-making and would have enjoyed the (admittedly slight) discomfort caused to Ron Bury by this incident.

Postscript

When I started this chapter in 2011, early on, amongst the thousands of pages of correspondence, including minutes of meetings, police interviews and various court papers, I came across a document written by Aubrey that gave a detailed background to the case. This document formed the basis of the

---

[185] Several Interviews with Derek Mason, 2022.
[186] Ibid.
[187] Bury, R. Letter to Mary Hames. 12 May, 1978.

first of many drafts of this chapter, which was then re-written and added-to as more details were untangled.

Crucial to this document was evidence to back up the statements he made. Initially, before examining this evidence, I removed much detail that Aubrey had included that seemed to me too subjective and far-fetched. Ultimately however, as I began to explore the evidence, nearly everything that I had removed found its way back. Nothing I could find the evidence for was untrue, and I had no reason to disbelieve the few things that I could not find the evidence for.

One crucial aspect for which I could find no evidence was Aubrey's belief that the BT Police had been criminally incompetent and that they may have acted in collusion with the BTDB. My initial thoughts were that the investigation was clearly incompetent (with evidence suppressed, statements tailored, and crucial evidence that could undermine the prosecution not submitted or obtained) but despite this, as previously mentioned, there was, at the time, no statutory requirement for the prosecution to disclose material that either undermined their case or assisted the defence. As for any collusion between Maurice Woodman and Keith Stuart, it was unlikely that there would be any written evidence of this, even if I could find it. John Innes had died some years before I started this research, and when I talked to Maurice Woodman, I never would have asked these questions. There was also the small matter that I was unprepared for the interview with him because he rang me unexpectedly; his interview was therefore carried out with no preparation on my part and the only one that was carried out on the phone (aside from the ones undertaken during the pandemic). As for Keith Stuart, he was decent in replying to my emails, but he had no interest in talking to me or answering any questions. Other evidence might have come from people who worked with Keith Stuart or people from the BT Police who either worked on, or knew of, the investigation. However, of the many letters and emails that I sent out, only Keith Stuart and Maurice Woodman replied. Much of this correspondence may have gone to the wrong person, or to individuals who were unable to respond for good reason, but I know from talking to Maurice Woodman and Graham Satchwell that many current and former members of the BT Police did not want anybody to talk to me. Some even actively conspired to stop people talking to me. Without doubt, this was to protect the institution of the BT Police for reasons outlined below. As for the BTDB, as well as BRS, it was more difficult to find and identify who to talk to, and generally those involved were a lot older and therefore less likely to still be around; but many who were around did not respond and at least one person deliberately made efforts to hinder my research.

The fact that Aubrey took his complaints against Maurice Woodman and John Innes to the European Court of Human Rights suggested that it was still appropriate to look for evidence for wrongdoing by the BT Police – and Maurice Woodman and John Innes in particular – as well as Keith Stuart. Consequently, every few months I carried out speculative searches for something based either on a hunch or something I had heard or read. Many of these searches highlighted the frightening levels of corruption in many of the police forces in London in the 1970s, as well as the (usually successful) attempts to hush them up – usually by moving the relevant individual police officers to different positions, pensioning them off, or asking them to resign rather than face a criminal prosecution. For several years, I came across nothing related to the BT Police and their activities in the 1970s, let alone Maurice Woodman and John Innes. All I found in relation to Keith Stuart was a chance discovery of a newspaper article in 1976 where he uniquely singled out the boost that the citrus trade received via Cardiff Docks – trade that had been made possible by Lihu Ichilov.[188]

However, this started to change in November 2016 when the latest speculative search turned up an autobiography of Graham Satchwell, who worked with Maurice Woodman, and was later to serve as the most senior investigative officer with the BT Police. This was the same post that Maurice Woodman held at the time he investigated Aubrey's case. I contacted Graham Satchwell, and he was more than happy to meet me as well as to read the draft of this chapter as it was at the time.

This meeting with Graham proved to be invaluable. Not only did it enable me to find out more about the personalities of Maurice Woodman and John Innes, but it also gave me the opportunity to question someone who served as a senior investigative officer of the BT Police around the time of Aubrey's case. The fact that Graham Satchwell offered to read what I had written also gave me the unexpected opportunity to gain the perspective of someone who knew the investigative officers but did not know Aubrey. Graham felt that the conclusions I had drawn from the evidence presented were logical, and crucially, that the investigation had been incompetently carried out. A couple of years later, Graham Satchwell also discussed this case informally with John Jones, Head of Investigations of the Criminal Cases Review Commission. Subsequentially this gave me the opportunity to talk to John Jones and to identify specific details of the law as it stood at the time of Aubrey's case.

Then, on 5th December 2019, four men who had received prison sentences of two years in November 1972, for assaulting BT Police officers and for

---

[188] "Optimism as docks future brightens." *South Wales Argus*. 1 July, 1976.

attempted theft, saw their convictions quashed by the Court of Appeal. The following day, one of these men, Winston Trew, who had led the campaign to overturn these convictions, and who had written a book on the case, was interviewed on BBC Breakfast News. Watching this interview, I became interested in Winston Trew's case; it was the first evidence that I had come across of serious corruption in the BT Police in the 1970s.

Winston Trew's book, together with the various newspaper reports of his case, known as the "Oval 4", brought my attention to a certain corrupt detective by the name of Derek Ridgewell.[189] Derek Ridgewell's modus operandi was to dress in plain clothes and to confront primarily young black men and falsely accuse them of theft. If they resisted arrest, he or members of his team would assault them, and make up false confessions which he would force them to sign. If they refused, they would be repeatedly beaten until they signed. Several young men ended up in prison in the 1970s as a result – convicted of spurious charges that were only being quashed in the Court of Appeal forty or more years later. Indeed, the day before I started this postscript, another one of his cases, known as the Stockwell Six, was quashed.[190]

Although Winston Trew's book introduced me to the corrupt activities of certain officers in the BT Police in the 1970s, it did not at the time provide me with any further details that I could link to Aubrey's case. With a bit of lateral thinking on my part, I might have realised who Derek Ridgewell's boss was, but this was to be revealed after Winston Trew's second book was published. This book, *Rot at the Core*, was written in collaboration with Graham Satchwell, and much of the material in this postscript is based upon this book as well as on a further interview carried out with Graham Satchwell in December 2021 and on follow-up correspondence.

I was probably one of the first people to be aware of Graham Satchwell's new book, as he emailed me in March 2021 to tell me that he had a new book out about police corruption in the BT Police in the 1970s, and would I like a copy when it was published. This book, published in May 2021, and based on extensive investigations, gave a detailed account of Derek Ridgewell's activities as a member of the BT Police. Almost from his first day as a probationary police officer he had demonstrated his dishonesty. He then left for a spell in South Africa and was, perhaps surprisingly, allowed to rejoin the BT Police a year later despite that fact that it was well known he could not be trusted. Despite his reputation, he was treated favourably

---

[189] Trew, W. *Black for a cause... not just because.* 2021.
[190] "Stockwell Six: Three men have 1972 convictions quashed by Court of Appeal." *BBC News.* 6 July, 2021. Available at: https://www.bbc.co.uk/news/uk-england-london-57735027.

by his senior officers and was soon promoted to a uniform sergeant who acted as supervisor to other police officers. In this role, he was unpredictable and violent, and not adverse to administering a severe beating to any police constable under his control that he took a dislike to. It is this role that enabled him to undertake the crimes that he has now become well-known for; fitting up innocent members of the public, usually young black men, for crimes that didn't exist and had no victims. As noted, many of these were subsequentially overturned as a miscarriage of justice and it is believed that he is responsible for more miscarriages of justice cases than any other police officer in British history.[191] But Ridgewell did not work on his own – many other members of the BT Police force took part in these acts. Many were willing to take part when they heard of his reputation for "fitting up" young black men. Others were framed with false evidence of corruption, to be exposed if they refused to take part in his activities or threatened to expose him.

This period of Derek Ridgewell's life in the BT Police was to end in 1973 when a case involving two Jesuit students from Oxford University was halted by the judge who felt that the evidence of the police could not be trusted. Despite concerns raised by, among others, the National Council for Civil Liberties (now Liberty) and the Labour spokesman on race, John Fraser MP, the response to the embarrassment caused to the BT Police was to promote Derek Ridgewell to the role of Detective Sergeant, and to move him to a new role in the detection of parcel and mail thieves, working primarily at the Bricklayers Arms depot.[192] It was here that Derek Ridgewell's criminality probably reached a peak. The detection of parcel and mail thieves increased, innocent people were charged for crimes mainly carried out by Derek Ridgewell and his team; the CID office at the Bricklayers Arms depot was full of stolen property. Stolen items were then disposed of by local villains working with Derek Ridgewell, sometimes with a police escort. By the time he was finally arrested in 1978, he was probably involved in organised thefts of goods from heavy goods vehicles across London, and evidence obtained from the CID offices at the Bricklayers Arms depot indicated that he was planning to move into armed robberies.

It is astonishing that Derek Ridgewell was allowed to operate to this level of criminality under the umbrella of a police officer for more than a decade, and it begs the questions as to why nothing was done sooner, and who was

---

[191] A real Line of duty: the London police officer who 'went bent.'" *The Guardian.* "1 May, 2021. Available at: https://www.theguardian.com/uk-news/2021/may/01/a-real-line-of-duty-the-london-police-officer-who-went-bent.
[192] Hall, S., Critcher, C., Jefferson, T., Clarke, J. and Roberts, B. *Policing the crisis: Mugging, the state and law and order.* London. Bloomsbury, 2013.

ultimately responsible for allowing him to continue. The answer to the first question is difficult to answer, and not the purpose of this chapter, but the second question is a lot easier; it was Maurice Woodman. Others were implicated to different degrees including John Innes as Maurice Woodman's deputy, as well as Roger Mayers, who was also part of the investigation team in Aubrey's case. It is possible that the other two (unknown) members investigating Aubrey's case were also implicated.

When Derek Ridgewell rejoined the BT Police in December 1965, he already knew Maurice Woodman and when he was promoted to an attachment at CID Headquarters of the BT Police three years later, he was managed by Maurice Woodman, who was a Detective Inspector at this time. This promotion, which included a key role in investigating corrupt detectives, was surprising considering the reasons for his unpopularity amongst many police officers who had previously worked with him. However, this seemed to carry little weight with the senior police officers. Indeed, when he got married in 1973, Maurice Woodman was best man at Ridgewell's wedding.[193] At this time, it was unheard of for a Detective Inspector, or other senior officer, to be best man at a very junior officer's wedding. Maurice Woodman was his boss when he started fitting up young, usually black, men for non-existent crimes on the London Underground. Woodman was also his boss when Ridgewell lost a case known as the Waterloo Four in April 1972 because the judge felt that he and the other officers involved could not be trusted – yet no action was taken against him. Four months later, when a trial known as the Tottenham Two was halted by the judge who saw the two people on trial as innocent victims of Derek Ridgewell's unethical police methods, his punishment (as noted earlier) was to be promoted to a Detective Sergeant by Maurice Woodman.

Following his promotion to investigate the detection of parcel and mail thieves, and the corresponding marked increase in the occurrence of parcel and mail theft, his boss, Maurice Woodman, did not note or want to note this as suspicious, and if any suspicions were raised, they were clearly suppressed.

In 1976, Maurice Woodman became a Detective Chief Superintendent, and head of CID. A year later he was in charge of the investigation into Aubrey's case at the same time as one of his officer's was arguably the most corrupt police officer of 1970's Great Britain, and while at least a dozen other of his officers were involved in well-established and organised thefts from the Bricklayers Arms Depot (the proceeds of the latter to Ridgewell

---

[193] Derek Ridgewell appears to have been married at least three times by his early 20s, although no wedding certificate for any of his marriages can be found.

alone are estimated to be at least £1 million).[194] Some officers under Maurice Woodman's control were blackmailed to either take part in these robberies or to keep quiet about them. They were typically blackmailed by planting stolen goods on them which Derek Ridgewell would make sure they handled for fingerprints. Yet in Maurice Woodman's eyes, Derek Ridgewell could seemingly do no wrong.

When Derek Ridgewell was arrested in 1978, the investigation was led by the head of CID, his friend Maurice Woodman, assisted by John Innes and someone called John Parker. He was ultimately caught when his criminal associates filmed him and his officers removing lorry loads of goods after they had a falling out, and under these circumstances it was probably impossible for Maurice Woodman to protect him any longer. However, several senior police officers still urged Maurice Woodman not to investigate the case too closely, and ultimately only junior officers were charged and convicted. Only junior officers faced internal disciplinary proceedings, and only junior officers were required to resign. No officer above the rank of Sergeant was ever accused or sanctioned.

Maurice Woodman was a very intelligent man, and there is little doubt that he was aware (at least to a degree) of Derek Ridgewell's criminal activities during his time on the BT Police. Whether it was a friendship, a desire to protect the reputation of the BT Police, a combination of the two, or some other reason, there is no doubt that Maurice Woodman's actions, or lack of them, allowed Derek Ridgewell's activities to flourish. Ridgewell's actions led to several young innocent men being sent to prison with the resultant loss of their freedom, livelihoods, and dignity. Woodman's investigation of Derek Ridegwell, and the resultant action only against junior officers, was (at its politest) negligent. A thorough investigation should have identified several senior officers in connection with Derek Ridgewell's crimes, and the investigation should have been carried out by an outside body rather than by Woodman himself (although he would have made sure that this didn't happen).

As for John Innes, he was also likely aware of the crimes as he was Maurice Woodman's deputy. Even though he was not primarily responsible for

---

[194] Corruption in the Metropolitan Police and the City of London Police was endemic in the 1970s. This resulted in Sir Robert Mark, Commissioner of the Metropolitan Police from 1972 to 1977, to famously say that he wanted to "arrest more criminals than we employ." As a result, under his tenure as commissioner, 478 police officers retired early, and 50 officers were prosecuted. A later investigation known as Operation Countryman resulted in further resignations and prosecutions, but no criminal convictions, mainly due to the deliberate obstructions put in place by many members of the police service.

protecting Derek Ridgewell, he, like Woodman, took no action when Derek Ridgewell's activities were revealed and failed in his duty as a serving police officer to report these crimes. In the case of Roger Mayers, he was part of Derek Ridgewell's team when a teenager by the name of Stephen Simmons was arrested and sent to Borstal for 8 months in 1976 for mailbag theft. At the trial, Roger Mayers made a potentially spurious statement that if known about at the time may have resulted in him serving a prison sentence instead of being free to investigate Aubrey's case; he was the only police officer directly involved in the case of Stephen Simmons who did not end up going to prison for corruption.[195] Simmons' sentence was another of Derek Ridgewell's cases that was quashed by the Court of Appeal, in 2018 – over 40 years after he was convicted.

It is easy to see why Aubrey believed that Maurice Woodman and John Innes were criminally incompetent; it should have been clear early on in their investigation that there was no case to answer. The question to be asked therefore is why did they pursue an investigation when (as in the Derek Ridgewell cases) they knew no crime had been committed? And ultimately, why did they charge Aubrey, Lihu Ichilov and Derek Mason? Evidence from the operations of the BT Police and Maurice Woodman's career in the force, does reveal some clues.

Maurice Woodman joined the police force in Bristol in 1951 and became a detective the following year at the age of 23. This was remarkable progress, and with progress in the police force typically linked to arrests, it is likely that he had a very high and successful arrest record. As already stated, he was a clever and determined detective, and this may explain his initial rapid rise through the ranks. However, unsubstantiated rumours in the latter part of his career – that some convictions were secured via dubious means – meant that many officers mistrusted him. That he was very proud of his police record, and keen to be seen as successful, became clear when I interviewed him in 2012. During the interview, he claimed that Aubrey's case was the only case he had ever lost – something that was later established to be untrue.[196] Other claims about the number of successful prosecutions that he had been involved in were also dismissed as significant exaggeration by Graham Satchwell. There is no evidence that Maurice Woodman was corrupt from a

---

[195] Mayer, R. Witness statement in Stephen Simmons case. 6 June. There is reason to believe that this statement was written by a third party, probably Derek Ridgewell, which was then signed by Roger Mayers, 1975.

[196] The first case aside from Aubrey's that I could find that involved Maurice Woodman was from 1961, where a youth accused of assaulting him was cleared at the Magistrates Court (*Taunton Courier and Western Advertiser*. "Youth cleared of assault." 11 March, 1961).

financial perspective, but his dealings with Derek Ridgewell suggest that his interest lay in protecting his personal and institutional reputation at all costs; and his friendship with the *Daily Mail* reporter, Peter Burden, suggests that his real interest lay in his own promotion and fame. It is possible that this was also true of John Innes who later succeeded Maurice Woodman.

Based on the way the investigation into Aubrey's case was carried out, and the lack of investigation by Maurice Woodman (and to a lesser extent John Innes) into Derek Ridgewell's corrupt practices, it would be difficult to conclude that the only criminal behaviour in Aubrey's case was carried out by them. It appears that the main aim of their investigation was the achievement of the institutional fame that would have resulted from their conviction of a high-profile politician. But a charge of Misfeasance in Public Office against them would have stood little chance of succeeding – particularly if any part of the investigation had been carried out by the BT Police.

Aubrey's accusation that Maurice Woodman and John Innes may have acted in collusion with Keith Stuart cannot be easily dismissed. Although no evidence for this has been uncovered, BT Police operations on BTDB property were funded by the BTDB. With the BT Police being pushed to achieve better and better results in the 1960s and 1970s in the face of threatened job cuts, removing a member of BTDB staff who was causing "operational difficulties" for their paymaster may therefore have been quite convenient.

CHAPTER 9

CONSTITUENTS AT THE CENTRE

The leader

By the time Aubrey became leader of the council in 1974, there had been a feeling in national government for several years that a reform of local government was required. The Local Government Act of 1972 therefore introduced new county authorities aiming for populations of between 250,000 to 1,000,000 people.[1] It was felt that with greater staff numbers and better resources, the newly-formulated authorities would be able to provide better services. These became effective in April 1974, at the same time as Aubrey took over the leadership of the council. The main role of governing Newport was now undertaken by the newly-formed Gwent County Council, and Newport itself became a second-tier government in what was now known as a "district" council.

With many councillors on the new Newport District council wanting to serve as county councillors, a number of these now stood for election in the new county council. Seventeen councillors were elected to represent Newport on the first Gwent County Council, and all bar two of these were existing Newport District council members.[2] None of these fifteen relinquished their role as district councillors. Among these was Aubrey who was to become Gwent County Council's first chairman of the finance sub-committee, and consequently responsible for managing two of the largest public purses in Wales.

---

[1] Buxton, R.J. *Local government*. Volume 4. Puffin, 1973.

[2] One of these was later to become a district councillor in Newport.

However, with a Gwent county councillor covering an area about five times larger than a Newport District councillor – including some areas with which they were unfamiliar – many of the newly-elected county councillors began to find their dual roles onerous. This was not helped by the fact that many employers were starting to restrict time-off for public duties at this time. This effected Aubrey who found his time off reduced by half by the British Transport Docks Board.[3] As a result, Aubrey was to stand down from Gwent County Council in 1977 after serving only one term. Many others were to follow him, and within 10 years of being formed, only one councillor remained on Gwent County Council who also served as a district councillor in Newport.

Despite only serving one term on Gwent County Council, Aubrey's time there introduced him to a wider political audience where he was to garner great respect due to his knowledge and expertise in local government –particularly in the area of finance.[4] He was subsequently elected as the leader of the Welsh Committee of District Councils, and by the time he retired from local politics in 1987, he was generally regarded as the best-known politician in Wales who was not a member of either the British or European Parliament.[5,6]

The Conservatives regained the control of Newport for one year in May 1976 and this was followed by Aubrey's year as mayor in 1977. As a result of two years away, when he returned as leader of the council in Newport in May 1978, it was in a fundamentally different position. Up until May 1976, he was leader of the council in Newport, a county councillor, and assistant docks manager at Cardiff. By May 1978 as a result of giving up his role on Gwent County Council and his sacking by the British Transport Docks Board, he was now just the leader of the council in Newport. Able to dedicate his time solely to local politics in Newport he therefore became one of the few essentially full-time councillors in Wales, and probably the forerunner in Newport of what was to become the full-time councillor.[7]

---

[3] "Time-off reduction makes councillor quit." *South Wales Argus*. 8 September, 1976.

[4] This is based on several interviews, but predominantly interviews with Paul Murphy and Don Touhig, 2021.

[5] "Aubrey steps out of the hot seat." *South Wales Argus*. 29 April, 1987.

[6] Almost without exception, everybody interviewed had the same opinion of Aubrey's standing in Welsh local politics, including past and present political figures from authorities other than Newport.

[7] Approximately half of local councils at this time had at least one councillor whose sole source of income was their council allowance (Leach, S., Game, C., Gyford, J. and Midwinter, A. *The Conduct of Local Authority Business, Research Volume I*. The Political Organisation of Local Authorities, 1986). Interview with Sir Harry Jones, Aubrey's successor as leader of Newport Borough Council. 3 March, 2013.

Famed for his ability to find a solution to a problem, and to take others along with him, his most notable achievement as leader of the council was probably the building of the Newport Centre.[8,9] Built during a time when Margaret Thatcher's Conservative government was waging a war against local government spending, Aubrey was to become a master of the intricacies of something called rate capping.[10,11] To the annoyance of many government officials, particularly the Welsh Secretary Nicholas Edwards, Aubrey's ability to find loopholes in government regulations and maximise government grants meant that over half the cost of the Newport Centre was covered at no cost to the ratepayers despite massive cuts to local government spending and heinous interest rates. While other local authorities were cancelling major capital projects and increasing council rates above the rate of inflation, the Newport Centre was built when Newport had one of the lowest council rates in the UK, and the increases that occurred while it was paid for were kept below the rate of inflation.

Extravagant, grandiose and a folly

By the end of the 1970s, the threat of house demolition had been replaced with the hopefulness of house improvement, and there was a feeling among many council members that Newport needed more from their bricks and mortar than just somewhere to live. Just twelve miles to the west, Cardiff had the national rugby stadium with a seating capacity of 60,000, and as a consequence of hosting the 1958 Commonwealth Games, an Olympic-sized swimming pool and various venues capable of holding large sporting and cultural events. It also had a host of leisure centres that were either already built, or under construction, or planned for the next few years. By comparison, there were few current or planned leisure facilities for the people of Newport, and with the Celtic Manor resort yet to be built, no venue capable of holding large sporting or other events of significance.

The process to provide Newport with sporting and leisure facilities fit for the upcoming 21st century had a fairly inauspicious start; on the 24th July 1979, a meeting of three council members – of the rather vague-sounding "Indoor recreation provision sector working group" – made a proposal for a large

---

[8] Interview with Bob Bright, 2013.

[9] Based on Aubrey's Freedom of Newport speech, 19/02/98.

[10] Rate capping is a government-imposed limit on the level of tax, or rates set by a local authority. Before the Conservative government came to power in 1979, local authorities were solely in charge of the level of local taxes to be charged.

[11] "Goodbye old friend." *South Wales Argus.* 1 May, 1987.

sporting and cultural centre in Newport. These proposals were laid before the monthly meeting of the council on 29th January 1980 where they were met with what could at best be described as indifference, and where most councillors expressed outright opposition to the scheme. Most councillors were still focused on housing and felt that Newport could not afford a project of this magnitude – especially as it was likely to saddle Newport ratepayers with a debt that would take 30 years to repay.

Considering the response to this proposal, it could have been expected to suffer the same fate as a similar idea for a leisure centre in Newport in 1963 which was defeated by government cutbacks.[12] However, this scheme had two major advantages over the 1963 scheme. The first was Ron Jones, a councillor in Pill who was a passionate and vociferous advocate of the scheme and who had made the initial proposal; and the second was Aubrey – the most persuasive member of the council and someone who recognized that Newport needed to do more for its citizens than just build houses. Over the next two to three years, there were plenty of arguments both within the Labour group and in the council at large (and not always within the confines of a meeting room) about the need to build a sporting and cultural centre.[13] Critics described the plans as "extravagant," "grandiose," and "a folly," and its supporters, as a prestige venture that would help boost the town and help to cultivate what it lacked most – civic pride.[14]

Show me the money

During the course of the first 80 years of the 20th century, local government spending increased significantly with the needs and demands of an increasingly affluent society. People were living longer, made greater use of local services and facilities, and stayed longer in school; a rise in council rates was the natural consequence of these increased demands.[15] With local government spending reaching a peak relative to public spending in the early 1970s, this became a bête noire for many Conservative MPs who had the widespread conviction that local councils were out of control and costing voters a fortune in the process.[16] As a consequence, when the Conservatives

[12] "Leisure centre for Newport – yes or no?" *South Wales Argus*. 8 September, 1981.

[13] "Newport Centre supplement, end of year review," *South Wales Argus*. circa December, 1985.

[14] "Act faith – or folly?" *South Wales Argus*. 31 January, 1984.

[15] Stoker, G. *The politics of local government*. London. Bloomsbury, 1991.

[16] Campbell-Smith, D. *Follow the money: a history of the Audit Commission*. Penguin UK, 2008.

became the party of government in May 1979, their manifesto made it clear that they were determined to cut council spending, and to spend less on housing, social services and education (all services under the control of local authorities) and more on defence, law and order, and social security (the services under the control of government).

So a proposal to build a major sporting and cultural centre within the first three months of Margaret Thatcher's first Conservative government was, on paper, not the most obvious suggestion. With interest rates running at 15-20% per year, and cuts of £300 million to local authorities in the new government's first budget, most local authorities were looking at ways to save money and had started to cut capital spending.[17] Despite this, Aubrey agreed with his fellow councillor, Ron Jones, that it was possible to build a major sporting and cultural centre in Newport with minimal impact on local taxation. Working with council officials, Aubrey therefore started looking for weaknesses and loopholes in the new regulations brought out under the new government, in order to secure more in government grants.

Analysing the complex methodology used to determine a local authority's government grant, Aubrey noted that the level of grant you received was related to your budget rather than what you actually spent. He therefore proposed to set Newport's budget to the maximum allowed at a time when the government was calling for a short-term freeze on local government recruitment.[18] Once the government-imposed freeze was lifted, he maintained a modified freeze in place for the next fifteen to seventeen months in order to maximise the surplus in Newport's budget. This surplus was then matched by unallocated grants from the government who were now trying to incentivise councils – thereby doubling the new money in Newport's reserves. Later in 1981, the government brought in a system of local government targets and penalties, with local authorities that spent above their targets having their government grant cut. With the system used to set targets changing every year, and sometimes more than once in a year, Newport set up what were known as special funds. These funds meant that money put into them in one year counted as expenditure, yet did not count as expenditure when taken out and spent in a later year.[19] This enabled Newport to manipulate spending in successive years and ensure that it spent up to its budget. This would maximise the grant it received from government, enabling even more

[17] Stoker, G., 1991.

[18] Hansard HC. *Rate support grant*. Volume 976. 16 January, 1980. Available at: https://hansard.parliament.uk/.

[19] Douglas, I.J. and Lord, S. *Local government finance: a practical guide*. Local Government Information Unit, 1986.

funding to go into its reserves.

As these various tranches of money built up, the arguments in favour of building a sports and cultural centre started to become more compelling. Ron Jones continued to bang its drum, and arguments between those who disagreed with him became more vociferous. And with Aubrey's success in manipulating government regulations and grants, he started to win over support for what was to become known as the Newport Centre.[20] Consequently, in March 1981, the Labour group half-heartedly agreed to build the Newport Centre in principle.[21] This agreement occurred despite the serious misgivings of several senior members of the Labour group – including Aubrey's current and previous deputy leaders, Harry Jones and Paul Flynn. Both felt strongly that any surplus money should be spent on housing and they were also concerned about engaging in such a large project at a time when they felt it could be scuppered by yet another change in government regulations. Others were also concerned because of Newport's poor track record with regard to major developments – such as the proposed construction of a major concert hall at the Civic Centre which had never been built due to lack of money.[22]

Over the next ten months, several hurdles (such as a deferral in September 1981) had to be overcome before the final decision was made at a council meeting in March 1982.[23] The decision came after a bitter debate when it was discovered that the reason for the deferral was because the cost to purchase the land for the Newport Centre (owned by a former mayor and alderman) had increased by almost 40%; many council members therefore felt they had been held to ransom.[24,25]

With the decision made to build the Newport Centre, the next problem was to work out the best way to raise the remaining funds. Even though Newport had accumulated considerable reserves since the proposal had first been mooted (which was to grow to more than £3 million by the time it was due

---

[20] Although originally proposed as a sporting and cultural centre, the Newport Centre was commonly thought of as just a leisure centre during initial discussions, and the name originally suggested was the Newport Leisure Centre. However, Aubrey proposed that it should just be known as the Newport Centre as it was meant to serve multiple purposes, not just those related to leisure.

[21] "Snags over planned £7m centre." *South Wales Argus*. 3 March, 1981.

[22] "Leisure centre for Newport – yes or no?" *South Wales Argus*. 8 September, 1981

[23] "Newport Centre supplement. End of year review." *South Wales Argus*. circa December, 1985.

[24] The name of the landowner has been deliberately omitted here, but he left the council after the local government re-organisation in 1974.

[25] "Extra cost leisure plan given go-ahead." *South Wales Argus*. 24 March, 1982.

to be built) about half the cost of the Newport Centre was for the various bits of plant and equipment needed.[26] In this case, Aubrey discovered that if plant and equipment was leased rather than bought, it did not count as capital spending; private sector funding could then be used taking advantage of their tax allowances.[27] This would result in significant savings due to lower interest payments. These various creative accounting techniques, together with the restructuring of payments in certain years, meant that the Newport Centre was fully paid for in eight years rather than the usual thirty years expected for this type of scheme.[28] During this period, the total capital and interest payments to the ratepayers was less than the cost of the Newport Centre at a time when loans for capital expenditure were of the order of 20% per annum. Even though rates went up to help pay for the remaining cost of the Newport Centre, one third of a million pounds per year was saved by closing Stow Hill baths, and (as mentioned) the overall increase in rates remained below the rate of inflation and was still one of the lowest in the UK.

Success or failure

The financing of the Newport Centre was a significant success at a time of astronomical interest rates, and unprecedented cuts in local authority spending. The various "dodges and wheezes" used to secure government grants – manipulating spending and securing preferential interest rates – could certainly be considered devious, but they were perfectly legal and little different to what many other local authorities were doing. At a time when spending targets and penalties were changing every year, and becoming increasingly more severe, it could be argued that it would have been negligent to avoid looking at every method available to help protect ratepayers from crippling government penalties. It was also a lot less devious than the system that let Conservative councils "off the hook" while at the same time imposing severe penalties on Labour authorities.[29] For example, penalties for Labour-controlled councils in 1983 to 1984 were almost ten times more than Conservative-controlled councils.[30]

With the proportion of local government spending that was supported by the government falling from 48.5% to 35.9% in the three years between when

---

[26] "Controversial leisure cash deal go-ahead." *South Wales Argus.* 3 March, 1984.

[27] Based on Aubrey's Freedom of Newport speech, 19/02/98.

[28] Ibid.

[29] Midwinter, A., Keating, M. and Taylor, P. *"Excessive and unreasonable": The politics of the Scottish hit list.* Political Studies. Volume 31. Number 3, 1983. pp.394-417.

[30] Stoker, G., 1991.

the Newport Centre was proposed to when it was approved, the success of Newport in not only raising the funds, yet keeping rate increases within levels of inflation was remarkable. Few local authorities undertook capital spending of note during this period, so much so, that by the end of 1982 the government was urging local authorities to increase their capital spending as they were concerned about the effect on the construction industry.[31] Aubrey was more than happy to remind the government that this was exactly what Newport was doing at a convenient meeting with the Federation of Civil Engineer Contractors in November 1982.[32]

Despite the success in financing the Newport Centre, it attracted widespread criticism, which was primarily politically driven. Within the pages of the *South Wales Argus*, this mainly came from Peter Davies – Aubrey's latest and most regular combatant who was the father of David Davies, the current Conservative MP for Monmouth.[33] Within government, criticism was led by Nicholas Edwards, the Secretary of State for Wales, and someone who was to have a fractious relationship with Aubrey during his time in post. Edwards' comments in parliament that implied that Newport had spent money for house improvements on the Newport Centre drew a furious response from Aubrey, who described him as a "liar and a nincompoop" – a school playground insult that I found very amusing when I read it.[34,35] Aubrey later regretted the language used, although there was also considerable anger from other councillors who described the accusations made by Nicholas Edwards as a "grotesque slur."[36]

As for the citizens of Newport, a survey by the *South Wales Argus* in 1982 indicated that 57% of the respondents did not want the Newport Centre if it meant paying more rates, despite most people indicating that they would be willing to pay more rates given a choice between cutting taxes or increasing services.[37,38] However, the vast majority of respondents were over fifty years

---

[31] Ibid.

[32] "Council are urged to spend, spend, spend." *South Wales Argus*. 30 November, 1982.

[33] Peter Davies was a prominent member of the Conservative Party who although he had never served on the council at this time, did get elected to the council in 1999, a year after Aubrey died.

[34] Hansard HC. *Small Firms Information Centres*. Volume 50. 12 December, 1983. Available at: https://hansard.parliament.uk/.

[35] "Edwards is a liar – council leader." *South Wales Argus*. 4 December, 1983.

[36] "Council hit at "grotesque slander". *South Wales Argus*. 6 December, 1983.

[37] "Act faith – or folly?" *South Wales Argus*. 31 January, 1984.

[38] Jones, G.W. and Stewart, J. *The case for local government*. Volume 1. Allen & Unwin Australia, 1983.

of age and among the younger members of the population there was an overwhelming desire for the Newport Centre to be built. It would also be fair to say that while most criticism was aimed at the cost and future interest payments, few seemed to be aware of the reserves built up to cover most of the cost. As for Nicholas Edwards, his criticism was ill-advised as the contract to sign the leisure centre had been signed six months before the government had initiated the programme of house improvement grants.[39]

The Newport Centre opened in July 1985. Despite the criticism, 110,000 people used it in its first two months, and by the end of its first year, Elton John had staged a concert there and Princess Diana had made an appearance.[40] Although it was envisaged that it would stage around one show per month when it first opened, within a year it was averaging one or two shows per week and hosting professional snooker tournaments one week and major music acts such as David Bowie, B. B. King, Genesis, and the Everly Brothers, the next.[41] There were also performances by the likes of Victoria Wood, the Vienna Boys Choir, Danny la Rue, and the Royal Shakespeare Company.

Without a doubt, the Newport Centre was a massive success both as a leisure and entertainment venue. Although it was to lose much of its lustre from the 1990s onwards as large indoor arenas in cities such as Sheffield (1991), Cardiff (1993) and Manchester (1995) were built, it remained the unofficial home of Welsh Snooker, and somewhere that still drew music and comedy acts that Newportonians could only have dreamt of half a generation earlier.

Few people realise that the Newport Centre was modelled on the Sun Centre in Rhyl, that opened five years before the Newport Centre. Treated with the same levels of scepticism amongst most councillors when it was first proposed, and facing the same battles to get built, it was ultimately as popular and successful as the Newport Centre.[42] The Sun Centre closed in 2014 for the same reasons that the Newport Centre was closed in 2022. It is difficult to accept that having learnt the lessons from the concept, building and promotion of the Sun Centre at the beginning of its life, lessons regarding the importance of maintenance were not grasped, and before the end of summer

---

[39] "Council hit at 'grotesque slander.'" *South Wales Argus*. 6 December, 1983.

[40] "Newport Centre supplement. End of year review," *South Wales Argus*. circa December, 1985.

[41] "Gig venue's 'black book' reveals piece of Newport's music history." *Wales Online*. 29 December, 2917. Available at https://www.walesonline.co.uk/lifestyle/nostalgia/david-bowie-elton-john-newport-14051119.

[42] "Rhyl Sun Centre: The fascinating story behind North Wales' famous 'tropical village.'" *Daily Post*. 27 August, 2016. Available at https://www.dailypost.co.uk/news/north-wales-news/rhyl-sun-centre-fascinating-story-11807201.

2023, the Newport Centre would be no more.[43]

Constituency leader

Although any politician, whether a member of parliament or a local council, should be judged by their actions, service, and value for money they provide to their constituents, it is probably fair to say that few are. Multiple opinion polls place politicians at the top of the list of people who are trusted the least – and there is a perception that many politicians pursue their goals for personal or selfish reasons. Indeed, it is interesting to note that an organisation set up to remember the memory of those who served in the Glider Pilot Regiment has previously stated that no politicians have earned the right to be mentioned in the same breath as the people they universally praise as heroes. No glider pilot I ever met considered themselves a hero, and all who knew Aubrey would have baulked at the suggestion that Aubrey the glider pilot could not be mentioned in the same breath as Aubrey the politician.

Considering this general attitude towards politicians, particularly those who reach a position of influence and control, the affection and fondness that people held for Aubrey during his time as leader of the council is remarkable. Described by the *South Wales Argus* on his retirement from local politics as "humble, approachable and always, fundamentally kind," these opinions didn't change in the last decade of his life after leaving the council, nor have they changed in the quarter of a century since his death.[44] Those whom I interviewed for this book – people who predominately worked with him on the council or within the Labour Party – talked about his great intellect, his sheer doggedness, and his original lateral thinking. Opinions of others that I have read from newspaper comment sections or on various social media sites invariably refer to him as a "gentleman," "a great man," or a "great people person." Even those who were children when they knew Aubrey remember him with great fondness – the most well-known man that most of them met, always playful, and the perfect person to play the role of Father Christmas.[45] Remarkedly, I have not read one negative comment about him, something that cannot be said about any council leader who has followed him.

The reasons for this affection and fondness are easy to understand. He was incredibly well respected for his achievements on the council, many of which

---

[43] "£11m needed to save Rhyl Sun Centre." *Daily Post.* 11 November, 2008. Available at: https://www.dailypost.co.uk/news/north-wales-news/11m-needed-save-rhyl-sun-2804510.

[44] "Goodbye, old friend." *South Wales Argus.* 1 May, 1987.

[45] This included at least one occasion when I was a recipient of a "present", and presumably didn't recognise him.

have been outlined in this book. However, it is those constituents who he helped in a personal way that hold or held the greatest affection and fondness for him. In his Freedom of Newport speech in February 1998 he was to say that his greatest enjoyment while serving as a councillor was in dealing with the problems of his constituents – problems that he described as "immediate and problematical to the people concerned."[46] The most obvious of these were the weekly shops for housebound constituents. But few people would have been aware of the almost daily visits by constituents to the family home, or the problems he dealt with on his ward rounds every Sunday, and the hours he would spend with constituents on problems that others would have seen as minor or irrelevant.[47] One of many incidents that I was party to was in 1986 when I helped him to clear out the home of three elderly sisters who had moved into a home. Their house had been burgled shortly after they had moved out. The thieves were later caught when it was discovered that they had found in excess of £20,000 wrapped up in newspaper and stuffed into several bags around the house. These had subsequently been converted into various items which included microwaves, cameras and a pick-up truck. These were returned to Aubrey in order that he could recoup the money for the sisters, and the first thing he did was to offer one of the microwaves to me, for which he would pay the full retail value. I refused, much to the annoyance of my flatmates who were denied the opportunity of a baked potato in 7 minutes. For me, this was a step too far in doing the right thing. It was not the sisters' fault that their money had been stolen, but it was also not Aubrey's responsibility to suffer the consequences. I do not know how much he ultimately recovered, but I suspect that he probably did end up buying some of the items himself at the full retail value (although I never saw the pick-up truck parked outside our house or the house of anybody I knew).

However, there was one resident of Newport who did not hold Aubrey in high regard, and that was a builder by the name of Abdul Ghafoor. Carrying out some building work at the family home in the early 1970s, Abdul Ghafoor felt that having formed a relationship with Aubrey, he would now exert some pressure within the council to secure certain contracts for his building company. When this did not happen, he was not impressed and started to make various accusations against Aubrey and regular phone calls to his home. Many of these calls were taken by Mary, and as some started to become abusive, Aubrey took him to court. A successful injunction meant

---

[46] Aubrey Hames Freedom of Newport speech. 19/02/98.

[47] After Aubrey was sacked from the British Transport Docks, the visits by constituents to the family home reduced significantly, presumably because he was now able to visit them during the day.

that he could no longer ring Aubrey's home phone number or pass within a certain distance of his house, but it did not prevent him from confronting Aubrey at meetings or making further accusations against him in the press.[48] It also did not prevent someone connected to him allegedly drawing a knife on Aubrey – something that would never have been mentioned to Mary, but a serious threat considering that the name of the person suggested to me is now serving a life sentence for killing someone with a knife.[49]

Every councillor I interviewed laughed or groaned when I mentioned Abdul Ghafoor's name, and all had stories of his various nefarious activities – particularly regarding his abuse of planning regulations. I also had reason to have a low opinion of Abdul Ghafoor as the phone calls happened when I was revising for my O levels. In the days of a single land line in every home and no mobile phones, the council leader's phone could not be taken off the hook even when he was not in. The phone rang hundreds of times when I was in the house on my own. If I answered, I was met with silence or some unintelligible rant on the other end even though he knew it was Aubrey's 16-year-old son he was talking to. If not answered, the phone rang for several minutes before ringing off, only to start ringing again a minute or two later.

Honour him

As Aubrey neared the end of his time on the council, there was a recognition amongst his fellow councillors that he should be recognized for all the work he had done for Newport over the years. Although he had previously resisted their attempts to nominate him for national honours, and had already turned an honour down, a proposal was made that he should be offered the Freedom of Newport.[50,51] This would have made him only the thirteenth person in Newport's history to receive this award. However, Aubrey wasn't interested in any acclaim for what he had done, so he turned it down saying that making him a freeman as a politician would "devalue that honour."[52] However, the members of the council were undeterred and without asking him, and probably using his own words against him, decided to award him the position of Honorary Alderman instead. He was not impressed by this,

---

[48] See for example: "Council is cleared in discrimination inquiry." *South Wales Argus*. 13 October, 1986.

[49] This was mentioned in an interview with a former prominent council member. Other councillors received dubious phone calls and various threats, with at least one other council member reporting Abdul Ghafoor to the press for a threat made to him.

[50] Interview with Ron Jones, former Newport Labour councillor. 25 May, 2013.

[51] Interview with Robin Hames, Aubrey's eldest son. 29 November, 2022.

[52] "Civic honour for politician." *South Wales Argus*. 28 May, 1987.

but nevertheless was made Newport's first Honorary Alderman on 28th May 1987. I believe he may have been the first person in the UK to be given this title.

Just over a year later, the Conservative group suggested that a new road in his ward should be named after him to further recognise his work for Newport and its constituents.[53] Much to the embarrassment of the Labour group, this was proposed by the Conservative group at the monthly meeting of the council the following day and passed unanimously. Again, they didn't ask Aubrey if he wanted a road named after him, and again given the choice he would have said no. Indeed, I only found out by reading about it in the *South Wales Argus*. When I asked him why he hadn't told me, without looking up from his paperwork he just muttered, "stupid idea". At the time, Aubrey was the only politician in the county to have a road named after them while still living – a remarkable achievement considering that, among others, this was a county of the likes of Nye Bevan who spearheaded the creation of the British National Health Service, and Michael Foot a former leader of the Labour Party.

Aubrey's youngest grand-children Alexandra and Samuel Hames on the left, and his eldest great-grandson Ralph Hames on the right, on Aubrey Hames Close. Both Samuel and Ralph share Aubrey as a middle name.

---

[53] Interview with Gerald Davies, former Newport Conservative councillor. 6 August, 2014.

CHAPTER 10

FREE MAN TO FREEMAN

"Retirement"

A few years after Aubrey left the council, Mary was interviewed by the *South Wales Argus* where she said that she hadn't realised he had retired until she read about it in the local paper. Aubrey may no longer have been a councillor, but he still took an active part in almost 50 organisations. This included taking on many roles normally reserved for sitting councillors such as chairman of the Newport Transport Board.[1] Entering his latter years, Aubrey therefore maintained an influence over certain council business, with one current member recalling his astonishment at how fellow councillors held Aubrey in such awe that they would often change their mind if they found that Aubrey disagreed with them. This included the first time this member attended a meeting with Aubrey where a proposal was rapidly overturned even though only one person, Aubrey, opposed it.[2]

The role that Aubrey was most passionate about after leaving the council was as chairman of Newport Action for the Single Homeless (commonly known as NASH).[3] Set up as a charity in 1983 by Aubrey and one or two others as a response to the Housing (Homeless Persons) Act 1977, its role was to

---

[1] Interview with Sir Harry Jones, 2013.

[2] This story was told to me when I went to pick up the copy of a speech made by Aubrey in India in 1946 which had been found in the Labour Party Headquarters on Stow Hill (see Chapter 3).

[3] Interview with Annette Hames, Aubrey's eldest daughter, 21 November, 2022.

take responsibility for Newport's single homeless and vulnerable people.[4] Employing Richard Frame as its first manager, Aubrey was to play the key role in guiding Richard Frame through his new role, teaching him the basics of management and providing him with access to different people within the Civic Centre if he needed specialist advice.[5] Richard Frame, who was to become close friends with Aubrey and Mary, was also given free rein to call on Aubrey whenever it was needed. When I came home for weekend visits in the 1990s, he was invariably sitting in my parents' lounge talking to Aubrey about one thing or another, often with a plate or cup and saucer in his hand. NASH was to become a tremendous success, the biggest and most successful charity in Newport; now rebranded as Solas, it provides homeless services across Wales. Richard Frame was later to become its first director, and after retiring became better known as a local historian, and the man who was to discover the grave and final home of the one former councillor and Mayor of Newport better known than Aubrey – one John Frost.[6]

Freebies on the rates

In September 1988 Aubrey and Mary went on holiday to North America where they met up with Lihu Ichilov, Aubrey's co-accused in his court case during his mayoral year. This was a trip that Mary in particular had been keen to do for a number of years and was the first holiday that Mary and Aubrey had been on since a family holiday to Denmark in 1976, 12 years earlier. Considering that fourteen-hour days for Aubrey were common, and there was rarely a day when he didn't do at least a few hours work, this may have been seen as a change in priorities for retirement, especially as trips to West Wales and Madeira were to become regular occurrences for the rest of Aubrey's life. However, it was less a change in priorities and more due to his pension from the BTDB kicking-in that year. When Aubrey was sacked from the BTDB and failed to secure another position, his sole source of income during his time as leader of the council had been his council attendance allowance. Accounting for inflation, this was less than half of what is now the national minimum wage, and even though he had no mortgage to pay, this income had to support not only himself, but Mary and his two youngest

---

[4] Interview with Richard Frame, former manager of Newport Action for Single Homeless (NASH). 15 November, 2022.

[5] Interview with Richard Frame, 2022.

[6] John Frost led the Newport Rising in November 1839 demanding the right to vote beyond those owning property. He was the last man together with two others sentenced to be hanged, drawn, and quartered in Britain for his role in the Newport Rising, although this was later commuted to transportation for life.

children, including myself. He also had to maintain a suitable supply of suits which would not normally have been expected of someone on such a low wage. The man responsible for managing the largest budget in Newport was also managing one of the smallest – which was less than what I was earning as an 18-year-old working for the council in Newport as a summer playscheme assistant. Aubrey had managed this budget from possibly the smallest office in the Civic Centre, despite many efforts by Harry Jones, rebuffed by Aubrey, to move him to a larger one.[7] Under these circumstances it is understandable how the occasional reference to councillors having "freebies on the rates" angered Aubrey. On one occasion he referred to one accusation as "sickeningly offensive and infantile."[8] Accusations of "freebies on the rates" also worked on the assumption that there was a perceived benefit. Indeed, I can remember my mother being aghast at Aubrey attending a meeting in China and returning to Newport the same day without taking advantage of at least one day's sightseeing. Having flown to China myself and spent a few hours working there before flying straight back out again, there is certainly no benefit beyond getting you from where you are to where you need to be quickly and efficiently.

If anybody was getting any freebies, it was the array of charities on which Aubrey served. Although the vast amount of material on Aubrey's charity work was lost in the immediate aftermath of his death, a list of the organisations he served on generally had a common theme – helping the vulnerable in society such as the elderly, the disabled, the lonely, or those with alcohol or drug problems. His former constituents also continued to benefit from his help with their daily problems whether big or small. The constituents I remember most clearly are Edna and Wilf Ford for whom Aubrey did a weekly shop, and a lovely old man I only ever knew as Mr Clifford. While these were the easiest and most visible problems that he solved, he spent considerably more time visiting people and undertaking daily letter writing at his dining room table. Indeed, I can remember little if anything about him ever doing anything for himself. He didn't drink, he didn't attend any social events that weren't linked in some way to his work, he rarely watched television (apart from the news), and never went to the cinema. He also didn't make a point of watching rugby matches despite his passion for the game – apart from attending the matches I played on a Saturday (when there was always something that I could have done better). His commitment to do all he could for others, and do nothing for himself, unfortunately likely contributed to his detriment towards the end of his life.

---

[7] Interview with Sir Harry Jones, 2013.
[8] "Council chief hits back." *South Wales Argus*. 22 October, 1985.

For your family

Sometime towards the end of 1994, Aubrey was diagnosed with prostate cancer. It is not known when or how advanced his cancer was, but on 20th December 1994 he made what was to be the first of several visits to the Velindre Cancer Centre in Cardiff – which meant that his cancer had metastasized.[9] These visits were to continue for another three and a half years. His many visits to the centre between January and March 1995 suggest that he was probably receiving radiotherapy to treat the cancer – with evidence suggesting that treatment was unsuccessful.[10] He kept his cancer diagnosis to himself, and almost three years later my parents came to stay with me in Liverpool, where I had recently bought my first house, for what was to be their first, and ultimately last, visit together. During this visit, my father was limping badly and, anticipating my concern (or more likely to avoid a question he didn't want to answer) he told me that this was due to arthritis. With my mother seemingly unaware of his diagnosis and treatment, my youngest sister Janine was concerned enough to insist on accompanying him on one of his visits to hospital. Here she found out that he had prostate cancer and that it had spread to his bones. He probably only had months left to live. As Aubrey's condition worsened noticeably towards the end of 1997, Ruth (who is now my wife) and I visited Newport more often. At the start of the New Year, Aubrey was spending increasing periods of time in bed as his illness worsened and the pain intensified. Despite this, his day was still centred around his "duties". He still did the weekly shopping for both himself and Mary, as well as for Edna Ford (her husband Wilf had by now passed away) who was now considerably more mobile than Aubrey. This included one occasion when he deliberately left the house early when he realised I was going to help him on a shopping trip. He never accepted help, and when he returned, he said I would have slowed him down, although I struggled to see how I could have walked any slower even if I tried.

As news spread about his condition, he started to receive regular visits from former colleagues on the council, including his predecessor, and his successor, as leader of the council – Steward Watson and Harry Jones respectively.[11] Council business was the main topic of conversation, including the council's desire to award Aubrey its highest honour (and as mentioned, something

---

[9] Cancer that spreads from where it started to a distant part of the body.

[10] This is based on Aubrey's diary entries and discussions with Aubrey's daughter-in-law, Dr Ruth Asher, Consultant Dermatopathologist, University Hospital of Wales.

[11] Interview with Patricia Watson, wife of Stewart Watson. 21 June, 2014.

he had refused several times before) – the Freedom of Newport.[12] Aubrey continued to refuse to accept the honour, but with Mary pressurising him to accept it, he finally agreed when Harry Jones asked him to consider accepting it for the sake of his family rather than for himself.

Aubrey was awarded the Freedom of Newport in the council chamber in Newport on 19th February 1998. It was the first time that Newport had awarded its highest honour to an individual for over 40 years. Aubrey was also the first man to receive the honour since 1945 when Field Marshall Montgomery received it in recognition for his command of the Allies in their first major land victory during the Second World War.

However, unlike Field Marshall Montgomery who was given the Freedom of Newport for winning his greatest battle, Aubrey, with his health deteriorating, was given his honour whilst losing his. Consequently, there was an expectation that the ceremony would be short with considerably less pomp and circumstance than was given to Field Marshall Montgomery. Aubrey was expected to speak for no more than five minutes, and with concern for his condition, a bed was installed in the mayor's parlour in case he needed to lie down at any point.[13,14] During the ceremony, I spent most of my time watching my father, concerned more by his health than the accolade of the award – especially as I knew it was something he didn't want. He never admitted he was in any pain and would do everything to hide it. However, the way he blew out as he sat down, and occasionally hid his eyes as he stroked his forehead, indicted that he was suffering. This was despite a visit to the hospital to ensure he was on suitable painkillers to see him through the evening. Yet, despite all this, when he came to speak he was a revelation. Given free rein to talk about what he loved, and with the pain possibly eased rather than made worse by standing throughout his speech, he went on to talk without a break for over half an hour. He dedicated his award to the women of the Labour Party who worked so hard for him when he first stood as a councillor in the 1950s. All those who were present that night, and who I was to later interview for this book, commented on what a wonderful speech he gave, with some saying that it was the best speech they had ever heard in the council chamber. Some may have said this out of politeness, but almost 20 years later the speech was described as "astonishing" in an article in the *South Wales Argus* by Councillor Allan Morris, who is still a serving

---

[12] This had been discussed in council meetings several times since Aubrey originally turned it down on his retirement (see Chapter 10).

[13] "Community news in Lliswerry and Nash." *South Wales Argus*. 23 May, 2017.

[14] Interview with Dame Rosemary Butler, 2012.

councillor over 40 years after he was first elected.[15]

Although this was Aubrey's last large public appearance, he continued to carry out the weekly shopping for a few more weeks until my brother Robin had to take over, and he still maintained an active interest in organisations where he could contribute from his bed. Stewart Watson visited Aubrey once or twice a week, so he was also kept abreast of council business, including the next council elections due in May. Aubrey played an active part in canvassing for these elections and canvassed for votes with Geoff Lee in late March and early April, at a time when he could hardly walk and where the pain of his cancer kept him in bed for up to 22 hours per day. I was completely unaware of his canvassing at this time and astonished when I found out about it. What made it more interesting were the circumstances of the person who told me – Matthew Evans, leader of the Conservative Group and a former leader of the council in Newport.[16] Accompanying Matthew Evans back to his car as mayor after he had attended an event that I had sponsored in 2015, he told me how my father had canvassed him in 1998 (when he just happened to live twelve doors away from Aubrey). This had been during the time when Mathew Evans had first stood as a candidate in Newport – and it involved a past leader of the council canvassing a future leader when one's council career had finished and the other's had yet to begin. Considering Aubrey's mantra when canvassing was to "not wake up the opposition" he probably failed as spectacularly as he could on this occasion – although I suspect that Matthew Evans' mind had already been made and that he needed no encouragement to vote.

The End

The last time I saw my father was on the weekend of 23rd of May 1998. I had spent the weekend with my parents and Ruth, primarily to spend time with my father, but also to get hold of details for a holiday to Madeira that we were going on in my parents' place. By this time my father rarely left his bed and had to spend most of the time lying on his side due to the intense pain in his back. Even though he knew he could no longer do anybody's shopping, or in the days before Zoom attend any meetings, there were certain things he could still do with limited help. So for most of the Sunday I walked up and down the stairs correcting and editing letters on the computer I had bought him a few months earlier. This included removing all the carriage returns at

---

[15] "Community news in Lliswerry and Nash." *South Wales Argus.* 23 May, 2017.

[16] Based on several communications with Matthew Evans, current Conservative Group leader, January 2015.

the end of each line for a man still used to using a typewriter. Two weeks before he was to take his last breath, he was still taking an active role as secretary for an organisation called Pant Glas Hall Management Committee and was due to appear in court to give evidence soon after – an appearance brought forward due to his illness although it is likely he did not attend.

Leaving that weekend, I knew that I might never see him again, even though we planned to return to Newport after returning from Madeira. On Thursday 4th June, while Ruth and I were on a mountain walk thinking how wonderful it would be if he was on the walk with us, back in Newport, my father finally accepted that he couldn't cope with the pain anymore and he was admitted to the Royal Gwent Hospital. My father died on the evening of 8th June 1998, less than half a mile from the road that bears his name. At the time of his death, I was on a plane over the Midlands watching a red sunset over South Wales oblivious to events underneath. Returning home, I was greeted with a message to ring Robin as soon as I got in, regardless of the time. I knew what that meant.

Returning to Newport the following day, I arrived during that time in the aftermath of someone's death when those outside the immediate family start to find out. The first person to contact was the funeral director, so my sister Annette rang Lyndon Bassett, a well-known funeral director in Newport. On telling him that our father had died he immediately broke down in tears and slammed the phone down. On the second attempt the same thing happened, and it wasn't until Annette rung for a third time that he managed to compose himself enough to take the call. Still crying, and apologising profusely while talking, we had possibly the unique situation of the relative of the deceased comforting the funeral director. Lyndon Bassett also struggled to discuss the funeral arrangements in follow-up calls, but refused to discuss costs beyond charging the minimal price for a funeral yet provided the best coffin and service.[17] As news of my father's death spread, the Civic Centre offered to take on all the arrangements for the funeral, including the offer of a civic funeral. I had never heard of a civic funeral before, however my mother turned this down as she wanted a Catholic funeral. When the accountant, Alan Shewring, was contacted to deal with all the necessary legal work, he refused to be paid and said that it would be an honour to do something for Aubrey after everything he had done for others in his life.[18] Other offers poured in, many from former constituents including one from dockers in

---

[17] Interview with Robin Hames, 2022.

[18] Alan Shewring was a family friend who had helped set up St. Joseph's school with Aubrey and was its first governor.

Newport who said it would be an honour to carry the coffin.

My father's funeral took place on the same day as William 'Bunner' Travers' funeral – one of Newport's most famous rugby players – and their deaths were reported on the front page of the *South Wales Argus* under the headline "A farewell to legends."[19] In a funeral service lasting an hour, there was no eulogy and anybody attending this service out of curiosity would have had no idea who Aubrey was. However, they would have been intrigued by the one reference to him made by Fr. Scanlon, the priest who led the service, who said, "some people have said he was the best-known person in Newport, but I can't comment on that." Throughout most of his life Aubrey was the best-known and most highly respected person in Newport, described by the *South Wales Argus* when reporting on his funeral as "the citizen who perhaps above all others, etched his name upon the town's heart."[20] Aubrey didn't need a eulogy. Everyone present knew who he was and what he had done, and all knew that no eulogy could ever have done him justice.

Aubrey was buried in St. Woolos cemetery at the bottom of the road where he lived, and where he now lies with his wife Mary who died 12 years later. His name lives on not only with the road named after him, but with my son, his youngest grandson and his eldest great-grandson who both bear his name. They, together with my daughter Alex and his other great grandchildren never met their great relative, but when one day they ask what their grandfather and great-grandfather was like, I can finally tell them.

---

[19] "A farewell to legends." *South Wales Argus*. 13 June, 1998.
[20] Ibid.

CHAPTER 11

OPPORTUNITY AND CIRCUMSTANCE

Not destined for the mines

When my children were born they entered a world of relative prosperity – "cradle to grave" healthcare provision, warm centrally-heated homes, and multiple means of entertainment from various digital devices. Although this life is a complete contrast to their grandfather – born in poverty in a slum over ninety years earlier – both Aubrey and his grandchildren were born into the norm for the place and time they were born into, and their experiences would have seemed little different from those who grew up with them. Similarly, my experiences as a child would have appeared to be little different from those I grew up with. I went to a comprehensive school like every other child I knew, played football in the street, and disappeared for hours on end either to my best friend Peter's house, or on some adventure such as a search for the remains of Allt-yr-yn lido, or Rexville, the former football ground of Lovells Athletic. Opportunities were also mainly defined by the area and era you grew up in. In South Wales in the 1920s, a university education was in the main the domain of the privileged. When I was a child, it was a realistic goal for many who were often the first in their families to go to university. In the interim, university became more of an expectation, and the argument now is whether or not it is a necessity.

With university education little more than a pipedream, the likely career path for Aubrey growing up in the 1920s was defined by where he was born and bred. Born in Sebastopol and brought up in nearby Griffithstown, he was destined for a career on the railways. However, if he had been born a short walk up the road in somewhere like Abersychan, a career down the mines beckoned. This was the career path of Ronald Murphy and Fred Touhig who were of a similar age to Aubrey, and the fathers of future Abersychan born MPs Paul Murphy and Don Touhig.[1,2]

However, not everyone born in Abersychan around the same time as Aubrey was destined for a career down the mines. Opportunity and circumstances were to dictate that one young man born two years before Aubrey would never have to go anywhere near the mines, and regardless of ability or application, was almost uniquely destined for the career of his choice. That young man was Roy Jenkins, future Chancellor of the Exchequer and Home Secretary, and Britain's only ever President of the European Commission. He was also destined to have the third longest parliamentary career in the last 200 years, surpassed only by William Gladstone and Winston Churchill.[3]

"A pampered young man"

Roy Jenkins was born in Abersychan on 11th November 1920, and like almost everyone born in Abersychan, he was the son and grandson of a miner. By the time Aubrey was born two years later, Roy Jenkins was living with his parents in a relatively large house 3 miles from Aubrey where, supplemented by his father's rather comfortable wage, they had a live-in maid and the use of a motor car, together with a house stacked full of books.[4]

Jenkins grew up in a very political household; his father, Arthur, was chairman of the Pontypool Labour Party and a Monmouthshire County councillor, and he was to become Pontypool's MP in 1935. Roy's mother, Hattie, was a magistrate, a school governor, and in later life also became a county councillor.[5] Roy was an only child who was cosseted, somewhat spoiled, and grew up in the 1920s seemingly unaffected and to a great extent unaware of the poverty and depression that affected nearly every other child in the area. This was probably not helped by the gold sovereign given to him by his father every birthday.[6] He was studious and obsessively numerate and regularly attended political meetings in Pontypool with his father, as well as union conferences and parliamentary sittings when his father was an MP. He

---

[1] Interview with Lord Don Touhig, 2021.

[2] Interview with Lord Paul Murphy, 2021.

[3] Campbell, J. *Roy Jenkins*. London. Random House, 2014.

[4] Ibid.

[5] Jenkins, R. *A life at the centre*. London. Macmillan, 1991.

[6] Ibid.

was also an excellent swimmer and although keen on all sports, he was more "enthusiastic" than talented.

By 1937, following his father's new position as Clement Attlee's parliamentary private secretary, the Jenkins' had moved to a large house with twelve rooms near to the railway station and a stone's throw from where Aubrey was born. Here, Clement Attlee, as well as many other major parliamentary figures of the day such as Arthur Greenwood, Herbert Morrison, Hugh Dalton and Wedgewood Benn, became regular weekend visitors.[7]

Leaving school at sixteen, Roy didn't get the grades he needed for admission to Oxford University, but with the drive of his mother and the determination of his father, he secured a place there after studying at University College Cardiff for a year. At Oxford he led a privileged existence; on the verge of the Second World War he was living in rooms with great open fires being waited on with hot luncheons in the winter, and lobster in the summer, all washed down with fine wines. This was all funded by his father although Roy seemed apparently oblivious to this.[8]

In 1941, during a time when his most pressing concern was his failure to become president of the Oxford Union, he was called up to the army and joined the Oxford University Senior Training Corps. However, thanks again to his father, he secured what he described as an idyllic existence working at the American Embassy in London while travelling to Oxford twice a week. This "pampered young man" was to get a major shock to his political ambitions in 1942 when he was summoned to an officer cadet training unit, but thanks yet again to his father and his Master at Balliol College, this wasn't to last long and he managed to secure a posting to Bletchley Park at the end of 1943.[9]

Keen to follow his father into the House of Commons as soon as possible, he (just) failed to secure the candidacy of two safe Birmingham seats – Aston and Sparkbrook – at the 1945 General Election. He did succeed in gaining the candidacy in Solihull, another Birmingham seat, but this was a seat he had no chance of winning. However, having flown the Labour flag in 1945, he was rewarded with selection for the safe seat of Southwark Central at a by-election in 1948. He was then welcomed into parliament as the "Baby of the House" by one of his sponsors, and the future godfather of his first child

---

[7] Campbell, J., 2014.

[8] Jenkins, R., 1991.

[9] Campbell used this phrase to describe Roy in his biography on him published in 2014., Campbell, J., 2014.

– Prime Minister Clement Atlee.[10]

Compare and contrast

Roy Jenkins and Aubrey were born two years and three miles apart and both had fathers named Arthur. They were both keen and talented mathematicians as children, both award-winning swimmers, and both were strongly influenced by the socialist ideals of the area they were born into. They also both spent a lot of time at Pontypool Railway Station – Roy Jenkins collecting train numbers and Aubrey spending with his father who worked there.[11] However, in nearly all other aspects their lives were completely different.

Roy Jenkins led a sheltered life in a comfortable and safe family home. He was protected by his mother and guided politically by his father and by a mentor who was later to become Labour's first Prime Minister. He had ample opportunity for study and grew up in an interesting and stimulating environment. He secured a position at Oxford University, with little if any effort on his part, where he ate good food and drank fine wine with no regard for where the money came from. He then enjoyed a comfortable life in the army before securing the nomination for a safe Labour seat, becoming the youngest member of the House of Commons. Aubrey on the other hand was born in poverty in a slum to a sixteen-year-old mother and a father who could hardly afford to feed and clothe him. With a father who struggled to look after himself let alone Aubrey, and a step-grandfather who would spend all his earnings down the pub given the opportunity, he had no obvious male role model, and probably limited reading material in his house. For the first eleven years of his life he lived in a household where his mother hated his father and spent most of her time trying to leave him. Involved in a tug-of-war between his mother and father at a crucial time of his educational development, he never had the chance of a scholarly career, and by the time he became a teenager, he had taken on much of the family responsibility for looking after his brother Russell as well as his father. With a career on the railways beckoning, he joined the army on his sixteenth birthday where he continually sought out the most challenging and demanding roles, finally volunteering for a regiment that had the highest casualty rate in the Second World War and whose members were murdered as spies by the Nazi's if they were caught. However, despite his considerable efforts to engage with the enemy, like Roy Jenkins, he never fired a shot in anger during the war, although for completely different reasons. As for his political career, he

---

[10] Ibid.
[11] Ibid.

could not even consider this until he left the army, which was a year after Roy Jenkins had become an MP. Only ever interested in representing his hometown, it wasn't until 1966 that he had his first serious opportunity, by which time Roy Jenkins was Home Secretary. Without the Prime Minister of the day in his corner, he failed to secure the nomination despite being the favoured candidate. By the time a second opportunity arose in 1983, Roy Jenkins had also been Chancellor of the Exchequer and President of the European Commission and was now leader of the Social Democratic Party with, albeit for a short period, a realistic chance of becoming Britain's next Prime Minister.

A stellar parliamentary career

Considering the difference between the two men's careers, one might wonder what would have happened had their childhoods been reversed. Roy Jenkins admitted that without the support of his father he would never have attended Oxford University.[12] With almost half of Harold Wilson's first cabinet of 1964 being Oxford graduates, he may have consequently struggled to get a cabinet position. He may also have struggled to gain recognition as a serious candidate to replace Harold Wilson as Prime Minister when he resigned in 1976. Of the six candidates standing, five (including Roy) were Oxford graduates, although the winning candidate, James Callaghan, wasn't.

Regardless of whether he secured a cabinet position or not, would Roy Jenkins have got into parliament in the first place? With no money, he could not have bought a Labour seat such as the one at Newport (a nomination which he sought in 1945).[13] It's also unlikely that he would have secured a nomination in a safe Labour seat against a sponsored union candidate. As a boy from Abersychan, with war nearly three years away when he turned sixteen, he may also have been unable to escape an early if not permanent career down the mines, as well as conscription into the army. If he had become a trade unionist like his father, a future parliamentary career may well have ensued but it probably would have started in the mid-1960s rather than the late 1940s.

Nevertheless, Roy Jenkins was an exceptionally clever man, and even without Arthur Jenkins as a father and Clement Attlee as a mentor, he may have succeeded in becoming an MP based on his own merits regardless of any union backing. However, he would have become an MP for the first

---

[12] Jenkins, R., 1991.
[13] Bloxsome M., 2004.

time later in life, and with no grammar school education (which would have been his fate had he been born to Aubrey's parents) he may not have gained a ministerial or cabinet role; he may also have found out, as Aubrey did in 1966 and in 1983, that ability or intelligence had little to do with securing a candidacy, or even a nomination.

As for Aubrey, it is a lot more difficult to predict his political career had he been given the same opportunities as Roy Jenkins. Aubrey did not have the academic career that Roy Jenkins had, but this had everything to do with his lack of opportunity rather than his lack of ability. In both local and national politics, Aubrey was renowned for his intellect, particularly in the field of political economics. He regularly outmanoeuvred the national government of the day taking advantage of various loopholes for the benefit of Newport. Without prompting, nearly every person I interviewed, whether a former member of the UK or Welsh Government, ex-councillors, or people who knew Aubrey in some other capacity, all mentioned his exceptional intellect. Even twenty years after his death, an article in the *South Wales Argus* by Councillor Allan Morris referred to him as "having the brain the size of a planet." [14] In terms of talent and intellect, there is little doubt that given the same opportunities as Roy Jenkins, Aubrey would have had the ability to have a stellar Parliamentary career.

In Parliament, Aubrey would have been among the group of MPs who were not seen as politically ambitious, which represents about a third of MPs. [15] Unlike every Prime Minister from Margaret Thatcher to Liz Truss, he would not have fought and lost multiple seats in multiple constituencies that he struggled to find on a map; he did not possess that type of ruthless personal ambition. He would perhaps therefore not have been seen as a threat to the Prime Minister or party leader of the day, and they in turn may have been more amenable to giving him a government or shadow government role. Without exception, every major political figure I interviewed who addressed this question thought he would have excelled in a ministerial role, including the only former Cabinet Minister I interviewed, Paul Murphy. [16] His chances may also have been significantly improved by spending considerably more time with the various party leaders than most; the train journeys from the constituency homes of James Callaghan, Michael Foot and Neil Kinnock – leaders of the Labour Party between 1976 and 1992 – all stopped at Newport.

---

[14] "Community news in Liswerry and Nash." *South Wales Argus*. 23 May, 2017.

[15] Sieberer, U. and Müller, W.C. "Aiming higher: the consequences of progressive ambition among MPs in European parliaments." *European Political Science Review*. Volume 9. Number 1, 2017, pp.27-50.

[16] Interview with Lord Paul Murphy, 2021.

Aubrey and Roy

An intriguing question to ask at the end of this chapter is whether Aubrey and Roy Jenkins knew each other. I have gathered no evidence that suggests that they did, but I have never had any reason to look. I was unaware that Roy Jenkins was from Abersychan until I bought a copy of his biography a few years ago on a whim. Reading the first few chapters of his biography, I was initially surprised that he was from Abersychan (as would anybody who remembers his accent), and then intrigued by the similarities and contrasts between his life and Aubrey's. Unfortunately, anybody who would have been likely to know whether they had any relationship is no longer alive, and there was nowhere obvious to look. However, when I interviewed Paul Murphy and Don Touhig in 2021, I was able to put together the pieces of many jigsaws that I had been trying to complete since I started this book eleven years previously. One of these was to emphasise that Aubrey really was a well-known and respected politician. Every leader of the Labour Party from at least Harold Wilson to Neil Kinnock, knew him, and he was widely known across the party not just within his locality. Roy Jenkins and Aubrey were both renowned for their friendly nature, and even though Roy Jenkins drank considerably more fine wines and ate more good food than Aubrey, they would have got on. They both knew Leo Abse well, who represented the constituency where they were both born from 1958 to 1987, and Aubrey knew Roy Jenkins' mentor Clement Attlee, even though his stellar parliamentary career was finishing as Aubrey's political career was just starting. It would therefore seem extremely unlikely that they didn't know each other, and if Aubrey knew Clement Attlee, how could he not have known Roy Jenkins? Indeed, if opportunity and circumstance had operated differently, perhaps there would have been no need for this book, and I would have been reading the many books written about Aubrey, rather than writing the first.

Bibliography

Personal correspondence and memoranda

Aubrey's personal diaries were sourced from his private collection and are now in the possession of the author along with items such as Aubrey's speeches, logbooks, school reports, police witness statements, BTDB memorandums, articles from the *The Eagle* and *Glider Pilot's Notes,* and letters (including Mary Hames' letters).

Newport Labour Party minutes

The Newport Labour Party Minutes can be accessed via the West Glamorgan Archive Service or the National Library of Wales. A copy is held by the author.

Interviews

All interviews, unless otherwise state, were carried out by the author between 2010 and 2013.

Newspaper articles

All articles from the *South Wales Argus* and the *Weekly Argus* can be found in Newport Reference Library. *The Montgomery County Times and Shropshire and Mid-Wales Advertiser* was sourced in Newtown Library, and all other newspaper articles were sourced from The British Newspaper Archive at www.britishnewspaperarchive.co.uk.

With thanks to the following archives and registries:

Alford Library and Focal Point
Army Personnel Centre
British Newspaper Archive
Dorset History Centre
General Register Office
Grantham Library
Gwent Archives
Hansard Parliamentary Debates, UK Parliament
Imperial War Museum Collections
London Metropolitan Archives
London School of Economics and Political Science
Ministry of Defence service personnel records (via National Archives)
The National Archives
National Library of Wales
Newport Reference Library (South Wales Argus and the Weekly Argus)
Newtown Library
Plymouth and West Devon Record Office
Probate Research Office

Printed Primary and Secondary Sources

Abrams, F. and Little, A. "The young activist in British politics." *British Journal of Sociology*. Volume 16. Number 4, 1965.

Addison, P. *Now the war is over*. British Broadcasting Corporation, London, 1985.

Addison, P. "Why Churchill lost in 1945." BBC website, 2011. Available at: http://www.bbc.co.uk/history/worldwars/wwtwo/election_01.shtml. Date accessed: 08/11/15.

Ahrenfeldt, R.H. *Psychiatry in the British Army in the Second World War*. London: Routledge and Kegan Paul, 1958.

"Albert Booth obituary." *The Independent*. 11 February, 2010. Available at: https://www.independent.co.uk/news/obituaries/albert-booth-principled-labour-mp-who-served-as-secretary-of-state-under-james-callaghan-1895853.html.

"A real Line of duty: the London police officer who 'went bent.'" *The Guardian*. 1 May, 2021. Available at: https://www.theguardian.com/uk-news/2021/may/01/a-real-line-of-duty-the-london-police-officer-who-went-bent.

Armstrong, E. *A Pontypool childhood in the 1920s*. Gwent County History Association, 2001.

Baldwin, P. Baldwin, R. and Evans, D.I. *The motorway achievement-building the network in Wales*. Chichester. Phillimore, 2010.

Benn, T. *The Benn diaries: 1940-1990*. London: Random House, 2013.

Bethell, N. The Palestine triangle: The struggle between the British, the Jews and the Arabs 1935-1948. London: Futura Publications Limited, 1980.

Biddiscombe, P. DeNazification of Germany 1945-1950. Tempus, 2007.

Bloxsome, M. The green Casanova: An affectionate biography of Peter Freeman, Maverick MP. Talybont, Y Lofla, 2004.

Bochel, J.M. and Denver, D.T. *The impact of the campaign on the results of local government elections*. British Journal of Political Science. Volume 2. Number 2, 1972, pp.239-244.

Branson, N. and Heinemann, M. *Britain in the nineteen thirties*. Harper Collins, 1973.

Brunner, H.G. and Winter, R.M. *Autosomal dominant inheritance of abnormalities of the hands and feet with short palpebral fissures, variable microcephaly with learning disability, and oesophageal/duodenal atresia*. Journal of Medical Genetics. Volume 28, 1991, pp 389-394.

Buxton, R.J. (1973) *Local government*. Volume 4. Puffin, 1973.

Caldero, M.A., Dailey, J.D. and Withrow, B.L. *Police ethics: The corruption of noble cause*. London: Routledge, 2018.

Campbell, J. (2000) Margaret Thatcher, volume one: The grocer's daughter. London: Jonathan Cape, 2000.

Campbell-Smith, D. (2008) Follow the money: a history of the Audit Commission. Penguin UK, 2008.

Campbell, J. (2014) *Roy Jenkins*. London: Random House, 2014.

Chandler, D. and Beckett, I. (1994) *The Oxford history of the British Army*. Oxford: Oxford University Press, 1994.

Clamp, A.L. *The blitz of Plymouth 1940-44*. Plymouth. P.D.S. Printers, 1984.

Clarke, C. Condition of Britain, 1937.

Cloughley, B. Trumpeters: The story of the Royal Artillery's boy trumpeters.

Bognor Regis: Woodfield Publishing, 2008.

Collingham, L. *The taste of war: World War Two and the battle for food.* London: Penguin Books, 2012.

Cook, *C. and Ramsden, J. eds., By-elections in British politics.* 2nd edition. London: Macmillan, 1997.

Cooper, A. *Wot! No engines? Military gliders, RAF pilots and Operation Varsity, 1945.* Bognor Regis: Woodfield Publishing, 2002.

Crang, J.A. *Politics on parade: army education and the 1945 general election.* History. Volume 81. Number 262, 1996, pp.215-227.

Darlow, S. D-Day bombers: The veteran's story. Bounty Books, 2004.

Davis, H. *The history of the Borough of Newport.* Pennyfarthing Press, 1998.

Davies, J. *A history of Wales.* London: Penguin, 2007.

Donnison, D.V. *Housing policy since the war.* Codicote Press, 1960.

Douglas, I.J. and Lord, S. *Local government finance: a practical guide.* Local Government Information Unit, 1986.

Dunleavy, P. The politics of mass housing in Britain: 1945-1975. Oxford: Clarendon, 1981.

Feickert, D. *Britain's civil war over coal: An Insider's view.* Cambridge: Cambridge Scholars Publishing, 2021.

Flynn, P. "It must be Christmas," blog post. 4 July, 2008. Available at: http://paulflynnmp.typepad.com/my_weblog/2008/07/it-must-be-christmas.html. Date accessed: 14/05/15.

Flynn, P. "My vote," blog post, 13 August, 2015. Available at: http://paulflynnmp.typepad.com/my_weblog/2015/08/my-vote.html.   Date accessed 22/11/15.

Foot, M. *Aneurin Bevan 1897-1945.* Volume 1. Harper Collins, 1962.

Foot, M. *Aneurin Bevan - 1945-1960.* Volume 2. Granada Publishing Limited, 1975.

Foote-Wood, Chris. T. Dan Smith, "Voice of the North," Downfall of a Visionary. Northern Writers, 2010.

"Gig venue's 'black book' reveals piece of Newport's music history." *Wales Online.* 29 December, 2017. Available at https://www.walesonline.co.uk/lifestyle/nostalgia/david-bowie-elton-john-newport-14051119.

Gill, C. *Plymouth: A new history*. Devon Books, 1993.

Glider Pilot's Notes. "The making of a total soldier - part one: glider pilot selection." *The Glider Pilot Regiment Society Magazine*. Summer 2018.

Glider Pilot's Notes. "The making of a total soldier - part two: Tilshead and Fargo." *The Glider Pilot Regiment Society Magazine*. Winter 2018/19.

Hall, S., Critcher, C., Jefferson, T., Clarke, J. and Roberts, B. (2013) *Policing the crisis: Mugging, the state and law and order*. London: Bloomsbury Publishing, 2013.

Harrison, M. Trade unions and the Labour Party since 1945. London: Ruskin House, 1960.

Haythorne, I. "A study based on the Arthur Marwick 'model' of the effect of the Second World War on the Alford district of Lincolnshire." MSc. Sheffield Polytechnic. June, 1989.

Hobbs, A. *The Story of Bryn-Glas House*. Newport: Brynglas Community Education Centre, 1989.

Hollis, P. *Jennie Lee: A life*. Oxford: Oxford University Press, 1998.

Hoffman, B. Anonymous soldiers: The struggle for Palestine, 1917-1947. New York. Alfred A. Knopf, 2015.

Hopkin, D., Tanner, D. and Williams, C. eds., *Labour Party in Wales 1900-2000*. Cardiff. University of Wales Press, 2000.

Hopkins, T. *A history of Griffithstown Baptist Church 1875-2000*. Griffithstown. Griffithstown Baptist Church, 2000.

Hughes, D. *Pontypool memories 1929-1947*. Bristol: Azimuth Print, 2010.

Hughes, R. *Seek fairer skies*. Spennymoor. The Memoir Club, 2003.

James, L. Raj: The making and unmaking of British India. London: Abacus, 1998.

Jarvis, D. "The Conservative Party's recruitment of youth." In: Orsina, G. and Quagliariello, G. eds., *La formazione della classe politica in Europa: (1945-1956)*. Volume 3. Rome, 2000.

Jenkins, R. *A life at the centre*. London: Macmillan, 1991.

"Jewish agency condemns deed." *Palestine Post*. 1 August, 1947. Available at: https://www.nli.org.il/en/newspapers/pls.

Jones, G.W. and Stewart, J. *The case for local government*. Volume 1. Allen

& Unwin Australia, 1983.

Jones, G.W. and Norton, A. eds., *Political Leadership in Local Authorities*. Birmingham. Institute of Local Government Studies, University of Birmingham, 1978.

Kandel, I. and Merrick, J. "The birth of a child with disability. Coping by parents and siblings." *The Scientific World Journal*. Volume 3, 2003, pp.741-750.

King, R. Brittle with relics: a history of Wales 1962-1997. London: Faber, 2022.

Knapp, M.G. Grantham: The war years 1939-1945. A pictorial history. Lincolnshire Books, 1995.

Lamb, M. "Young Conservatives, young Socialists and the great youth abstention: Youth participation and nonparticipation in political parties." Doctoral dissertation. University of Birmingham, 2002.

Layton-Henry, Z. "Labour's lost youth." *Journal of Contemporary History*. Volume 11, 1976, pp 275-308.

Leach, S., Game, C., Gyford, J. and Midwinter, A. The Political Organisation of Local Authorities, Research Volume I, Committee of Inquiry into the Conduct of Local Authority Business. London: HMSO, 1986.

Leonard, R.L. and Mortimore, R. *Elections in Britain*. London: Van Nostrand, 1968.

Lewis, G. Corporate strategy in action. The strategy process in British Road Services. London: Routledge, 1988.

Lowe, E. *Forgotten conscripts: Prelude to Palestine's struggle for survival*. Trafford Publications, 2007.

Lloyd, W.G. *Sebastopol. A local history*. Newport: Starling Press, 1992.

Marquand, H. *The second industrial survey of South Wales*. Cardiff: National Industrial Development Council of Wales and Monmouthshire, Office for National Statistics, 1937.

Mathevet, J.C. *Flying drama in the Pyrenees: Pic de la Camisette (Ariege),* December 5th, 1944 Available at: https://the24sec.files.wordpress.com/2009/06/flying-drama-dakota-fl-588.pdf. Accessed 10/07/23

Merrett, S. *Owner-occupation in Britain*. London: Routledge, 1979.

Midwinter, A., Keating, M. and Taylor, P. "'Excessive and unreasonable':

The politics of the Scottish hit list." *Political Studies*. Volume 31. Number 3, 1983, pp.394-417.

Moore, C. Margaret Thatcher, the authorised biography, Volume One: Not for Turning. London: Penguin Books, 2013.

Morgan, K.O. *Rebirth of a nation: Wales, 1880-1980*. Oxford: Oxford University Press, 1982.

Niven, D. *The Moon's a Balloon*. London: Hamish Hamilton, 1971.

"Obituary of Peter Burden." *Press Gazette*. 19 October, 2017. Available at: http://www.pressgazette.co.uk/they-trust-me-and-i-trust-them-how-police-contacts-took-daily-mails-peter-burden-who-has-died-aged-77-to-the-top/. Date accessed: 15/03/17.

Osborn, B. and Pasley, D. *I just wanted to Fly: The story of WWII Glider Pilot Bernard Osborn*. (The Airborne Memoirs Book II). Baverstock and Pasley, 2019.

"Palestine: The Jewish war." *Empire Warriors*. Episode 4, TV mini-series. 2004.

Pilgrim Trust. *Men without work*. Cambridge. Cambridge University Press, 1939.

Pugh, D. "The Second World War in Newtown." *The Newtonian*. Volume 22. Autumn, 2005.

Pugh, M. Speak for Britain!: A new history of the Labour Party. London, Vintage, 2011.

Rallings, C. and Thrasher, M. *Local Elections in Britain*. London: Routledge, 2013.

Ranney, A. Pathways to Parliament. Candidate selection in Britain. London: MacMillan, 1965.

Reese, P. *Homecoming Heroes*. London: Leo Cooper, 1992.

"Rhyl Sun Centre: The fascinating story behind North Wales' famous 'tropical village.'" *Daily Post*. 27 August, 2016. Available at https://www.dailypost.co.uk/news/north-wales-news/rhyl-sun-centre-fascinating-story-11807201.

Rose, N. *A Senseless Squalid War*. London: Pimlico, 2010.

Rush, M. The Selection of Parliamentary Candidates. London: Nelson, 1969.

Seth, R. Lions with Blue Wings: The story of the Glider Pilot Regiment

1942-1945. London: Victor Gollancz Ltd, 1955.

Shaw, E. Discipline and Discord in the Labour Party: The Politics of Managerial Control in the Labour Party, 1951-87. Manchester University Press, 1988.

Short, J.R. Housing in Britain: The Post-War Experience. London: Methuen, 1982.

Sieberer, U. and Müller, W.C. "Aiming Higher: The Consequences of Progressive Ambition among MPs in European Parliaments." *European Political Science Review*. Volume 9. Number 1, 2017, pp.27-50.

Skinner, J. Images of London – Hillingdon Cinemas. Stroud: Tempus, 2002.

Smellie, B. *A History of Local Government*. London: George Allen & Unwin. Third Edition, 2002.

Smith, C. *History of the Glider Pilot Regiment*. Barnsley. Pen and Sword. 1992.

Stevenson, J. Social History of Great Britain. British Society 1914-1945. London: Penguin, 1984.

Stevenson, J. and Cook, C. Britain in the Depression: Society and Politics, 1929-1939. London: Longman, 1994.

"Stockwell Six: Three men have 1972 convictions quashed by Court of Appeal." BBC News. 6 July, 2021. Available at: https://www.bbc.co.uk/news/uk-england-london-57735027.

Stoker, G. *The Politics of Local Government*. London: Bloomsbury, 1991.

Stott, L. "Looking Back." *The Newtonian*. Volume 24. Spring, 2006.

Street, S. *British National Cinema*. London: Routledge, 1997.

Tanner, D., Thane, P. and Tiratsoo, N. eds., *Labour's First Century*. Cambridge. Cambridge University Press, 2000.

Tanner, D., Williams, C. and Hopkin, D. *The Labour Party in Wales 1900-2000*. Cardiff. University of Wales Press, 2000.

Taylor, A.J.P. *English History 1914-1945*. Oxford: Clarendon, 1965.

Taylor and Bogg. Children's Memories of Alford 1920s-1950s, 2007.

The Eagle: The Glider Pilot Regiment Magazine. Volume 1. Number 1. July, 1946.

The Eagle: The Glider Pilot Regiment Magazine. Volume 1. Number 4. June,

1947.

The Eagle: The Glider Pilot Regiment Magazine. Volume 1. Number 5. December, 1947.

The Eagle: The Glider Pilot Regiment Magazine. Volume 2. Number 2. June, 1950.

The Eagle: The Glider Pilot Regiment Magazine. Volume 13. Number 6. December, 2013.

Thorpe, A. *Britain in the 1930s.* (Historical Association Studies). Oxford: Blackwell, 1992.

Thorpe, A. Parties at war: Political organisation in Second World War Britain. Oxford University Press, 2009.

Timbers, K. *The Royal Artillery Woolwich: A celebration.* London: Third Millennium Publishing Limited, 2008.

Trew, Winston, N., Black for a Cause... Not Just Because, 2021.

Von Papen, F. *Franz Von Papen memoirs.* London: Andre Deutsch Limited, 1952.

"Wales this week," documentary, HTV Wales. 24 March, 1983.

Wasley, G. Plymouth, a Shattered City: The Story of Hitler's Attack on Plymouth and its People 1939-1945. Wellington. Halsgrove, 2004.

Watson, J. "Some notes on post-war development at Plymouth." *Journal of the Royal Sanitary Institute* (Great Britain). Volume 69. Number 2, 1949, pp.71-78.

Weber-Newth, I. and Steinert, J. *German Migrants in Post-War Britain: An Enemy Embrace.* London: Routledge, 2006.

Williams J. Digest of Welsh Historical Statistics. Volume 1, 1985.

Wilson, D. "The Day War Broke Out." *The Newtonian.* Volume 22. Autumn. 2005.

Wilson, D. With 6th Airborne Division in Palestine 1945-1948. Barnsley: Pen and Sword, 2008.

Wintle, F. *The Plymouth Blitz.* Bodmin: Bossiney Books, 1981.

Wragg, D. *Wartime On The Railways.* Stroud: The History Press, 2006.

Wrigley, C. ed., *A Companion to Early Twentieth-Century Britain.* Oxford: Wiley-Blackwell, 2003.

Yelling, J. "The incidence of slum clearance in England and Wales, 1955–85." *Urban History*. Volume 27. Number 2, 2000, pp.234-254.

Young, J. "Newport wraps up improvement package." *ROOF*. July, 1979, pp. 116-117.

Zmith, Z. Eugene Di Villa – a friend to Underwood, 2014.

Milton Keynes UK
Ingram Content Group UK Ltd.
UKHW020013101123
432275UK00011B/160